Gulls Simplif

A Comparative Approach to Identifi

Pete Dunne and Kevin T. Karlson

Gulls Simplified

A Comparative Approach to Identification

Princeton University Press

Princeton and Oxford

DEDICATION

We dedicate this book to the many gull aficionados who spend countless hours in the field studying these fascinating birds without the usual appreciation given by the general birding community for ID breakthroughs. We hope this book will change that.

We also dedicate this book to our wives, Linda Dunne and Dale Rosselet, for their invaluable help and patience with this and all our previous projects.

ACKNOWLEDGMENTS

The authors would like to thank the following individuals for their helpful review of the text and/or photos: Michael Brothers, Rene Buccinna, Cameron Cox, Don Freiday, Paul Lehman, Derick Lovitch, Dennis Paulson, and Dale Rosselet. Special thanks to the following people for inspiring and influencing us to appreciate gulls in a new way and to bring that appreciation to this book: Harold Axtell, Amar Ayash, Michael Brothers, Cameron Cox, Jon Dunn, Steve Howell, Alvaro Jaramillo, Richard Kane, Hans Larsson, Klaus Malling Olsen, Martin Reid, Floyd P. Wolfarth. Added thanks to Jon Dunn, Steve Howell, and Houghton Mifflin Harcourt publishers for permitting us to use the excellent maps from *Gulls of the Americas* (2007), and to Tom Johnson for his review of the Quiz photos. A true debt of gratitude goes to Cameron Cox for his very thorough review and comments on the final draft.

Published by Princeton University Press
41 William Street, Princeton, New Jersey 08540
6 Oxford Street, Woodstock, Oxfordshire OX20 1TR

press.princeton.edu

Library of Congress Control Number: 2018930944

ISBN (pbk.): 978-0-691-15694-1

British Library Cataloging-in-Publication Data is available

Editorial: Robert Kirk and Kristin Zodrow
Production Editorial: Ellen Foos
Text Design: D & N Publishing, Wiltshire, UK
Cover Design: Carmina Alvarez Geffen
Jacket images (front and back) courtesy of Kevin T. Karlson
Production: Steven Sears
Copyeditor: Laurel Anderton

This book has been composed in Brandon Grotesque

Photograph previous page: Franklin's Gull, adult breeding, Texas

Printed on acid-free paper. ∞

Printed in South Korea

10 9 8 7 6 5 4 3 2

CONTENTS

GREAT BLACK-BACKED GULL

LESSER BLACK-BACKED GULL

GLAUCOUS GULL

WESTERN GULL

YELLOW-FOOTED GULL

ICELAND GULL
(THAYER'S SUBSPECIES)

BLACK-HEADED GULL

HEERMANN'S GULL

IVORY GULL

LAUGHING GULL

FRANKLIN'S GULL

BONAPARTE'S GULL

Shown here are twenty-two species of gulls that breed in North America, which includes one species (Iceland Gull) that has two distinct subspecies (Thayer's and Kumlien's subspecies). Some are rare and are encountered only in distant locations, so fewer than twenty species of

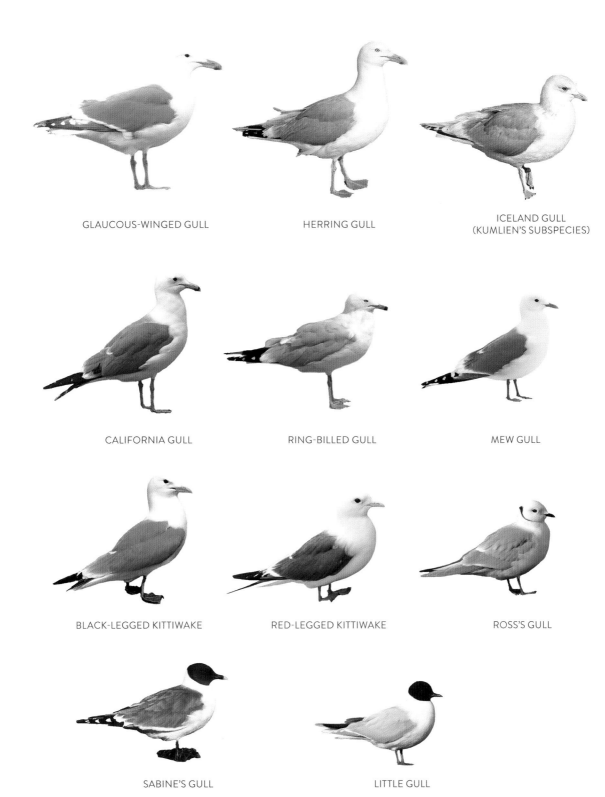

GLAUCOUS-WINGED GULL

HERRING GULL

ICELAND GULL
(KUMLIEN'S SUBSPECIES)

CALIFORNIA GULL

RING-BILLED GULL

MEW GULL

BLACK-LEGGED KITTIWAKE

RED-LEGGED KITTIWAKE

ROSS'S GULL

SABINE'S GULL

LITTLE GULL

gulls are regularly seen throughout North America—not so many when compared to the number of warblers or shorebirds. These gulls are shown as adults, scaled to size, and arranged to allow for direct comparisons of size, shape, and structural features as well as plumage.

GREAT BLACK-BACKED GULL

LESSER BLACK-BACKED GULL

GLAUCOUS GULL

WESTERN GULL

YELLOW-FOOTED GULL

ICELAND GULL
(THAYER'S SUBSPECIES)

BLACK-HEADED GULL

HEERMANN'S GULL

IVORY GULL

LAUGHING GULL

FRANKLIN'S GULL

BONAPARTE'S GULL

These silhouettes of the gulls on the previous pages allow you to assess the differences in size, shape, and structural features more easily, since you have to use your right-brain skills to work with these gull silhouettes that have no details to analyze.

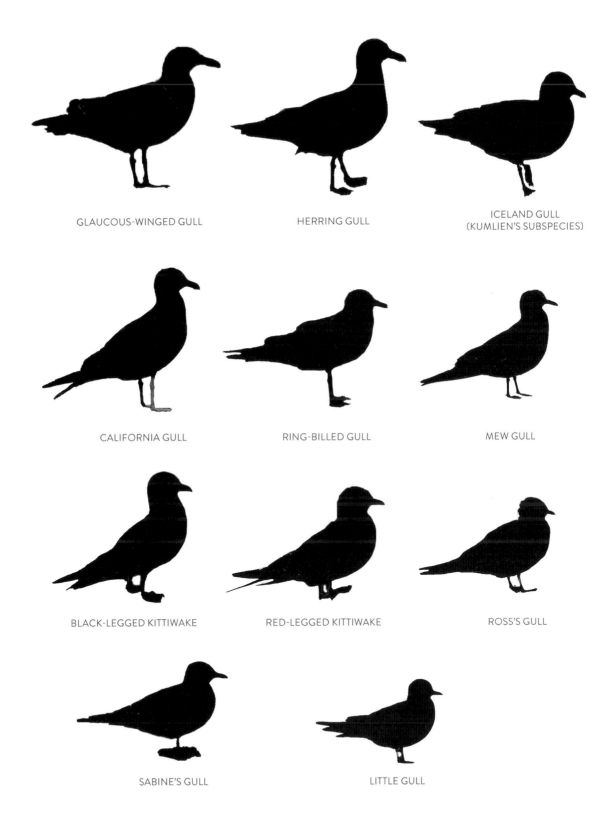

GLAUCOUS-WINGED GULL

HERRING GULL

ICELAND GULL
(KUMLIEN'S SUBSPECIES)

CALIFORNIA GULL

RING-BILLED GULL

MEW GULL

BLACK-LEGGED KITTIWAKE

RED-LEGGED KITTIWAKE

ROSS'S GULL

SABINE'S GULL

LITTLE GULL

BASIC ANATOMICAL TERMS

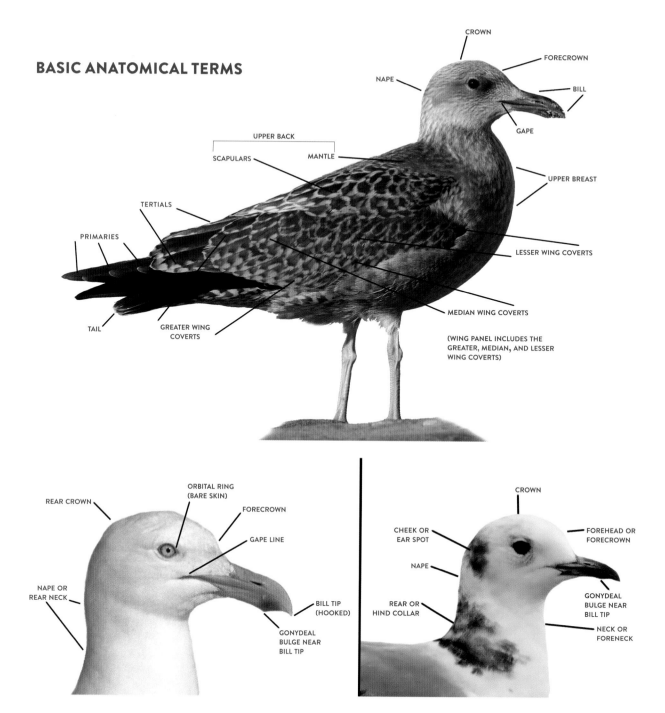

CROWN
FORECROWN
NAPE
BILL
GAPE
UPPER BACK
SCAPULARS
MANTLE
UPPER BREAST
TERTIALS
PRIMARIES
LESSER WING COVERTS
TAIL
GREATER WING COVERTS
MEDIAN WING COVERTS
(WING PANEL INCLUDES THE GREATER, MEDIAN, AND LESSER WING COVERTS)

REAR CROWN
ORBITAL RING (BARE SKIN)
FORECROWN
GAPE LINE
NAPE OR REAR NECK
BILL TIP (HOOKED)
GONYDEAL BULGE NEAR BILL TIP

CROWN
CHEEK OR EAR SPOT
FOREHEAD OR FORECROWN
NAPE
REAR OR HIND COLLAR
GONYDEAL BULGE NEAR BILL TIP
NECK OR FORENECK

GLOSSARY

Bleaching (sun bleaching) – the whitened, faded, or colorless appearance of feathers due to exposure to strong sunlight.

Breeding – the overall appearance of a gull as typically seen in the breeding season.

Ear spot (or cheek spot) – a contrasting dark spot or mark on a gull's cheek.

Inner primary window – the outer exposed section of the innermost primary feathers, which on some large gulls show paler shading than the rest of the primaries and secondaries creating a moderate to strong contrast with the rest of the trailing edge of the spread wing (see Herring Gull 11, p. 91, for a visual example).

Lower wing panel (greater wing coverts) – the lower portion of the folded wing on standing birds, comprising the greater wing coverts.

Mirror – a white spot or bar within the dark outer portion of the outer primaries of a gull's wing.

Nape – the back of a bird's neck just below the rear crown.

OUTER PRIMARIES

GREATER WING COVERTS

MEDIAN WING COVERTS   UPPER WING COVERTS

LESSER WING COVERTS

TERTIALS

TAIL   UPPERTAIL
COVERTS   RUMP

UPPER BACK (SCAPULARS AND MANTLE)

GAPE LINE

BILL

TAIL
BAND

CHEEK

SECONDARIES

INNER PRIMARY WINDOW

PRIMARIES (10)

Nonbreeding – the overall appearance of a gull as typically seen in the nonbreeding season.

Orbital ring – bare skin that encircles a gull's eye. Orbital rings often show color during the breeding cycle and may be dull or lack color in fall and winter.

Primaries – the ten visible feathers on the outer half of a gull's wing.

Secondaries – the feathers on the inner half of the wing, which in gulls number from 16 to 23 feathers.

Subspecies – a term that reflects a taxonomic category below the level of a species and refers to populations that can be distinguished by differences in plumage or measurements but are not considered distinct enough to be treated as species.

Tertials – the innermost secondary feathers, which act as coverts, or protection, for some of the closed wing feathers.

Wing coverts – feathers that cover the upper portions of the flight feathers on a gull's spread wing on the under and upper sides. On a standing gull, wing coverts comprise much of the visible wing on the sides of the bird, and they protect crucial flight feathers from harmful weather elements, including the harsh sun.

Wing panel – the visible wing on the sides of a standing gull, which includes the lesser, median, and greater wing coverts. We use this nonscientific term to simplify the terminology of the three sets of wing coverts, and we often specify upper wing panel or lower wing panel.

Wing tip – the exposed tips of the outer primaries on a standing bird, or the outer portion of the spread wing on a flying bird. Outer wing tips often contain pale to dark shading on the wing, and small to large white spots near the tip.

1st summer – a plumage condition that shows a mix of older feathers (often very worn) of a gull's 1st winter plumage and new, fresh 2nd winter feathers.

1st winter – a plumage condition related to the postjuvenile appearance of a gull until the end of its first plumage cycle, which may occur up to one year after hatching.

2nd summer – a plumage condition that shows a mix of older, worn 2nd winter feathers and newer, fresher 3rd winter ones.

2nd winter – a plumage condition that is related to the appearance of a gull in its second winter after its worn 1st winter feathers have been replaced with fresh 2nd winter ones. This plumage may be seen during late summer months and continues to the following spring/summer.

HEERMAN'S GULL,
adult breeding

INTRODUCTION

OVERVIEW—BY PETE DUNNE

GULLS? No Waaaayyeeeeeeeeeeee!!!!!!!!!!!!!!!!!!!!!!!!!!!

Ask any bird-watcher to name the bird group that is most intimidating, and to a man, woman, and tour leader they often shout: "GULLS!"

So daunting is this family that one accomplished field trip leader of my acquaintance, a person who can identify any North American warbler in three notes or less, categorically asserts: "I don't do gulls."

Sadly, such unconditional dismissal renders birders incapable of becoming acquainted with one of the planet's most fascinating bird groups. No other birds are so adept at foraging on land, in the air, and in aquatic environments. In addition to being panglobal in distribution, gulls are intelligent, inquisitive, and socially complex, and these superior aerialists are able to acclimate themselves to a wide array of habitats, from Arctic cliffs to tundra ponds, inland waterways, city streets, South American deserts, lakes, landfills, and of course coastal beaches. Ironically, one habitat most gull species have not adapted to is deep, open marine environments, the place that puts the "sea" in "seagull." Kittiwakes and Sabine's Gulls are the only true "seagulls," spending their nonbreeding months over deep ocean waters. In the balance, most gull species rarely stray beyond sight of land.

Distributed as breeders across the planet's colder regions for the most part, gulls as a family largely surrender tropical regions to their close relatives the terns.

Ranging in size from the dove-sized Little Gull to the greater-than-Osprey-sized Great Black-backed Gull, these

INTRO 1 Gulls often roost together in small to large flocks on beachfronts and in other open spaces. This flock contains Herring and Great Black-backed Gulls of various ages. New Jersey, August

INTRO 2 Two birders consult their field guide while looking at a mixed flock of gulls and terns, including the Black Skimmer flying toward them to warn them not to come any farther. New Jersey, July

INTRO 3 A subadult 1st winter Ring-billed Gull (*right*) stands on a Florida beach next to a Royal Tern. These birds are roughly the same size and often roost together on beachfronts. Both are commonly found on southern beachfronts of all coasts and in some tropical regions of the Caribbean. Florida, March

carnivorous birds feast on a variety of food sources, including mostly aquatic fare on coastal beaches and insects and larvae for inland breeders. The hooked bills of the larger gull species are well suited for tearing flesh from large carcasses, or rending starfish, crabs, and other tidal-zone fare (literally) limb from limb from limb. Smaller gull species are equally adept at snapping insects out of the air or foraging for them on foot. Unlike terns and many aquatic seabird species, gulls are nimble afoot, their legs and webbed feet positioned for efficient biped locomotion as well as swimming.

In the air they excel at soaring, and many are fast and agile enough to rob other seabirds of their prey. Where skill fails, ingenuity reigns. Several gull species are known to carry mollusks, urchins, and other armor-plated food aloft and drop them upon hard surfaces, forcefully decanting the gastronomic delights within. The Ivory Gull, a rare snow-colored Arctic species that specializes in attending polar bear kills, is reported to investigate anything red on the snow. The adaptive Ring-billed Gull, a common and widespread North American species, has in recent decades successfully exploited the culinary riches of America's fast-food culture, eschewing coastal beaches and tide-borne fare in favor of french fry–strewn parking lots farther inland. In short, if there is a meal to be had, there is almost certainly a gull suited to exploit it.

I was once interviewed by a reporter who was interested in the "gull problem," which she defined as the french fry and pizza

INTRO 4 Ring-billed Gulls are often found in parking lots near fast-food restaurants or in Dumpsters with food waste. They are quick to exploit a Good Samaritan who stops to give them a few morsels of food, like Kevin did with this small flock in southern New Jersey. Note the two larger gulls in this flock. What species do you think they are? Answers are in the appendix, p. 205. New Jersey, April

pilfering predilections of Laughing Gulls, especially in coastal boardwalk locations. My response was to point out that the "problem," as she defined the interaction, was not the gulls, but was instead the result of the poor food husbandry practices of humans. With gulls in the vicinity, you guard your lunch or lose it. Kleptoparasitism (one species taking food from another that has acquired it) is a practice right out of the gull basic playbook.

This truism was once forcefully brought home to me while I was standing in a parking area in Denali National Park, Alaska, with a freshly made ham sandwich in hand, unaware that the parking area was haunted by Mew Gulls. Raising binoculars to my eyes, I foolishly used my sandwich-bearing hand to steady the elevated instrument, thus triggering the kleptoparasitic instincts of a bird that had become habituated to the misguided food-offering habits of tourists. In July in Alaska, this inland-breeding gull had young to feed and I, through a lack of caution, had egg on my face.

Gulls typically breed and roost in large groups from hundreds to many thousands. Like egrets, gulls were once persecuted and killed for their feathers to fuel the fashion trade, with the result that some gull populations a century ago were only a fraction of the numbers we know today. In fact, Herring Gull was once extirpated as a breeding bird along the coast of Maine, where its keening cry is now iconic. Now protected and established as a breeder on small offshore islands, Herring Gulls thrive in Maine and elsewhere. Other gulls nest on Arctic cliffs, on shores of inland rivers and lakes, or in vegetation of freshwater and tidal wetlands. One species, Bonaparte's Gull, even nests in trees on the edges of the vast boreal forests, where it uses twig platforms lined with moss to deposit its eggs.

INTRO 5 Gull numbers in Daytona Beach, Florida, are estimated at close to one million birds in winter, many of which are Laughing Gulls. Larger gulls typically roost together, but a few different species can be found in this large flock. Hint: Ring-billed Gull and Herring Gull. Daytona Beach, Florida, January

INTRO 6 Bonaparte's Gulls are very comfortable perching in trees near their nest sites in boreal regions, where they survey the landscape. They often nest in these trees as well, using a nest of loose sticks to deposit their eggs. Churchill, Manitoba, June

INTRO 7 Herring Gull size and structure differences. Determining the sex of a gull is not possible in most gulls because of broad overlap in measurements between the larger males and smaller females. However, the very large bill, bulky body, and large head with a flat-topped crown on the immature bird (*right*) suggests a male Herring Gull. The 1st winter immature Herring Gull (*left*) has a tiny bill for this species, as well as a rounded crown and a slender, long-winged profile, which suggests a female. However, it is best to say "probable" because there can be extreme variation in body size, wing length, and bill size in the larger gulls. Sexing is best done with mated pairs of gulls, where even subtle differences in bill size, head shape, and body bulk are sometimes obvious because of the direct comparison. Florida, January (both birds)

Gulls are mostly monogamous and pair for life, and both members of the dyad care for the two to three young produced during a nesting cycle. If the young survive, adulthood is attained in two to five years, depending on the species. Once mature, gulls may lead long lives, resulting in a high proportion of adults in a population of a given species. While males and females have identical plumage, determining the sex of members of a breeding pair is sometimes possible, especially with larger, white-headed gulls. Males average larger than females and have slightly to distinctly bigger bills and larger heads with flatter crowns, differences more easily noted when birds are standing together, especially in mated pairs. These differences are often much harder to notice in the smaller gull species.

WHY THIS BOOK, NOW?

Since Roger Tory Peterson published the first field guide to birds in 1934, the identification process has been mostly plumage driven. With bird species whose plumage possibilities are limited to a manageable three to five options, this plumage-driven approach works fine. But gulls go through a series of plumages en route from their juvenile feather coating to adulthood, compounding the complexity of plumage-based identification. This paves the way for a more fundamental size- and structure-first approach, which is then augmented with plumage details to reach a more holistic ID conclusion.

This is a book that begged to be written, and for years I tried to get someone else to write it—a treatment of gulls

that presents them in the simplified, straightforward way in which we regard other bird groups, most notably raptors.

Ultimately, I came to understand that I was precisely the person to write this book, an epiphany prompted by two things: first, by my realization that I am better able to isolate and identify Lesser Black-backed Gulls at two hundred yards than at twenty feet; and second, by the complementary working relation I developed with author and photographer Kevin Karlson while working on a book treating North America's birds of prey. Kevin, coauthor of *Birding by Impression*, is the image-driven complement to my wordsmithing and has spent many years perfecting a way to simply explain a more complete, holistic ID process.

Also supporting my standing to write this book is that, while I am an experienced birder, I harbor no deep fascination with gulls. I accord gulls the same level of interest I bestow on any other bird group. What's more, my approach to identification hinges mostly on traits easily noted in the field, which are characteristics relating to size, shape, behavior, structural features, habitat, distribution, range, and direct comparative assessment. This approach has been honed by many years of hawk-watching, and it sidesteps, where feasible, the mostly plumage-centric approach embraced by gull mavens that differentiates species based largely on distinctions related to successional age classes or molt "cycles" (for example, 1st winter, 2nd winter, or 1st cycle, 2nd cycle, 3rd cycle). These determinations are for the most part feather deep.

INTRO 8 Herring Gull plumage variation by age. This photo array shows the variation in plumage in Herring Gulls from fresh juvenile plumage (*upper left*, New Jersey, late July) to full adult plumage (*lower left*, New Jersey, March). Immatures in the first two years are mostly brownish gray, with variable gray upper back feathers, while subadults and adults have gray upperparts and white underparts. Streaking on the head of the *lower middle* subadult is nonbreeding plumage (shown by adults and subadults), while the clean white head in the *lower left* photo is a breeding-plumaged adult. *Upper middle* (immature, 1st winter, Florida, November); *upper right* (immature, late 1st winter, New Jersey, May); *lower right* (immature/subadult, 2nd winter, New Jersey, April); *lower middle* (subadult, 3rd summer, New Jersey, July).

When I am regarding a Sharp-shinned Hawk or a Black-and-white Warbler, it never occurs to me to ask how old it is beyond perhaps immature or adult. Why must gulls be treated differently? If your answer is that differences relating to transitional molt cycles make such determinations possible, that is indeed commendable, but it still does not explain why such involved determinations are desirable or necessary if your objective is simply to pin a name to the bird.

If another answer is that a working knowledge of plumage and molt patterns is essential to the discovery of rare vagrants, I point out that geography has pretty much already solved this problem for you, putting distance between North American

INTRO 9 Vega and Yellow-legged Gulls. These two rare vagrants to North America were both formerly part of the Herring Gull complex, but recent decisions by worldwide ornithological societies determined that Yellow-legged Gull is now a separate species, while Vega Gull is still a subspecies of Herring Gull that breeds infrequently in extreme northwestern Alaska but is rare anywhere else in North America. Vega Gull, adult, *left*, Kuparuk, Alaska, July; Yellow-legged Gull, adult, *right*, Germany, June

birders and birds like Yellow-legged and Vega Herring Gulls. Geographic isolation is, after all, fundamental to speciation. Yellow-legged Gull (not to be confused with Yellow-footed Gull) is found in Europe, Asia, and North Africa. An entire ocean lies between North American birders and this large, white-headed gull. As for Vega Herring Gull, I have never dreamed of seeing one of these Siberian subspecies in the continental United States. And yes, some gull species do present a persistent pattern of vagrancy, but persistent is not the same as pervasive, and in every generation a few individuals are hardwired to take the path less followed. This is one of the key tenets of evolution.

I am by no means trying to diminish the difficulty inherent in gull identification—a challenge already complicated by the sheer number of variables. In North America, there are twenty-two regularly occurring gull species and a handful of regular to rare vagrants and remote breeders, many similarly sized and plumaged, with younger birds for the most part clad in shades of brown, black, and dirty white, while many adults share gray or black upperparts and white underparts with black highlights. Then, as noted, gulls go through a multiyear succession of plumages en route from their juvenile plumage to adulthood, displaying in these transitional years plumages that are often fundamentally similar to the corresponding plumages of closely related species in similar transitional age classes.

Further complicating gull identification is the protracted and asynchronized (nonconforming) feather replacement evidenced by individual birds of the same species, so that some individuals in an age class advance rapidly through a molt (feather replacement) cycle and other individuals undergo a more delayed molt, making textbook examples of birds in any particular age class difficult. This variation challenges field guide authors and artists to depict representative birds and not include the different plumage conditions possible at that same age cycle. We try to show these variations in plumage in photo arrays that depict the possible plumages seen in a given year of a gull's life.

Small wonder that mere mortals, when confronted by some feathered brown miscreant loafing on a beach, shrug and walk away, or, as one celebrated North American field guide author and tour leader pronounced when apprised of this book's title and ambition: "Good luck."

Other experienced birders, after hearing the title of this book, commented that "gulls **cannot** be simplified". Our response: Perhaps, but at least the process of identification **can be simplified**, and that is what we hope to accomplish in this book.

And while it does take a measure of hubris and perhaps naïveté to try to bring a measure of practical sense to the challenge of gull identification, the most important element may indeed be humility. Not every gull encountered in the field is going to be identified, or at least identified correctly. Acceptance of this makes it easier to move forward and focus on broad commonality and consolidation as opposed to getting lost in feather-splitting differences related to plumage and molt.

INTRO 10 This messy, worn, brownish gull is one of the reasons that many birders are disinclined to identify many gulls, or even look at them. However, geographic location and other features, such as size, body and head shape, bill size and shape, and bare parts and eye color, may help solve this puzzle. This brown miscreant was photographed in July in New Jersey, when many gulls are undergoing a replacement (molting) of their older, worn feathers and acquiring new, fresh feathers for the winter months. This is a 1st summer Herring Gull, with a pulled-taffy front head shape; a large, straight bill with a bulge near the tip; a compact body with uniform brownish plumage and a whitish head; a pinkish-based bill and pink legs; and a dark eye typical of 1st year Herring Gulls. New Jersey, July

American Oystercatcher losing food to Ring-billed Gull. Florida, January

BY PETE DUNNE AND
KEVIN T. KARLSON

Why, then, has gull identification been presented as such a feather-splitting challenge?

First, we humans seem obsessed by the need to find and classify differences, whether these have a bearing on species differentiation or not—that is, we like splitting hairs, or in this case, feathers. Fine and well; who doesn't enjoy a challenge? But gulls, because of their complex plumage array, simply overwhelm most observers.

Also exacerbating the challenge of gull identification is the avocational focus on finding birds that are outside their conventional range—that is, "rare birds." By placing added

value on finding Slaty-backed Gulls or Yellow-legged Gulls among the ranks of far likelier but similar species, we at times complicate the identification challenge. This almost mandates that plumage be the foundation of gull identification insofar as differences between similar species, particularly those found within an evolving species complex, are mostly feather deep.

But if we embrace the nature of probability and accept that rare and unusual species are unlikely to be encountered, the challenge presented by North American gulls becomes greatly simplified, reduced to telling Ring-billed Gull from Herring Gull and California Gull, birds whose size and structural differences do readily distinguish them. Instead of fighting probability by aspiring to find birds outside their normal

INTRO 11   Herring and Ring-billed Gulls comparison. This photo shows two common species in the *left* foreground. While plumage is very similar, Ring-billed (*center* and *left front center*) is a smaller gull with a smaller, more delicate bill; a more slender body with proportionally longer wings; greenish to yellow legs versus pink in Herring Gull; and a smaller head with a more rounded crown. The larger Herring Gull *behind* the Ring-billeds has a bill pattern similar to that of the Ring-billed, but this occurs only in subadult Herring Gulls in their 3rd year, or in adult birds that are not fully sexually mature. Another subadult Herring Gull is sleeping at *center right*. The standing Ring-billed Gull is a 2nd winter bird with gray, not yellow, eyes; greenish versus yellow legs; immature diffuse scallop-like markings on the breast; and black wings that lack white spots, as in adults. The very large, dark-backed gulls at the *right rear* that have a huge yellow bill with a red spot near the tip are adult Great Black-backed Gulls, which are the largest gulls in the world. The black, white, and gray granite–patterned gull at the *left rear* is an immature Great Black-backed Gull, which is also larger than Herring Gull, and much larger than Ring-billed. These three species are the most commonly seen gulls on beachfronts on the Atlantic coast. New Jersey, March

ABOUT THE TIME Pete decided to write this book, a woman attending one of his regular bird walks asked of a gull standing on the beach, one that he had identified as a "Lesser Black-backed Gull," whether it was a 1st cycle or 2nd cycle bird.

To which he replied: "I have no idea," having no more interest in the bird's age than he did in knowing what side of the colony it fledged from or how it voted in the last presidential election. All Pete knew or cared about was that it was a certifiable Lesser Black-backed Gull, a determination made on the basis of size (smaller than a Herring Gull); its lean, trim, athletic proportions; its long wings; and its mostly uniform darkish plumage; and supported by the bird's more petite black bill and punched-in-the-eye bruised look that most immature and subadult Lesser Black-backeds often show.

INTRO 12 Immature Lesser Black-backed and Herring Gulls. These two species are very similar as immatures, but Lesser Black-backed Gull (*left*, 1st winter) has a more slender, athletic body structure with longer wings, a more rounded crown, and a typically smaller black bill that shows a small pink spot only near the lower bill base. The immature late 1st winter Herring Gull (*right*) has a bold pink bill with a strongly demarcated black tip; a stockier body structure; a pulled-taffy look to its front face; shorter wings that extend only slightly past the tail; and an overall brownish-gray plumage compared to Lesser's colder, grayer upperparts and whiter head and upper breast. New Jersey, early April

Also figuring in his determination was the assurance that nonbreeding Lesser Black-backed Gulls, while uncommon to rare across much of North America, are a fairly common summer bird on the beaches of southern New Jersey and so are something to be expected, and the possibility of any other medium to smallish black-backed gull (for example, Kelp Gull or Black-tailed Gull) was remote.

Pete and his group then studied another Lesser Black-backed Gull, this one showing the charcoal-gray back of a subadult as it flew in off Delaware Bay. Ignoring all the other gulls loafing on the beach, the newcomer landed right next to the first Lesser Black-backed. Birds of a feather tend to stand together. Pete could not say how the newly arrived bird established the identity of the first from so far offshore, but he was fairly confident it did not study the bird's molt pattern. He suspects it made its assessment in much the same way he did: on the basis of size, shape, and overall plumage characteristics.

At a distance, immature Lesser Black-backed Gulls appear overall leaner, long winged, and white headed and have a darker back, whereas immature Herring Gulls are often larger, more compact, and more uniformly brown. Immature Great Black-backed Gulls are conspicuously bulkier, heavier billed, paler overall, and more distinctly black-and-white patterned above.

INTRO 13 Lesser and Great Black-backed Gulls and Herring Gull, immatures. This great comparative photo shows these three species together, with the noticeably smaller Lesser Black-backed Gull (*left*, 1st winter) standing directly in front of the immature 1st winter Great Black-backed Gull, which is much larger and has a bigger, more oval-shaped head; granite-patterned upperparts of gray, white, and black; a much heavier, mostly black bill; and thicker, pink legs. The 2nd winter Herring Gull (*right*) is between the other gulls in size and shows a heavier bill than the Lesser, with a strong pink base and an overall brownish-gray plumage. Note the plumper-breasted body shape on the Lesser compared to the more slender upper breast but overall stockier body shape on the Herring Gull. New Jersey, early April

range, we advocate embracing probability and letting it work *for you, not against you.*

What all this means is that if you are in Morro Bay, California, in November and looking at a large, dark-backed gull on the beach, you are almost certainly looking at an adult Western Gull, the expected large, dark-backed gull of California coastal regions. You need not anguish about a possible Slaty-backed Gull, unless this is a challenge you want to undertake. One look at the range maps will assure you that geographic distribution has mostly solved this problem for you.

By relying on probability as opposed to fighting it (that is, accepting that rare birds are rarely encountered), birders are free to adopt a more simplified approach to gull identification. After learning the regularly occurring gulls in a geographic area, birders can then spend time studying the possible expected rarities with a working familiarity of the common birds. As for seeing gulls that are commonly found in Asia, Europe, or South America, it is more satisfying to see them in their native context, where you will become very familiar with them because you will have a larger sample group to study.

We are in no way trying to diminish the challenge presented by gulls or the advantages inherent in a plumage-centric approach to identification. All we are saying is that approaching the challenge of gull identification in a less plumage-centric manner may greatly simplify that challenge.

We also do not present this book as the final word on gull identification. It is more nearly a starting point, one that purports to offer birders a measure of confidence as they explore this fascinating bird group.

As for hybrids (that is, birds sired by two separate species, most famously Western Gull and Glaucous-winged Gull), they are simply labeled as "challenging." They have a variety of possible plumage and structural features taken from both species to create a bird that may show bits and pieces of both adults' physical and plumage profiles, or that mostly resembles one adult physically but has some plumage features inconsistent with that species but consistent with the other.

When you encounter a puzzling gull that defies identification, it is up to you to decide whether you want to try to figure out what species it is. Or you can turn and walk away. Run, if you like. Birding is a personal sport or hobby, and you have the final say on your ID approach. If your curiosity is piqued, by all means use your field guide to work out the dilemma as best you can, or take a few photos and show them to some gull aficionados to get their opinions.

If dissecting hybrid gulls is a challenge that fascinates you, we enthusiastically encourage you to delve deeper. Buy a copy of *Gulls of the Americas*, by Jon Dunn and Steve Howell (2007, currently out of print), or Klaus Malling Olsen and Hans Larsson's *Gulls of North America, Europe and Asia* (2004). Also note that David Sibley, in the second edition of his excellent field guide (*The Sibley Guide to Birds*, 2014), dedicates two illustrated pages to the subject of hybridization, and that the balance of his gull section is well conceived, lucid, systematic, and eminently user-friendly.

POP QUIZ I know, I know, it's hardly fair to pop a quiz now, insofar as you have not even gotten into the book yet, but with gull ID, so much is about comparison. So let's give it a

INTRO 14 Western Gull and hybrid Western × Glaucous-winged Gull. Shown here is an adult Western Gull (*right*) and a paler gray-backed Glaucous-winged-type gull (*left*). The hybrid gull has the gray upperparts of Glaucous-winged, although maybe a bit darker than usual, and blackish outer wings (primaries) that are typical of Western and very unlike the pale gray outer wings on adult Glaucous-winged, which are usually the same shading as the upper back. The body structure is a bit stockier than that of a typical Glaucous-winged as well, which usually shows a more slender, tapered body shape (except for some very large males). Herring Gull is eliminated on the *left* bird by the pale left underwing; a dusky, not yellow, eye; and the gray inner primary shading. These two species interbreed freely, and in certain areas on the coast of northern Oregon and southern Washington, hybrids are easily found in good numbers. California, November

try. Try to identify the immature gulls flanking the adult dark-backed gull (see Intro 15).

The adult's charcoal-gray back with contrastingly blacker wing tips and bright yellow legs are traits consistent with Lesser Black-backed. A Great Black-backed Gull would have a darker black back whose shading matched its wing tips, and it would be noticeably larger and bulkier than any other gulls on the beach.

Now for the immature gulls. Here's a hint: the bird on the right is an immature Herring Gull. Herring Gull ranks among the most widespread large gulls in North America, but in some locations it can be uncommon to scarce. You have almost certainly seen this bird. Note the overall compact profile and mostly uniform and coarsely patterned brownish plumage. Also note the ill-defined pinkish-colored base to the long, slender bill. This species also has a thin face that recalls pulled taffy.

Now compare the Herring Gull to the slightly smaller, slimmer, longer-winged bird on the left that has a slender, straight, mostly black bill. Observe the overall colder grayish-brown upperparts, the whiter head, and the upper breast, which is noticeably less spotted and is generally paler than immature Herring's uniform dusky-brown underparts.

Compare the size of the "unidentified" bird to the adult Lesser Black-backed Gull. If you concluded that our mystery bird is anything but an immature Lesser Black-backed Gull, you are wrong, but look how far you have come already. Only yesterday you wouldn't have even looked at the bird, and now you've progressed to misidentifying it. You are now one misidentification closer to getting it right next time. Congratulations!

INTRO 15 Pop Quiz – These three gulls were photographed in New Jersey in early April on the Atlantic coast. Refer to the nearby text to see the ID criteria for these birds and answers as to what species they are.

A BASIC APPROACH TO GULL ID

For all their inherent challenges, gulls do present students of birds with ID advantages.

Most gulls are readily distinguishable as gulls, members of the family Laridae, simplifying the identification process by eliminating the need to initially assign an unidentified bird to a broader grouping or family.

Gulls are mostly large enough to note key differentiating traits relating to bill and head shape, eye color, leg color, and overall plumage characteristics, such as the color of the bird's upper back (silver gray vs. charcoal gray). In addition, gulls typically stay in the open, where they are easily viewed. Insofar as they are often found in places people frequent, gulls are mostly habituated to us and allow prolonged scrutiny and close approach.

Gulls are gregarious, often gathering in mixed-species flocks that facilitate direct comparison between known species and less familiar ones—a boon to identification and one that supports a dynamic comparative ID approach. Knowing the identity of a gull standing next to a mystery gull presents observers with a point of reference for size, shape (slender vs. bulky), bill shape, back color (silver gray vs. charcoal gray vs. black), and body shape (plump breasted vs. slender bodied).

While gulls do present an array of plumages typically arranged by successive molts (replacement of feathers), we find that these plumages—especially among the larger, white-headed gulls—may be combined into three broad, manageable age classes. These age classes correspond to the terms that birders commonly use to organize other bird groups, most notably raptors, according to plumage. These age designations are immature, subadult, and adult (breeding and nonbreeding).

Further clarification can then be added to these basic age groups, such as immature/juvenile, immature/1st or 2nd winter, or advanced or retarded immature or subadult. The term "advanced" refers to a plumage state at a particular age that

INTRO 16 Gulls are typically found in open spaces, such as this beachfront in Daytona Beach, Florida (January), and often in areas people frequent on a regular basis. Thus, they are somewhat habituated to humans and often allow close approach. As long as beach walkers maintain their steady pace, gulls will show no concern. Stop, however, and the gulls will move away. This is a great comparison of two very common gulls on this beach in winter and one uncommon one. The *front* gulls with a

charcoal back are nonbreeding Laughing Gulls, while the largest pale gray–backed bird on the *right* is an adult Herring Gull. Try to identify the medium-large subadult gull at *rear left*. Note the emerging charcoal-gray back feathers for a hint. Answer is in the appendix, p. 205.

INTRO 17 Gulls often rest in mixed flocks, which allow you to use a familiar gull to establish general size and shape reference points. The smallest charcoal-backed gulls at *left* are the ubiquitous, very common Laughing Gulls, and while most are in nonbreeding plumage here in Florida in late January, note the two birds with completely black breeding hoods. Molt timing is not always consistent in gulls, which creates ID problems for some feather-centric birders who minimize other important features, such as size and structure. For a fun ID quiz, try to identify the other gulls in the photo. Hint: there are six Herring Gulls of various ages in the photo and two other species that are uncommon to rare on this beach in winter. Note body size, bill size and shape, and overall plumage to help with your ID. Answers are in the appendix, p. 205.

is more complete than usual for a species, and the term "retarded" means that the plumage is less complete than usual at a particular age.

Most smaller to medium-sized gulls take only two years to reach full or mostly adult plumage, and these species typically replace their juvenile upper back feathers in early fall with adultlike grayish feathers. Larger gulls typically take three to four years to achieve full adult plumage, and most typically acquire various amounts of adultlike upperpart feathers in their second or third year.

Immatures: These gulls have a mostly brown or grayish-brown body. This group includes juvenile birds, 1st winter, and in some larger species, 2nd winter birds. Give or take a bit of sun bleaching, feather wear, and bill coloration, we find the basic commonality shared by these brown- and gray-bodied types (ages one to two years) unifying, compelling, and simplifying.

INTRO 18 These three photos show Herring Gull in immature plumages. The *left* photo shows a fresh juvenile bird (New Jersey, August); the *center* shows a 1st winter immature that has replaced its juvenile upper back feathers with postjuvenile ones in fall (Florida, January); and the bird on the *right* is a 1st summer (one-year-old) immature Herring Gull (New Jersey, May) with a strong pink bill and demarcated dark tip. Some 1st year Herring Gulls have a pink bill with a black tip, and many of these represent central- and western-breeding birds. We label all these birds as immatures because of the uniform brownish-gray plumage and because they lack adultlike feathers on the back, and we further qualify them by age as juveniles or 1st and 2nd winter.

INTRO 19 Smaller gulls reach full adult plumage sooner than larger gulls, and this transition is shown in these four photos of Laughing Gull. Juveniles (*upper left*, New Jersey, August) are mostly brownish overall with strong, buff fringes to the upperpart feathers. First winter birds are labeled as subadults because of the adultlike gray feathers on the upperparts and lower wing panel, and these birds now show white feathers on the head and breast (either by feather wear or replacement) and grayish markings on the head and underparts. Retained worn, brown juvenile feathers are present on the wing panel (wing coverts) and lower rear back feathers (tertials) (*upper right*, Florida, November). Second winter birds (not shown: see Laughing Gull account) are very similar to adults but lack the white outer wing (primaries) spots and have a dusky wash to the sides of the upper breast. Full breeding plumage is acquired by the 3rd year (*lower left*, New Jersey, May), and adult nonbreeding plumage by the 3rd winter (*lower right*, New Jersey, September).

Subadults: These gulls show a mix of adult and immature plumage traits—for example, variable amounts of gray or black adultlike upper back feathers but with touches or patches of worn immature plumage (typically concentrated in the wings and tail). Species reach their subadult plumage classification at different times. Some examples include Mew Gull and Ring-billed Gull in their 1st winter; California, Iceland, and Glaucous-winged Gulls in their 2nd winter; and many Herring and Western Gulls in their late 2nd and 3rd winter. Smaller gulls, such as hooded gulls, move from a distinct darkish juvenile plumage to a somewhat adultlike plumage by early fall, except for retained juvenile brownish wings and tertials. We call these subadults, even though they are in 1st winter plumage, because of their gray upper back feathers.

Adults: Adult gulls show fully gray, white (Ivory Gull), or black upperparts; white underparts (except for Heermann's Gull); and for the most part, leg, bill, and eye colors consistent with those of adult birds. The presence or absence of white spots on outer wing tips or a touch of vestigial black on the bill or tail of less advanced adult birds is disregarded and does not undermine the unifying commonality evidenced by birds in these advanced plumage states.

Since gulls replace their feathers because of wear at various times of the year and may appear disheveled and messy, you can often see these newer, more neatly arranged feathers molting in to replace the older ones.

Gulls can also be categorized by "age class" or "cycle," which is the term used in today's popular classification of plumage conditions typically seen in the initial successive years of a gull's life.

In any winter gull population, the season when northern-breeding gulls are widely distributed across the United States, the most dominant age classes will be immatures and adults, since the ranks of immatures are bloated by the year's crop of juveniles. Many immature gulls encountered in winter are fresh-plumaged 1st winter birds whose feathers are neatly arranged and textbook distinctive, their plumage unaffected by the sun bleaching, molt, and wear that affect older birds. Adults also show textbook traits, including unique eye, bill, and leg color. There are fewer confusing subadult birds in these flocks because they have been whittled down over several years by natural attrition. Once a gull matures, it may lead a long life (some up to thirty years or more), accounting for the greater number of adults.

INTRO 20 California Gull plumage variation by age. This photo array shows a 1st winter California Gull (*upper left,* California, February) in its immature/1st winter plumage. The upper back feathers are typical of this age, with a gray background as in adult feathers but with dark centers. These feathers have replaced the dark brown feathers of juvenile plumage. The *upper right* bird (California, February) is a subadult with mostly completely gray upperparts, except for some worn, brown immature feathers on the wing, and a bill that is grayish with a black spot near the tip instead of a yellow bill with a black and red spot, as in adults. The *lower right* photo shows a bird in mostly adult nonbreeding plumage, while the *lower left* photo shows a breeding adult. Both of the lower photos were taken on the same day in California in February, which suggests that the *lower right* bird may be either a 3rd year bird that shows mostly adult plumage but is less sexually mature than full adult birds, or a less sexually mature adult that has not acquired breeding plumage yet.

INTRO 21 Ring-billed Gull plumage variation. Ring-billed Gull is one of two medium-large, white-headed gulls (Mew Gull is the other) that acquire adultlike upper back feathers in their 1st winter. The photo array here shows the plumage changes and corresponding feather wear of Ring-billed Gull from fresh juvenile plumage (*upper left*, Rhode Island, late July) to adult breeding plumage (*lower right*, Florida, March) during a three-year period. *Upper center* shows an immature/subadult 1st winter Ring-billed in November with fresh gray, pale-fringed postjuvenile upper back feathers and more white feathers on the underparts and head than juvenile birds. The *upper right* photo shows a similar 1st winter bird in January with worn, brown juvenile wing covert and tertial feathers, and with a more streaked head and paler underparts than the *upper center* bird. The *lower left* photo shows a late 1st year bird in April (Florida) with worn and bleached wing feathers and gray feathers on the back without pale fringes, which have worn off. The *lower center* photo (Florida, January) shows a 2nd winter Ring-billed that is similar to an adult but has a greenish-yellow bill and legs versus the bright yellow of an adult (*lower right* bird). The eye is also grayish, versus the yellow of adults. This 2nd year bird (*lower center*) also shows a handful of juvenile-like dark scalloped feathers on the breast, similar to those of early 1st winter birds, and it lacks the white outer primary wing tips that are present on adult birds.

INTRO 22 Examples of molt (feather replacement). Gulls replace their feathers because of wear at various times of year, and you can often see these different feathers in subadult and immature gulls. The *left* subadult Lesser Black-backed Gull has acquired charcoal-shaded upper back feathers that contrast strongly with its immature plumage on the wing panel (New Jersey, July), while the messy immature 1st summer Herring Gull (New Jersey, August) has replaced its worn upper wing panel (lesser and median wing coverts) with new immature 2nd winter feathers in July that are uniform and neatly arranged compared to the irregular, worn, 1st winter feathers. Instead of replacing all their feathers at once, which would compromise their health and safety, birds replace groups of feathers at strategic times to allow for a smooth transition to the next age-related plumage condition.

GULLS AND GULL-LIKE BIRDS

GULLS Gulls are relatively small to large birds with a pro-portionally large head and a narrow, pointy, or hook-tipped bill and are found for the most part in or near freshwater and saltwater habitats. With webbed feet, they swim readily and sit buoyantly high on the water. Some species are nimble on land, such as Ring-billed Gull with its quick, mincing steps, and others walk with a rolling sailor's gait (Herring and Great Black-backed Gulls). Awkwardness notwithstanding, no other bird group seems so admirably suited to exploit both an aquatic and a terrestrial life.

Highly social, gulls may forage or loaf in large aggrega-tions on land or in water, often in mixed-species flocks. In the air, they typically soar high on down-bowed, slender, pointy-tipped wings. When landing on water, most plop to the surface rather than dive headfirst (as do terns). On land, they lift off with a short, running, wing-flapping start. Typ-ical plumages are brown, grayish brown, and dirty white in younger birds, and gray, black, and white in adults.

Try to identify all the gulls in this photo quiz. Answers are in the appendix, p. 205.

TERNS Terns are small to medium-sized waterbirds that are smaller than the medium to large gulls, other than the large Royal and very large Caspian Terns. Sharing with gulls basic color and pattern similarities (a gray back and white underparts), most terns are on the whole more slender and paler overall, with black on the head restricted to the cap. Bills are mostly pointy and narrow and lack a hooked tip, except for several larger species that have thicker, heavier bills, and in flight the wings are acutely angled backward, not bowed downward. The tail of a few tern species is long and often splayed, extending slightly to or noticeably past the folded wings of standing birds (Roseate Tern; see Intro 24, below).

As social as gulls, terns may roost with similarly sized gulls on beaches. Even more than gulls, terns are bound to aquat-ic environments, where they plunge-dive headfirst into the water for fish or swoop low and snap prey from the land or water without landing. When taking off, terns loft into the air without a running start. Flight is more active and nimbler than that of most gulls, and they walk reluctantly.

INTRO 23 Quiz photo: Assorted gulls in early September in Queens, New York. This group of gulls was photographed at the Jamaica Bay Wildlife Refuge in New York City and represents the most common gull species found near coastal areas of the eastern United States. You have encountered all of these gulls in the introduction, so they should be familiar to you. Answers are in the appendix, p. 205.

INTRO 24 Terns are small to medium-sized close relatives of gulls that are even more attached to aquatic habitats. The *left* bird is the very large nonbreeding Caspian Tern, which is larger than the Ring-billed Gull and about the same size as a small California Gull. Breeding Roseate Tern (*center*) is a slender tern whose tail extends noticeably past the folded wings on standing birds. Nonbreeding Forster's Tern (*right*) is a medium-sized tern that is commonly found in marsh habitats.

INTRO 25 Terns have the same shading as many gulls, but their wings are more slender and pointed. Caspian Tern (*left*) shows the dark cap of breeding plumage, while Sandwich Tern (*center*) has the white forecrown of nonbreeding birds (this is a postjuvenile bird [Texas, September] that lacks the yellow bill tip and shows black markings from juvenile plumage on its wings). The Gull-billed Tern (New York, August) (*right*) is a freshly molted 1st winter/postjuvenile bird that closely resembles a nonbreeding adult, which would have an all-black bill. In breeding plumage, both this and the Sandwich Tern have black caps.

JAEGERS AND SKUAS These brigands of the open sea have gull-like bodies but pointy, tern-like wings. The bill is short and hook tipped like that of some gulls. Some jaegers are uniformly dark and recall juvenile Laughing and Heermann's Gulls. Others show plumage patterns similar to those of many gull species: dark above and whitish below (these light-morph jaegers also typically show white patches on the outer wing, except for Long-tailed Jaeger). Some tails on nonbreeding

INTRO 26 Jaegers are pelagic birds that spend much of their lives at sea, coming to land to breed in Arctic tundra habitats. An assortment of the three jaeger species (which are called "skuas" outside of North America) is shown here. *Top panel, from left*: Pomarine Jaeger, light morph; Parasitic Jaeger, light morph; and Parasitic Jaeger, dark morph. All these birds were photographed in breeding season (*top left*, Texas, May; *top center* and *top right*, Alaska, June). *Lower panel, from left*: Long-tailed Jaeger, juvenile (New Jersey, September); Parasitic Jaeger, adult light morph (Alaska, June); and Pomarine Jaeger, adult light morph (North Carolina, April).

jaegers are like those of gulls (Pomarine Jaeger), but all have much longer tails in the breeding season that project well past the folded wings on standing birds (see Intro 26, jaeger composite).

Outside Arctic breeding environments, jaegers typically forage well offshore in marine environments (many gulls are mostly coastal and typically remain within sight of land). Jaegers often pursue terns and gulls to steal fish. In mixed feeding flocks, the jaeger will be the pursuing bird. Caution: several dark-bodied gull species (especially juvenile Laughing Gull and Heermann's Gull) also chase other gulls and terns to pirate fish and may be confused with jaegers.

BOOBIES AND GANNET   These are large seabirds (most larger than gulls) with a tapered face; a long, strongly pointed bill; a pointy tail; and long, pointed wings that are angled backward or held stiffly straight in gliding birds. These birds are often seen flying single file, low over the water. Birds in this grouping plunge-dive for fish, often from great heights, or arrow into the water headfirst. Diving birds fully submerge themselves under the water and often swim quickly after fish (boobies), something most gulls do not do.

SHEARWATERS   Shearwaters are medium-sized, slender-winged seabirds specialized to glide low just above the water's surface on narrow-set wings, flapping sparingly and soaring rarely. Shearwaters are highly social and are generally found far from shore. In migration, flocks of some shearwater species may number in the many thousands and sometimes in the hundreds of thousands. Birds resting on the water often sit in densely packed "rafts." Shearwaters differ from gulls in their slender and straighter-winged profile, low gliding flight with spare wing beats, and tendency to dive for prey.

INTRO 27   Boobies are large seabirds that spend most of their lives in ocean habitats. *From left*: adult Brown Booby (Grand Cayman, March), immature/juvenile Brown Booby (Florida, May), and adult Masked Booby (Cuba, January).

INTRO 28   Northern Gannets are larger than boobies and are often seen closer to shore. They also breed in cold northern waters, while boobies are tropical species. Shown here are a 1st winter Northern Gannet (*left*, Florida, January) and a subadult (Florida, January).

FULMARS Fulmars are like stocky, large-headed shearwaters that glide on stiff, straight wings and are also found in marine environments. The plumage of light-morph Northern Fulmar resembles that of many large adult gulls, but the bill of fulmars is stubby and the wings are held straight, not crooked downward, as in gulls.

OSPREY This unique, crook-winged, black-and-white bird of prey is often mistaken for a gull but is broader winged and enters the water for prey talons first. Showing slotted wing tips (with individual outer feathers splayed), Ospreys are distinguished from gulls, whose outer flight feathers are fused to a point. Ospreys also carry fish in their talons, while gulls carry food in their bills.

INTRO 29 Shearwaters are highly pelagic seabirds that are often seen gliding low over waves on stiff wings. Shown here are Great Shearwater (*left*, Maine, June) and Galapagos Shearwater (*right*, Galapagos, October), which was formerly a subspecies of Audubon's Shearwater.

INTRO 30 Fulmars are pelagic seabirds that resemble gulls in shape and plumage. Shown here is a light-morph Northern Fulmar (New York, February).

INTRO 31 Ospreys are large birds of prey that are found near aquatic habitats, where they feed exclusively on fish. Their long, angled wings that bow down when they glide are very similar to the wings of some gulls, and thus Ospreys are often mistaken for gulls at a distance. Both photos were taken in New Jersey in October.

SPECIES ACCOUNTS

SIZE AND SEX GUIDELINES FOR GULLS

Two measurements for the length and wingspan of a gull species in the following accounts reflect variation in the size of gulls, with adult males having the largest measurements and 1st year females the smallest. However, a great deal of overlap occurs between the upper and lower measurements of gulls shown here, so exercise extreme caution when trying to sex a gull.

Noted gull authorities Klaus Malling Olsen and Hans Larsson, in their excellent book *Gulls of North America, Europe, and Asia*, give the following advice on this issue: "In gulls, males are larger with a heavier, deeper bill and flatter head than females. The larger the species, the more obvious the difference is. Also, first years are smaller than older birds. Therefore, in a given species, a first year female may look unexpectedly small compared to an adult male (this difference is again most obvious in the larger species) . . . Only by direct comparison—best in pairs—is sexing advisable".

Size measurements are from *Gulls of the Americas* (Howell and Dunn), while wingspan measurements are from *Gulls of North America, Europe, and Asia* (Olsen and Larsson).

The italicized sentence found just below the heading of each species account is Pete's lighthearted personal view, which includes humor, irony, and other nontraditional ID criteria.

Ring-billed Gull by John McNamara

BONAPARTE'S GULL,
1st winter

SMALL TO MEDIUM-SIZED GULLS and HOODED GULLS

Most of the birds in this group breed in northern or interior regions and winter mainly coastally (except for Laughing Gull, which also breeds in southern Gulf coast locations, the Caribbean, and the Gulf of California in Mexico; and Heermann's Gull, which also breeds in the Gulf of California).

LAUGHING GULL *Leucophaeus atricilla*

SIZE **15–17 inches long** WINGSPAN **37–47 inches**

It's the medium-sized, charcoal gray–backed, black-headed gull with the last of your boardwalk hot dog in its mouth and three noisy accomplices standing nearby. (PD)

PROFILE This lanky gull stands with a horizontal profile and shows *black wing tips that are acutely pointed and extend well beyond the tail. A long, slender bill droops near the tip. Long, typ*ically black legs are set moderately forward, with some birds showing dull to fairly bright red legs in the breeding season. The dark hood is replaced by a mostly white head with a dark ear patch and scattered dark markings on the crown in winter.

On beaches and in the water, they tend to gather in tightly bunched monotypic flocks away from larger gulls. In mixed-species flocks, Laughing Gulls often segregate to one side. Very agile and aerial, this species is adept at snapping insects out of the air and may gather in wheeling numbers over

LAUGHING GULL 1 Breeding adult pair. Classic adult Laughing Gulls in breeding plumage. Laughing is a medium-sized gull that takes three years to reach full breeding plumage. It is a slender, long-winged gull with a relatively long bill that droops slightly near the tip and can be mostly reddish in breeding birds or mostly black with a reddish tinge. It has charcoal-gray upperparts, a black hood, white eye arcs, and a clean white nape and underparts. Black outer primary tips may or may not show small to large white spots. While it is very difficult to sex single birds, a mated pair usually shows the larger size, moderately bulkier structure, and slightly larger bill of the male (*left*). Copulation confirmed the sexes. Florida, early May

LAUGHING GULL 2 First year plumage variation. This photo array shows the changes in plumage that a typical Laughing Gull undergoes in its 1st year from early August to the following summer, and then to its fresh 2nd winter plumage. **TOP:** Laughing Gulls transition rapidly from juvenile plumage (*left*, early August) to early 1st winter plumage (*right*, November), and then to late 1st winter plumage by early spring (*lower left*, April). The *center* photo shows gray 1st winter feathers already starting to molt in by early September. **BOTTOM FROM LEFT:** late 1st winter (April); worn 1st summer (New Jersey, July); 2nd winter (New Jersey, September) showing gray nape (white in adults) and a dusky wash on the sides of the upper breast and flanks that is absent on adults. Franklin's Gull does not typically show this dusky wash on the nape, upper breast, and flanks but instead has clean white feathering in these areas. Some early 1st winter Franklin's may show a dusky wash to the sides of the upper breast, however. Second year Laughing Gull typically shows no white spots on wing tips, but neither do some adult birds.

LAUGHING GULL 3 If books could reproduce sound, you'd have to close the book. The din of adult Laughing Gulls foraging on horseshoe crab eggs on Delaware Bay in May is deafening. Note the absence of juveniles, which in Cape May at this time are still in the formative process. First summer, sexually immature Laughing Gulls are absent as well, since many remain at wintering areas in their 1st summer. New Jersey, May

LAUGHING GULL 4 This adult Royal Tern is about to be relieved of its fish by this 2nd winter Laughing Gull (or not, if it has experienced this before). This Laughing Gull has at this point in its young life already learned the fine art of piracy. Usually it takes two or three Laughing Gulls to steal a meal from an agile Royal Tern, as the adolescent Laughing Gull learned the hard way. The all-brown juvenile Laughing Gulls are sometimes mistaken for jaegers when they engage in this type of piracy, but they are not as powerful and agile as jaegers. Florida, April

marshes and uplands when an insect hatch is in progress. They are also a threat to coastal tern colonies and beach-nesting shorebirds, since they can swoop in and grab an egg or small chick before the defending birds can react to their approach. The bird's loud, raucous (laughing) call is iconic, as much a part of a visit to coastal beaches and marshes as the sound of surf and the tang of salt-laden air. The sound of feeding flocks approaches the level of a din. Breeding colonies are noisy, even at night.

Skilled foragers, Laughing Gulls are adept at plucking food from human hands, whether the morsel is offered or not, and they seem to know all about picnic baskets, potato chip bags, and their contents. Very social and vocal, Laughing Gulls also forage offshore in large aggregations, usually within sight of land, where noisy feeding flocks hover and wheel over schools of baitfish. They commonly pursue other gulls and seabirds to steal food.

STATUS AND DISTRIBUTION This is a common, almost iconic gull of coastal environs and is the default "black-headed" summer gull of the Atlantic and Gulf coasts. They also frequent the southern coastal beaches and Gulf coast in winter. Northern-breeding birds typically migrate south no later than early December, and many others leave from October onward.

While most commonly found on sandy beaches, Laughing Gull also frequents tidal wetlands, plowed fields, parks, and picnic areas. You may also share your hotel swimming pool with these birds in coastal areas with warm climates as they drop by for a drink or a swim. Though mostly coastal year-round, individuals are occasionally found well inland, most commonly on freshly turned agricultural land, landfills, and the parking lots of food outlets.

ADULT BREEDING The back is all charcoal gray, with a black head and black wing tips, commonly showing small, inconspicuous to obvious white spots. Neck and underparts are gleaming white. Dark eyes are surrounded by a narrow to larger oval broken white orbital ring. The slender, drooping,

LAUGHING GULL
Rare to casual elsewhere in the United States and Mexico.

■ resident, breeds locally
■ seasonal, breeds locally
■ nonbreeding occurrence (can be year-round)

LAUGHING GULL 5 Late winter flock. When not foraging, Laughing Gulls often cluster in monotypic flocks on the high beach. This group of adults and subadults (two in 2nd winter plumage) includes two birds with breeding hoods and many birds transitioning into breeding plumage. The timing of transition to breeding plumage varies greatly in this species, with some birds acquiring full dark hoods in late January and others not until April. Note the two birds with grayish napes, slightly worn wing panels (wing coverts), and a dusky wash on the sides of the upper breast (2nd winter plumage). Florida, early March

LAUGHING GULL 6 Juvenile Laughing Gull (*left*) and nonbreeding adults are biding their time on the Atlantic shore of Stone Harbor, New Jersey, in early September. This is a typical scene on a late-summer beachfront as these gulls are preparing to migrate south in a few months or less. Bonus points for finding the three Ring-billed Gulls (hint: the ones with paler gray backs). The shorebirds? Sanderling in *front*; Western Sandpipers at *left* and *center*.

LAUGHING GULL 7 Adult breeding Laughing Gulls show a slender bill with a drooping tip and long, angled wings that have a relatively broad inner half and a slender, tapered outer half with a pointed tip. Note the extensive black on the outer wings, visible above and below, and the small white primary tips, which are larger and more prominent on Franklin's Gull. The white tail and rump on Laughing Gull (*right* photo) differ from Franklin's grayish outer tail and contrasting white rump. Legs may be dark red or blackish. New Jersey, May

LAUGHING GULL 8 Courtship display and copulation. Evidently a successful courtship display, where the birds throw their heads back and call loudly with characteristic laughing notes. Royal and Sandwich Terns behind the copulating pair seem unimpressed. Texas, April

LAUGHING GULL 9 Nonbreeding adults show a limited shadowy band across the head and a slender drooping bill tip. A whitish nape and underparts are typical in adult nonbreeding birds. Note the dusky flight feathers that contrast with the clean white underwing, and the extensive black shading on the outer wing above and below. Overall profile on standing birds is lanky. Texas, November (*left*); Florida, January (*center* and *right*)

LAUGHING GULL 10 Laughing and Franklin's Gulls comparison. **TOP PHOTO** shows breeding birds of both species, with the Laughing Gull (*center*) showing larger overall size; longer, more pointed wings; a larger, more drooping bill; longer legs; less prominent white spots on exposed primary wing tips; and smaller white eye arcs. Franklin's has a more compact body shape with shorter, more rounded primaries. This Franklin's shows a pink blush on the breast, which is often seen on breeding birds. For an expert-level quiz, can you identify the sleeping shorebird? Focus on the size compared to the gulls and the location and date of the photo to help with your ID. Answer is in appendix, p. 205. Texas, April. **BOTTOM PHOTO** shows adult nonbreeding Laughing Gulls (*center and right*) with only a shadow of Franklin Gull's dark rear hood, but since some Laughing Gulls will show a similar dark hood beginning in late January, it is more important to note obvious physical differences. Laughing Gull is larger overall with a bigger head; longer, pointier wings; and a noticeably longer, heavier, drooping bill. Adult Franklin's has larger, bolder white outer primary tips and eye arcs. In direct comparison to the other Laughing Gull, it is easy to see the larger size, bulkier body, bigger head, and heavier bill on the *center* Laughing Gull, which suggest a male, but nothing definite. Note the dark bills on both nonbreeding species compared to the reddish ones in breeding birds. Texas, November

reddish bill of breeding adults may appear black at a distance. In flight, *birds appear very slender winged and long tailed.* Legs range from black to reddish in breeding birds. White spots on outer primary wing tips are either very small or relatively large. The tail and rump of adult Laughing Gull are fully white, with adult Franklin's Gull having a pale grayish tail and white rump.

ADULT NONBREEDING (includes 2nd winter) These charcoal gray–backed birds show a shadowy impression of a partial hood in late summer, which changes to a white head creased by a single or double dark band crossing the crown and a dark ear patch that resembles earmuffs by September. *Incoming breeding head feathers form a partial rear helmet in January or February, which strongly recalls the black head pattern of nonbreeding Franklin's Gull (so use extreme caution with this similar plumage feature from January to March).* Legs are typically dark in nonbreeding birds. White primary wing tips range from small to large, with 2nd winter birds typically having limited to no white in the primaries.

LAUGHING GULL 11 Adult breeding, with odd color on bare parts. Don't let differences in the color of bare parts distract you from more important physical features and overall plumage patterns. This adult Laughing Gull has a bright orange (not dull reddish) bill and legs, which is an aberration of pigment distribution to these bare parts. Everything else points to Laughing Gull, so go with the obvious physical and plumage features and disregard the odd bill and leg color. Bare part color aberration occurs fairly regularly with Laughing Gull, but it is not often as bright as on this bird. Texas, late April

LAUGHING GULL 12 Laughing Gull behavior. A juvenile Laughing Gull (*left* photo, brown bird, New Jersey, August) is learning that this adult transitioning into nonbreeding plumage is no longer the meal ticket it used to be. Note the very slender, tapered, long-winged profile on the juvenile bird, which needs to fatten up before migrating south for the winter. A 2nd winter Laughing Gull (*right*) purports to salvage some stray fish scraps from this Brown Pelican as it siphons its catch through the porous membrane of its lower pouch. Texas, September (*right*)

Among gulls on Atlantic and Gulf coast beaches, Laughing Gull's charcoal-gray upperparts are conspicuously darker than those of adult Ring-billed and Herring Gulls, but not as black as those of Great Black-backed Gull. The charcoal-gray back is very close to the shading of the distinctly larger, yellow-legged subadult and adult Lesser Black-backed Gulls, which do not show a dark hood but instead have light to dense dark streaking on the head and nape in winter. While full breeding adult Lesser Black-backeds are usually absent from Atlantic and Gulf coast beaches in summer, subadult Lesser Black-backed Gulls are fairly common in July and August when Laughing Gulls are seen in large numbers, and these have a mostly white head with sparse dark streaks.

IMMATURE (juvenile) Juvenile Laughing Gulls have brown upperparts with strong buff fringes and a brownish head, neck, and upper breast that contrast with a whitish lower belly and under tail. Deep black wing tips contrast with the overall brown plumage, and a broad black band

LAUGHING GULL 13 Immatures. This photo array shows a fresh juvenile (*left*, New Jersey, August) and an early September juvenile (*center*, New Jersey) with a cooler overall plumage tone resulting from feather wear and sun bleaching. Older feathers on the upperparts have worn, and their rich, golden edges from fresh juvenile plumage are now muted and grayer. Note the overall slender wings as well as the dark tail that contrasts strongly with the white rump. The *right* photo (Texas, April) shows an immature/subadult that has replaced many feathers (mostly visible on upperparts) and has a whiter head and dusky to brownish wash on the nape, upper breast, and flanks.

trims the white tail. The slender, drooping bill and the legs are dark.

Juvenile birds begin their partial molt (feather replacement) to 1st winter/subadult plumage starting in late summer to early fall (depending on location) by molting small numbers of pale gray feathers on the upper back (see *upper middle* photo in Laughing Gull 2). A grayish upper back is typically acquired by midfall, and the brown head begins to show the white feathers of nonbreeding subadults at this time as well.

SUBADULT (includes 1st winter and 1st summer) First winter birds show a distinct gray upper back and worn brownish wings and tertials (feathers on rear upper back closest to wings; see Intro 19) by late fall, and by December, the brown head feathers are replaced by a sparse blackish rear helmet and a white forehead and throat with sprinkles of grayish feathers.

By spring, the head is either mostly white with a dark gray ear patch and thin gray streaks on the rear crown and nape, or more heavily streaked in more advanced birds, while the upper back and lower rear wing panel are mostly solid gray.

LAUGHING GULL 14 Immatures (juvenile/1st winter). When human beach traffic is high, birds also cluster and wait for the dinner bell in open water, as these juvenile birds are doing in Cape May Point, New Jersey, in September. The absence of adults is understandable. After a summer of parenting, the adults are all offshore, searching for baitfish. If they are successful, the juveniles will join them in the feeding frenzy in the Atlantic Ocean or adjacent Delaware Bay. Note the gray backs and dusky wash to the necks and sides of the breast on some of these juvenile birds already transitioning to 1st winter plumage. New Jersey, September 22

The head is black to grayish capped from mid-January onward, recalling the restricted black head pattern of non-breeding Franklin's Gull (see Laughing Gull 2, *upper right* photo taken on December 29). The long, slender bill is drooped and blackish. Black primary wing tips lack the white spotting of adults, including most 2nd year birds.

LAUGHING GULL 15 Adults and 1st winter. These three breeding adults and one 1st winter Laughing Gull are following a ferry in Texas waters in April, where passengers attract them by offering french fries or other tasty morsels of food. Note that the late 1st winter bird has replaced its secondaries (shorter inner wing feathers) at this early date, suggesting a nonmigratory local bird. Texas, April

LAUGHING GULL 16 Laughing Gull with Black Skimmer. Direct comparison with the unmistakable Black Skimmer allows you to save a mental picture of the general size and shape of Laughing Gull. The skimmer, which is now grouped in the same family as gulls and terns (Laridae), is more capped than hooded and lacks eye arcs. Its bill is also quite distinctive. Florida, late April

FRANKLIN'S GULL *Leucophaeus pipixcan*

SIZE **13.25–15 inches long**   WINGSPAN **33–36 inches**

It's the small, compact, inland-breeding, black-headed gull with the grasshopper in its mouth, and the gull that takes the "sea" out of "seagull." However, while Franklin's is mostly seen at inland locations from spring to fall, it spends four to five months in coastal marine habitats in winter off the coast of western South America. (PD)

PROFILE   This small, gregarious, petite-billed, and black-headed breeder of the western interior *suggests a smaller, stockier Laughing Gull, with a shorter, straighter bill, shorter legs, and conspicuously shorter, round-tipped wings.* Franklin's also has a rounder head with more prominent white eye arcs and boldly patterned black outer wings with large white spots (mirrors) near the tip of the outer primaries (adults). Franklin's are agile gulls, able to hop over obstacles and perch on cattails.

During the breeding season, they hawk insects over marshes, and in migration often forage on tilled agricultural land. When foraging for aquatic insects on lakes, they behave like a swimming phalarope, plucking insects from the surface. In some locations, migrating flocks may number in the thousands. Franklin's Gulls forage on beaches, inshore waters, lakeshores, and dry or flooded fields, and they nest in freshwater marshes. They are often found in small homogeneous flocks, but inland they may mix with California Gulls. In migration on the Gulf coast, they often roost and rest with Laughing Gulls.

STATUS AND DISTRIBUTION   Common in appropriate habitats, it breeds for the most part in small to very large colonies in inland marshes and lakes on the prairies, in the Great Basin, and in the northern Rocky Mountains.

Breeding colonies may number in the hundreds, or as many as twenty-five thousand pairs, which occurred at the Lake Alice National Wildlife Refuge in North Dakota in 2000 (North Dakota Game and Fish Department website, 2017).

During migration, Franklin's is common to abundant from August to October through its main migratory corridor south through the Great Plains, and also along the Texas lowland coastal areas from mid-October through November (*Gulls of the Americas*, Howell and Dunn, 2007). Migratory

broad white tertial tips

FRANKLIN'S GULL 1 Adult breeding. Note the overall compact physical profile, which is accentuated by the shortish wings with rounded tips. Franklin's also has a relatively small, mostly straight bill and short legs. The prominent spotting on its primaries combined with the white tertial tips (feathers visible just above the folded wings) gives them a banded appearance. Pinkish blush on the underparts is typical on many breeding Franklin's, and bold white eye arcs are more prominent than the thinner ones of the similar but larger, lankier Laughing Gull. Texas, April

FRANKLIN'S GULL 2 Adults breeding (*left*); adults nonbreeding (*right*). In the *left* photo, note Laughing Gull's (*left* bird) larger size and longer, pointier-winged profile. Also apparent in both photos is Laughing Gull's longer, heavier, and more drooping bill and Franklin's wider, more prominent white eye arcs; broader white tertial tips; and larger, bolder, white primary tips. The black hood is more restricted on breeding Franklin's, but fuller and more conspicuous on nonbreeding adult Franklin's. The nonbreeding Laughing Gull (*right* in *right* photo) is bulkier overall, with a larger head and noticeably bigger bill than the breeding Laughing Gull in the *left* photo, which reflects variation in size and structure. Texas, April (*left* photo); November (*right*)

FRANKLIN'S GULL 3 Franklin's and Laughing Gulls flock. Given the tight bunching and angled posture of some birds, the usually obvious size difference between these species is not immediately apparent. Better to focus here on Franklin's fuller, darker rear caps; more prominent white spotting on the wings (adults); and the broader, more prominent white eye arcs. The *front center* Franklin's is in fresh 1st winter plumage and shows neatly arranged, dark-centered feathers in the wing panel (wing coverts); a grayish wash on the sides of the upper breast (usually absent or much reduced in 1st winter Franklin's); and smaller white spots on the visible flight feathers (primaries). Adult Franklin's have a whiter hind neck compared to Laughing Gull, and bolder white eye arcs. Franklin's also has a noticeably smaller, straighter bill, which you can directly compare in the two birds in the *lower right* corner. Can you identify the bird above the *front center* Franklin's with its head tucked in the center of the photo? Answer is in the appendix, p. 205. Texas, November

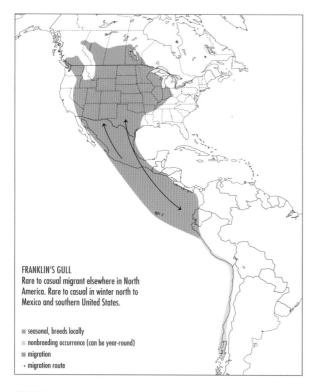

FRANKLIN'S GULL
Rare to casual migrant elsewhere in North America. Rare to casual in winter north to Mexico and southern United States.

- seasonal, breeds locally
- nonbreeding occurrence (can be year-round)
- migration
→ migration route

flocks at this coastal Texas location can number in the many thousands, and Kevin witnessed a flock of over six thousand birds at South Padre Island, Texas, in early November 2003. Migration through the interior is often spread out, with migrating birds widely dispersed until larger numbers gather at nighttime roosts on bodies of water. Winter range is primarily coastal regions of western South America.

This species has experienced a notable decline over the last fifty years (78 percent) according to North American Breeding Bird Atlas data, but population numbers and concerns vary according to individual research papers.

ADULT BREEDING Shows an all-black hood with *prominent white eye arcs*. White underparts are often blushed with pink. Folded wing tips show a bold, banded, black-and-white pattern. In flight, black outer wings are separated from the gray upper wings by a band of white. Pete has noted that in midsummer when adults are molting their primaries, wing tips on standing birds appear all white. Legs range from blackish to reddish.

ADULT NONBREEDING (combines 1st summer, 2nd winter, and nonbreeding adult) Birds in these age groups

FRANKLIN'S GULL 4 Franklin's and Laughing Gulls. In late fall, Franklin's may be seen in small to very large migratory flocks. This flock shows mostly adult Franklin's at a staging area on South Padre Island, Texas, with a number of nonbreeding Laughing Gulls whose longer, broader, and more pointed, tapered wings lack the bold white spots on the wing tips of adult Franklin's. Note that 1st winter Franklin's lack bold white spots on the wing tips and also show a dark tail band. They also lack the white band inside the black wing tips on adult Franklin's. A few 2nd winter Franklin's are also present, and they show gray upper wings with reduced white primary tips. The grayish tail with white outer feathers on Franklin's contrasts with a pale rump compared to Laughing Gull's all-white tail and rump. Try to find the Laughing Gulls in the photo. The number may surprise you. Also try to pick out the nonbreeding Forster's Tern. Answer photo is shown in the appendix, p. 205.

FRANKLIN'S GULL 5 Breeding (*left*); nonbreeding (*center* and *right*). These photos show the compact body shape and slender wings of this species as well as the dark hood of breeding adults and the rear-helmeted appearance of nonbreeding birds. The breeding bird's (*left*) upper wing shows the prominent white band that separates the black outer primary tips and the charcoal-gray inner wings, which are not present in Laughing Gull. Also evident are Franklin's Gull's mostly pale underwings. The bold white primary tips on adult Franklin's are larger than in Laughing Gull, and a grayish tail with white outer feathers that contrasts with a white rump on Franklin's differs from Laughing Gull's all-white tail and rump. Texas, April (*left*); November (*center* and *right*)

show charcoal-gray upperparts with a well-defined rear black cap with sparse white streaks *that resembles a partial helmet*, not the full hood of breeding adults.

IMMATURE (juvenile) Full juvenile plumage is held for only several months (July–September) and includes brownish upperparts with buff fringes; a brownish, lightly streaked nape; and contrasting black wing tips with small white spots. A blackish-brown partial rear hood contrasts with a white forecrown and throat, and a strong, broken white orbital ring is very evident. Neck and sides of upper breast are mottled and washed with brown shading. Tail is white with a black terminal band, *but the outer tail feathers are all white, which separates it from Laughing Gull, whose tail band is black from edge to edge in young birds.*

SUBADULT (1st winter) First winter birds differ from juveniles by having a gray upper back similar to that of adults,

FRANKLIN'S GULL 6 Franklin's and Laughing Gulls, adults nonbreeding. Franklin's (*front*) is smaller overall and has a more compact profile and a shorter bill. The darker and more extensive rear cap of Franklin's is obvious, but this partially hooded appearance can be similar to that of some Laughing Gulls from late January onward as they begin their molt into breeding plumage. White primary tips are almost similar in size between these two birds, which is not usually the case. Franklin's typically has larger, bolder white tips. Florida, January

FRANKLIN'S GULL 7 First winter/subadult. Even though all these birds are in their 1st winter, they are showing gray upper back feathers similar to those of adults, but they still have their worn, brown, juvenile wing feathers and tertials (feathers showing on the middle of the lower back on perched and swimming birds). The underparts on 1st winter Franklin's are mostly white and cleaner than in Laughing Gull, which has a strong gray wash to the upper breast and flanks, including many 2nd winter Laughing Gulls. Note the bold, wide, white eye arcs and blackish rear cap, which resembles a partial helmet (slightly grayer markings on 1st winter Laughing Gull are more restricted to smudges on the rear of the head but become similar after they molt in dark crown feathers from January onward). White spots on primary wing tips are much reduced or absent on 1st winter Franklin's. Small bills are also helpful for your ID. New Jersey, February (*left*); Texas, November (*center* and *right*)

FRANKLIN'S GULL 8 Nonbreeding and 1st winter with Laughing Gull. In migration, Franklin's Gulls are quite gregarious and are often seen in flocks numbering from a handful to many thousands of birds. This photo shows two 1st winter Franklin's in the foreground (*center* and *right*), with a much larger, paler nonbreeding Laughing Gull in the *rear upper left*. Note the smaller size; more slender wings; and more complete rear hoods on Franklin's. Also note the bolder outer primary white wing tips on the adult Franklin's Gulls. First winter Franklin's show an overall brownish-gray upper wing with strong black outer primaries and virtually no bold white primary wing tips typically present in adult Franklin's. Can you identify the tern in the background at *lower right*? Answer in the appendix, p. 205. Texas, November

mostly clean white underparts, and a whitish hind neck with sparse gray streaks. Since this species winters primarily along the Pacific coast of South America, this plumage is seen in North America mostly during southbound migration during the fall months. First winter birds show few to no white wing tips on the primaries, but older subadults may show more obvious white outer primary wing tips similar to those of adults, or very small white tips that are hard to see on the black wings.

FRANKLIN'S GULL 9 Nonbreeding and late fall flock with other species. Final exam: This photo in November shows mostly adult nonbreeding Franklin's Gulls, with a few 1st winter birds present. Also shown are several species of terns and a few Laughing Gulls. Try to find the Laughing Gulls and then, for a tougher quiz, try to identify the tern species shown. Answer photo is shown in the appendix, p. 206. Texas, November

BONAPARTE'S GULL
Chroicocephalus philadelphia

SIZE **12.3–13.8 inches long** WINGSPAN **30–36 inches**

It's the very small, tern-like gull flying into the wind just above the water with what appears to be nothing in its bill, since its food includes tiny aquatic invertebrates that it picks from the water surface, and sand fleas. (PD)

PROFILE Bonaparte's is delicately proportioned overall, with a long-winged profile; a small, round head; and a petite, short, thin, straight, pointy, tern-like bill. In feeding flight, they often impart a potbellied profile when dipping down to the water's surface to gather food. *Initial confusion with terns is not just possible but likely because of their size, physical resemblance, and buoyant flight style.* Legs are relatively short compared to those of other North American hooded gulls other than Little Gull.

In flight, adults show a flashing white triangle on the leading edge of the outer wing, while 1st winter birds have reduced white on the underwing primary tips and black shafts and markings on a white outer wing triangle. Adults have uniformly pale silvery-gray upperparts and white underparts, making the black trailing edge to the outer wing and the black bill stand out.

BONAPARTE'S GULL 1 Adult breeding. Bonaparte's is a small, petite gull with a dainty black bill. This complete breeding plumage is not regularly seen in parts of North America and is seen only briefly at normal migratory locations from April to May. Note the all-black hood (brown in Black-headed Gull), bold white eye arcs, and petite black bill (reddish to black in Black-headed). These nimble gulls commonly perch on elevated platforms, where the pink legs of adults are evident. Churchill, Manitoba, June

BONAPARTE'S GULL 2 *From left:* adult breeding; adult nonbreeding; subadult (1st winter). Note black tail tip and dark bar on upper wing on the 1st winter bird. White flash on leading edge of adult's wing is bold and obvious, above and below. On 1st winter birds, the white outer upper wing feathers are mottled with black, and feathers on the underwing are duller with some dark markings, compared to the mostly pale underwings of adults. Nonbreeding adults and immature birds show a dark cheek spot and limited black on the crown. This pattern differs from the nonbreeding Black-headed Gull's heavier vertical blackish bar or smudges on the crown. Texas, April (*left* and *right*); Florida, January (*center*)

BONAPARTE'S GULL 3 This photo, taken at Rollover Pass, Texas, shows a typical tightly clustered feeding flock of Bonaparte's Gulls flying over fast incoming tidal waters. Possibly because of the late date of mid-April, this flock comprises mostly 1st winter birds, with just five adults mixed in. These adults are acquiring dark breeding hoods. The 1st winter birds show a dark bar on the inner forewing; a dark trailing edge to the wings; variable dark markings on the white outer wing feathers; and a dark tail band. Comparably sized terns would show a forked rather than blunt-tipped tail and more slender wings. Feeding flocks are often vocal, emitting peevish rasping and squealing sounds. Texas, April

Bonaparte's are often found in *large, vocal flocks that hover and wheel over food-rich (often flowing or turbulent) waters*, or on large lakes, where they sit in concentrated groups while foraging with short, low flights. Feeding birds emit a conversational series of soft snorts, squeals, quacks, and raspy snarls. Wheeling flocks resemble an animated collage of black, white, and silver.

Unlike terns, Bonaparte's does not dive headfirst into the water but plops to the surface and bobs, picking at the water like a large phalarope. Birds standing on beaches cluster tightly.

STATUS AND DISTRIBUTION Typically a commonly seen small gull on or close to water (salt or fresh), especially from October to April. Flocks may range from small to very large. Bonaparte's is a common to abundant migrant in the eastern half of North America and along the Pacific coast, but uncommon to rare in the Great Basin and western Great Plains (*Gulls of the Americas*, Howell and Dunn, 2007).

Bonaparte's breeds in the boreal forests of Alaska and Canada east to southern Hudson Bay and winters coastally along the Pacific from Vancouver to Baja California, Mexico, as well as on the Atlantic coast from Maine to the Caribbean and Cuba. Bonaparte's winters widely along the Gulf coast into Mexico, and well inland in adjoining states, including Texas, Oklahoma, Arkansas, Mississippi, Louisiana, and Alabama. It also migrates through and winters on some Great Lakes (open water permitting), primarily Lake Erie and adjoining inland locales. Smaller numbers can be found

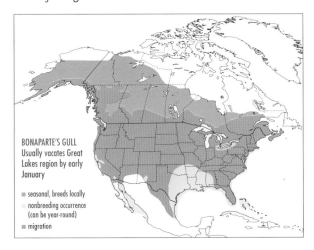

BONAPARTE'S GULL
Usually vacates Great
Lakes region by early
January

■ seasonal, breeds locally
  nonbreeding occurrence
  (can be year-round)
■ migration

BONAPARTE'S GULL 4 Feeding style. Low, slow, fluttery, foot-pattering behavior is typical of feeding Bonaparte's Gulls, which often forage in small to very large flocks. When food is sighted, birds plop to the surface and pick small fish or aquatic invertebrates from the water. Note the potbellied appearance of the birds when they are pattering along the water's surface, accentuated by the raised heads. All the birds here are 1st winter individuals except for the one at *lower right*, which is an adult transitioning to breeding plumage. Texas, April

BONAPARTE'S GULL 5 Adult, winter. This photo shows the delicate nature and features of this small gull as it feeds on small fish or aquatic invertebrates in quiet freshwater pools. A dark cheek spot; diffuse black marks on the head; and a small, thin, black bill are all classic features of this species in winter. Florida, January

BONAPARTE'S GULL 6 Adult, winter. Bonaparte's often forages over turbulent water that ferries food to the surface. This individual shows a double earmuff slash more typical of Black-headed Gull, but note the petite black bill and lack of dusky to blackish shading on the outer half of the underwing, which is present on Black-headed. Also note the thin black trailing edge on the outer wing, which would be more extensive on Black-headed, and a noticeable gray nape (rear neck), which would be whitish on Black-headed. New Jersey, January

in central and southern New Mexico and the Salton Sea in California (*Gulls of the Americas*, Howell and Dunn, 2007).

At inland locations, Bonaparte's often frequents sewage-treatment impoundments as well as large lakes in southern states where water remains open in winter. During migration, Bonaparte's concentrates on inland lakes and rivers. It is typically found in large monotypic flocks that rest on beaches, jetties, and sandbars, or on open water.

BONAPARTE'S GULL 7 Adult nonbreeding, with adult Ring-billed Gull. A Ring-billed Gull dwarfs the petite Bonaparte's Gull in direct comparison, although Ring-billed is only a medium-large gull. Bonaparte's likes to swim when foraging in shallow water, while Ring-billed prefers to walk. Florida, January

ADULT BREEDING (April through August, including 1st summer) Adults have an all-black head, while 1st summer birds have a black hood with scattered white feathers in the forecrown. Away from the gull's subarctic breeding areas, many viewers typically see the birds in nonbreeding plumage, with white-headed birds showing a dark ear spot. However, in some spring locations where Bonaparte's are common in migration, transitional or mostly breeding-plumaged birds are seen on a regular basis (see Bonaparte's Gull 4, *lower right* flying bird). Eyes are black, and legs are pink to orange, with breeding birds showing rich orange legs.

ADULT NONBREEDING Standing birds in winter recall a portly, longish-legged tern (with which they commonly associate). In flight, Bonaparte's show silvery-gray upperparts and black trailing edges to the outer portion of their gray wings, with a bright white triangle near the wing tip. Underparts are white; bill is black; legs are pinkish to orange; and a dark round ear spot and shadowy vertical smudge are present over the eye.

BONAPARTE'S GULL 8 Adult breeding. Flying birds show a white flash on the leading edge of the outer wing and crisp, narrow, black trim on the trailing edge. Bonaparte's flight is tern-like, with agile changes in direction and nimble dips and dives to the water's surface to feed. Similar to slightly larger in size compared to Forster's and Common Terns, Bonaparte's are often mistaken for these species at a distance. Churchill, Manitoba, June

BONAPARTE'S GULL 9 Bonaparte's and Black-headed Gulls, adults nonbreeding. Nonbreeding Bonaparte's Gull (*left*) shows a dark cheek spot, petite black bill, and pink to orange legs. Nonbreeding Black-headed Gull (*right*) is overall more robust, with a slightly heavier, more reddish bill and dark red legs, although the bill and legs of some birds are so dark red that they appear black at a distance or in poor light. Note the faded double earmuff slash on the crown over the eye and a whitish nape (rear neck) and paler gray upper back on the *right* bird. This Black-headed has a relatively small bill, but most members of this genus typically show a noticeably larger, heavier bill compared to Bonaparte's. New Jersey, March

BONAPARTE'S GULL 10 Bonaparte's and Black-headed Gulls, nonbreeding adults. This digitized photo shows both species in nonbreeding plumage. Both photos were taken on the same day and put together digitally to compare them directly. Black-headed (*right*) shows a heavier body structure and bigger head, a larger bill, and broader wings. Underwing on Black-headed is dusky to blackish overall compared to Bonaparte's paler underwing, and the black in the primaries (outer wing feathers) is much more extensive than Bonaparte's thin black trailing edge on the outer wing. Nape (rear neck) is noticeably whiter in Black-headed, and dusky markings on the head are more pronounced in Black-headed. New Jersey, early March

BONAPARTE'S GULL 11 Bonaparte's Gull with two other species. Flanked by two adult nonbreeding Ring-billed Gulls, Bonaparte's (*center*) small size is apparent, a characteristic reinforced by the equally petite nonbreeding Forster's Terns (*rear*). This adult nonbreeding Bonaparte's Gull shows an all-gray upper back and wings with no black on the tail, as in immature birds. Note also a single dark cheek spot. New Jersey, early March

BONAPARTE'S GULL 12 Bonaparte's and Herring Gulls. Two adult nonbreeding Bonaparte's Gulls are dwarfed by this immature 2nd winter Herring Gull, which also shows a much bigger, heavier bill typical of large gulls. New Jersey, March

IMMATURE (juvenile) Fresh-plumaged young juvenile (not shown in photos) has white underparts and head with a dark crown and dark ear patch that connects to the crown. Upper back is brownish with a strong blackish upper wing panel and grayish lower one, creating a strongly contrasting pattern on the upperparts. Flight feathers are black with pale whitish tips. This plumage is mostly similar to that of subadult/1st winter birds but differs in a brownish versus a gray upper back.

Older juveniles show a white head with a dark ear spot and diffuse black on the crown and brownish-centered light upper back feathers. A white tail, usually hidden beneath folded black wing tips on standing birds, shows a dark tip, which is best seen in flying birds. In flight, a bold black M-shaped upper wing pattern is eye-catching, but this trait is shared with several other smaller gull species.

SUBADULT (1st winter) Early 1st winter birds show a black "M" pattern on the upper wings, which are mostly gray with a white wedge near the tip that contains black edges and internal markings. A complete, neat, thin, black trailing edge to the wing and a black band on the white tail finish the contrasting appearance of the upperparts of this species in flight (see Bonaparte's Gull 2). First winter Black-headed Gull has a broader dark trailing edge to the outer upper wing (see Bonaparte's Gull 10). Legs are pinkish to pale orange; bill is black; and a black ear spot is present on a white head. The petite all-black bill helps distinguish it from the noticeably larger 1st winter Black-headed Gull, which shows an orange bill with a dark tip (see Bonaparte's Gull 13).

BONAPARTE'S GULL 13   Bonaparte's and Black-headed Gulls, subadults/1st winter. First winter Bonaparte's (*left*) shows a more petite, black bill and pinkish legs compared to those of the more robust Black-headed (*right*), which has a larger, orange bill with a black tip and orange legs. Black-headed's browner-toned, retained juvenile wing and tertial feathers (broad feathers just above the base of folded wings) are also evident here. Heavier, dusky markings on the head of Black-headed have mostly worn off by this late winter date. This Bonaparte's shows relatively brownish versus blackish upper wing coverts due to feather wear at the late date of April, but note blacker tertials. Texas, April (*left*); New Jersey, March (*right*)

BLACK-HEADED GULL
Chroicocephalus ridibundus

SIZE **14.5–17 inches long** WINGSPAN **39–43 inches**

It's the larger, Bonaparte's-like gull foraging at the business end of an open sewage or storm drain pipe along with Bonaparte's Gulls, snapping up tiny unmentionables. (PD)

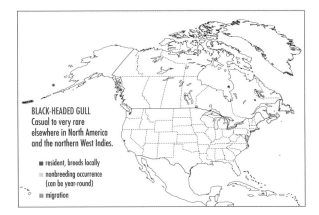

BLACK-HEADED GULL
Casual to very rare elsewhere in North America and the northern West Indies.

■ resident, breeds locally
▨ nonbreeding occurrence (can be year-round)
■ migration

PROFILE Black-headed is an Old World vagrant that breeds locally in only a handful of known northern Atlantic locations. *It closely resembles a robust Bonaparte's Gull with a red, blackish-red, or pale-based bill.* The name is also something of a misnomer, insofar as the hood of breeding adults is brownish, not black, as in Bonaparte's Gull. *Black-headed is slightly smaller than Laughing Gull, with paler gray upperparts.* Black-headed Gull's bill is straighter and shorter than that of the much darker-backed Laughing Gull, and longer and often more robust than the petite all-black bill of Bonaparte's Gull.

Black-headed's bill is reddish to very deep red, with a small black tip in nonbreeding or breeding adults, though it may appear black at a distance or in poor light. In comparison, Bonaparte's has a black bill at all ages. Because of their longer legs, Black-headed Gulls stand taller among Bonaparte's Gulls, but this is often hard to see in a tight flock.

STATUS AND DISTRIBUTION Locally common in Newfoundland in winter and an increasingly regular fall to spring visitor along Atlantic coastlines from Newfoundland to North Carolina (*Gulls of the Americas*, Howell and Dunn, 2007). It is very rare elsewhere, with scattered sightings inland. Regular in spring in the Aleutians, but probably represents a different subspecies.

Breeding locations include a small area at the tip of Greenland, and in North America several locations in Newfoundland, where it is a regular breeding species. Small numbers have bred in Nova Scotia, Maine, and Massachusetts, and some continue to attempt to breed in these or other

BLACK-HEADED GULL 1 Adults breeding. A medium-sized, relatively slender gull with long wings and neck. Slightly to noticeably larger and more robust than Bonaparte's Gull, with a larger, reddish to blackish-red bill and dark reddish to blackish-red legs. Note the more restricted hood (ending at the crown), whereas Bonaparte's Gull's hood extends to the nape. Germany, June

BLACK-HEADED GULL 2 Subadult, 1st winter with other gulls. A subadult (1st winter) Black-headed Gull (*center*, with brownish wing feathers) is flanked by four adult nonbreeding Bonaparte's Gulls (*left* and *rear*) and two larger nonbreeding Ring-billed Gulls (*left rear* and *center right*). Note Black-headed's larger size; longer, orange bill; and more robust proportions compared to the more delicately proportioned Bonaparte's, which has a more petite, black bill. *Also note Black-headed's paler gray upper back.* Can you identify the flying gull? Answer is in the appendix, p. 206. New Jersey, March

BLACK-HEADED GULL 3 Subadult (1st winter) Black-headed Gull (*right*) with Forster's Tern. First winter Black-headed Gull shows an adultlike pale gray back but retains the brownish wing feathers from juvenile plumage throughout the winter. It also retains the brown tertials from juvenile plumage. The yellowish-orange bill and legs are classic for this age group. Many individuals show a double shadowy band of feathers across the head, but this has mostly worn off in this late-winter bird. This Black-headed Gull is noticeably larger than the nearby Forster's Tern (*left*), whereas Bonaparte's Gull would be only slightly larger (see Bonaparte's Gull 11, p. 55), and the Forster's Tern shows the thinner, pointier bill typical of most terns. New Jersey, March

BLACK-HEADED GULL 4 Size differences in Black-headed Gulls. Yes, Virginia, these are the same species! Male gulls can be slightly to distinctly larger and also show a larger bill, head, and overall proportions compared to small females. These photos show a very large 1st winter Black-headed Gull and a smaller 1st winter Black-headed. Either the larger bird is a very big male or the smaller bird is a very small female. *Definite sexual determination by size of nonmated gulls (especially in smaller gull species) is very difficult* because of overlap in measurements in males and females. However, comparisons like this of extreme-sized birds help with understanding the size range variation in gull species. New Jersey, March

BLACK-HEADED GULL 5 Adult Black-headed Gull transitioning to breeding plumage. This bird is acquiring the all-dark hood present in breeding adults and appears much smaller than the nonbreeding Ring-billed Gulls seen in both frames. Note Black-headed's dull reddish bill and legs. The bird in flight shows the classic wing pattern, with white outer primary feathers and dark tips on the upper wing and dark shading on a number of flight feathers just inside the white outer feathers on the underwing. New Jersey, March

northern Atlantic coastal areas (*Gulls of the Americas*, Howell and Dunn, 2007).

In winter, Black-headed is found around harbors, inlets, sewage outlets, and wherever Bonaparte's Gulls are concentrated. However, this larger hooded gull will also join flocks of (similarly sized) Laughing Gulls and Ring-billed Gulls. In Europe, they often forage in plowed fields and are commonly found in suburban and urban areas along rivers. In North America, they are mostly aquatic, found close to shore and in estuaries.

ADULT BREEDING (1st summer and adult) Adult has a pale ice blue–gray back and wings (paler than in Bonaparte's), a broad, black trailing edge to the outer primaries, and normally four white outer flight feathers (primaries). Breeding adults have a brownish hood and a partial white eye ring near the rear section of the eye. Breeding adults show a dull reddish bill that can appear black in bad light or a fully black bill. First summer (one-year-old) birds show the gray back, brown hood, and reddish bill of adults, but they have 1st winter-like wings and tail patterns (see Bonaparte's Gull 13, p. 57).

BLACK-HEADED GULL 6 Adults breeding. Note the long, slender wings (the longest of all hooded gulls, along with Laughing Gull); fairly short, wedge-shaped tail; and small bill. Black-headed has slightly paler gray upperparts compared to Bonaparte's. A heavier bill differs from the more petite black bill of Bonaparte's. A brownish cast to the hood is apparent, as are the blackish underwing feathers in the outer wing (*left* photo). The black trailing edge on the outer primaries is more extensive than on Bonaparte's. Germany, June

BLACK-HEADED GULL 7 Subadult (1st summer). Note the pale gray back (similar to that of adults); a brownish hood; prominent white eye arcs; and a slightly drooping, reddish bill. First summer Black-headed Gull retains many brown wing feathers and a banded tail from last year's juvenile plumage, but it acquires (molts in) pale gray adult feathers on the back and the dark hood of a breeding adult. Subadults may show a complete brown hood, but with some white feathers scattered throughout. England, May

The all-brownish hood is less extensive than in Bonaparte's Gull, terminating at the rear crown. The legs are reddish and in direct comparison, noticeably longer than those of Bonaparte's Gull.

In flight, the undersides of the outer flight feathers (primaries) are dusky to black and contrast strongly with several white outer primaries. A black trailing edge to the outer wing is obvious on white outer primaries and gray inner primaries on the upper side, but these black tips blend in with the blackish flight feathers on the outer underwing (see Bonaparte's Gull 2, p. 50). This upper wing pattern is similar to that of adult Bonaparte's, but the underwing on Black-headed is

BLACK-HEADED GULL 8 Adults nonbreeding. The combination of a reddish bill (sometimes blackish-red) and reddish legs in nonbreeding plumage distinguishes this species from other hooded gulls, with Bonaparte's having pink legs and a black bill. Black-headed also has a paler grayish-white upper back than Bonaparte's, and a more robust body structure. The bird on the *left* is acquiring the dark hood of breeding plumage, which accounts for the partially capped appearance, but a dark ear spot and eye patch are still apparent, which are more easily seen on the *right* bird in flight. New Jersey, March

quite different and shows black outer primaries. However, the black on the underwings of Black-headed is more restricted than on the mostly blackish underwings of the much smaller adult Little Gull.

ADULT (nonbreeding) Like breeding adult, but the now-white head sports two shadowy, thin earmuffs, one

terminating at the black eye and the other at a black ear spot. Note that earmuffs are typically more prominent on Black-headed than on Bonaparte's, but they are reduced or absent on late-winter birds.

IMMATURE (juvenile) This plumage is rarely seen in the United States, with a molt of 1st winter feathers starting to

BLACK-HEADED GULL 9 Fresh juvenile. Note the extensive brownish feathering on the back and wings. By late summer, birds replace the brown feathers on the back with adultlike gray ones, but they will retain the brown wing feathers for about a year. The pink bill base will also change to a more yellowish-orange color by fall. Germany, June

BLACK-HEADED GULL 10 Subadult/1st winter. First winter birds have a mostly orange bill with a black tip and yellowish-orange legs. Note the brownish markings on the upper wing, which are blacker on 1st winter Bonaparte's Gull (some late winter Bonaparte's may show worn, brownish markings). Bonaparte's Gull has pink legs in the 1st winter and shows an all-dark bill. The dark trailing edge to the upper wing on 1st winter Black-headed is broader and not as sharply defined as that of 1st winter Bonaparte's (see Bonaparte's Gull 4, p. 52). New Jersey, March

BLACK-HEADED GULL 11 Adult breeding. This bird stretching its wings shows the classic dusky to blackish underwing pattern on Black-headed Gull, which is all white with a thin black trailing edge on Bonaparte's. Note the robust dark reddish bill and legs. Laughing Gull's bill is much heavier and more drooping, and its upper wings are charcoal gray with extensive black tips, not pale gray with black-and-white outer wings, as in Black-headed. New Jersey, March

appear relatively soon after fledging. Brownish above (darker brown than Bonaparte's), with a brown-collared nape, a white rear collar, and a more extensive brownish hood plus a dark ear spot, which contrasts with the straight, thickish, pinkish bill with a black tip (unlike the black bill of juvenile Bonaparte's).

SUBADULT (1st winter) Combines pale ice-gray back of adult with strongly contrasting brownish upper wing pattern of juvenile. Differs from Bonaparte's in the orange-red to pinkish bill with a dark tip and the more distinct double-earmuff slashes creasing the crown and extending from eye to eye and from ear patch to ear patch. Birds in later winter may lack this pattern because of feather wear (see Bonaparte's Gull 10, p. 55). The dark trailing edge to Black-headed's upper wing is broader and less neatly arranged than the thinner, neater black trailing edge to Bonaparte's Gull's upper wing (see Bonaparte's Gull 4, p. 52).

LITTLE GULL *Hydrocoloeus minutus*

SIZE **10.25–11.5 inches long** WINGSPAN **29.5–31.5 inches**

Aptly named "Little Gull," since it is the smallest gull in the world. (PD)

PROFILE *A tiny, compact, petite-billed gull with pigeon-like proportions.* Nonbreeding Little Gull resembles a baby Bonaparte's Gull with a dark cap and ear spot. It is slightly smaller than Rock Pigeon and distinctly shorter than Bonaparte's Gull, with which it readily associates (see Little Gull 4 and 7).

Little Gull feeds like a Bonaparte's Gull by floating on the water and picking food from the surface, phalarope fashion. Blackish brown–backed juveniles (late July–November) stand out when roosting in a flock of gray-backed immature Bonaparte's (September onward), and *the dark underwings of adult Little Gull are very eye-catching when birds are flying.* Wing beats are quick, deep, and somewhat fluttery. In winter Little Gull is distinguished by its dark skullcap, and in flight by shorter, *blunt-tipped, mitten-like wings* flashing a white-tipped dark underwing.

STATUS AND DISTRIBUTION Migrates primarily through the Great Lakes region, where good numbers may remain until early January. Winter range has historically been the mid-Atlantic coast, where it associates with Bonaparte's Gulls, but recent trends indicate fewer birds in this area and more birds seen on the Great Lakes. In warm winters, varying numbers may remain on the Great Lakes.

Breeds sparingly in Canada adjacent to Hudson and James Bays and has formerly bred along borders of the Great Lakes,

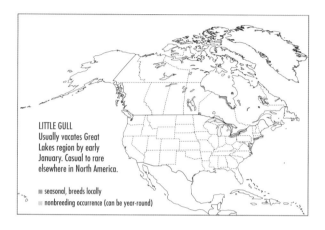

LITTLE GULL
Usually vacates Great
Lakes region by early
January. Casual to rare
elsewhere in North America.

■ seasonal, breeds locally
■ nonbreeding occurrence (can be year-round)

LITTLE GULL 1 Adult breeding, in flight. Our smallest gull (and the smallest gull in the world) shows a compact body; a slender, straight, black bill; and reddish legs (pink to orange on Bonaparte's Gull). Note the small head and short, rounded, blunt-tipped wings. Hard to overlook are Little Gull's mostly black underwings, which highlight the bold white outer primary wing tips and broad white trailing edge on the wings, a trait also visible on the upper wing, but with gray versus black shading. This species has historically been a rare, local breeder around Hudson Bay and the Great Lakes (the first nest was found in 1962), but its present-day status is incompletely known. Little Gull winters casually along the upper Atlantic coast, where numbers have declined in recent decades. It also winters on the Great Lakes, where numbers seem to be increasing. Sweden, late June

LITTLE GULL 2 Adult nonbreeding, with Bonaparte's Gulls. This is typically how you find them in a crowd: blackish underwings contrasting strongly with the silver and white wings of Bonaparte's Gulls. Note the prominent gray rear neck and shorter, more rounded wings. You would instinctively search for another Little Gull in the flock, which would distinguish itself by its smaller size and dark cap (seen on adults and immatures). But you can stop looking, since there is only one Little Gull in this shot. Flight is light, buoyant, nimble, and erratic, with quick wing beats. New Jersey, February

LITTLE GULL 3 Adult nonbreeding. Little Gull is a small (dove-sized), compact gull with a petite black bill, dark ear patch, and dark skullcap in winter. Note the rounded white primary tips, which are black in Bonaparte's and Black-headed Gulls. The *right* bird was photographed in late February, and much of the dark cap has worn off, but note the deep gray on the hind neck and the sides of the upper breast, which is absent in other hooded gulls, except for some much larger 2nd winter Laughing Gulls. With its short, rounded wings, its flight is quick and buoyant. This gull is highly sought after by birders in North America. Europe, January (*left*); New Jersey, late February (*right*)

LITTLE GULL 4 Adult nonbreeding, with Bonaparte's Gulls. Among these nonbreeding Bonaparte's Gulls, the Little Gull's smaller size; much shorter, deep pink legs; and compactness are apparent. The gray cap also differs from Bonaparte's mostly whitish crown in late winter. New Jersey, February

LITTLE GULL 5 Adult nonbreeding, with Black-headed and Ring-billed Gulls. Little Gull appears positively diminutive in comparison to the adult nonbreeding Black-headed Gull (*left*) and adult Ring-billed Gull (*right*). Note the white primary wing tips on Little Gull compared to the black ones on Black-headed (Bonaparte's is similar), and the darker remnants of its black cap compared to the sparse black spots on Black-headed. The strong gray nape and sides of the upper breast of Little Gull differ greatly from the white nape and underparts of Black-headed. Ring-billed Gull, which is a medium-sized gull, looks quite large in comparison to both hooded gulls. Anyone having problems understanding why this bird is called "Little" Gull? New Jersey, February

LITTLE GULL 6 Adult, with nonbreeding Forster's Tern. Little Gull (*left*) shows only a shadowy gray cap, but its very small size; short, rounded wings; and uniformly gray upper wings with a white trailing edge give you plenty of information to identify it in the field. Although the flight style is similar to that of nonbreeding Forster's Tern (*right*), Little Gull stands out because of its very small size and short, rounded wings. New Jersey, February

LITTLE GULL 7 Adult nonbreeding, with Bonaparte's Gulls. The adult nonbreeding Little Gull (*front*) shows a more compact body structure; shorter, white-tipped wings; paler back; shorter, redder legs; and black cap, which the duo of adult winter Bonaparte's Gulls lack. North Carolina, February

but no nesting records have been confirmed in the United States since 1989 (*Gulls of the Americas*, Howell and Dunn, 2007).

In winter and migration, Little Gull is typically found among Bonaparte's Gulls, where it often segregates to the perimeter of resting flocks. Also associates with Black-headed Gulls. In winter, it may be found well offshore. Nonbreeding birds (typically subadults) are occasionally found among flocks of terns in summer along the mid-Atlantic coast.

ADULT (combines 2nd winter and adult) Ice gray above, white below (with occasional pinkish blush); short, rounded, whitish wing tips extend slightly beyond the white tail on standing birds. Head has a black hood with no white eye

LITTLE GULL 8 Immature (1st winter). In this plumage, which includes retained juvenile wings, tail, and crown, Little Gull shows short, round-tipped wings and a dark, M-shaped upper wing pattern that lacks the white wedge on the outer primaries as in immature Bonaparte's and Black-headed Gulls. The dark cap is also unique to this species among hooded gulls. Observers are struck mostly by the tiny size and overall compactness of Little Gull. Europe, January

LITTLE GULL 9 Nonbreeding, with Common Terns and immature/juvenile Laughing Gull. Nonbreeding Little Gull (*front center*) shows a small head, compact body, reddish legs, extensive black cap, and white wing tips. Nonbreeding Common Terns are slightly larger, longer winged, and longer billed, and the medium-sized juvenile Laughing Gull *behind* looks huge compared to these birds. The dark primary tips on the far underwing might suggest a 2nd winter Little Gull, but it is hard to say without seeing spread wings. New Jersey, September

crescents in breeding plumage, and bill is black throughout the year.

ADULT NONBREEDING Birds show a dark cap with a shadowy earmuff and black ear spot. Shortish legs are dark red.

IMMATURE (includes juvenile and 1st winter subadult) Distinctly dark blackish brown above, whitish below (juvenile, not shown). First winter plumage is similar but has gray back, similar to that of adults. A dark cap and dark smudge on the side of the neck distinguish it from the larger, paler-backed, juvenile Bonaparte's Gull. Shorter wings give birds a compact profile unlike the slender tern-like proportions of Bonaparte's Gull.

SUBADULT (1st summer) Like breeding adult with pale gray back and mostly all-black head but retains the dark upper outer wings and strong black bar of 1st winter birds on the wing panel.

SABINE'S GULL *Xema sabini*

SIZE **12.5–14 inches long** WINGSPAN **35.5–39 inches**

Arguably our most beautiful gull! (PD)

PROFILE A small, trim gull that is smaller than a kittiwake or Mew Gull and most commonly seen in flight over ocean waters (less commonly found sitting on beaches with similarly sized gulls). In flight, Sabine's appears short bodied, with broad-based, angular wings and a fairly long, *uniquely forked tail.*

The bold tricolored upper wing pattern (black, white, and gray) is somewhat similar to that of other species but is distinctly bolder on Sabine's and thus more visually grabbing. Stiff, shallow, steady wing beats reveal flashes of the bird's wedge-like white wing patch. Flight is overall lofting and buoyant, but not as nimble or tern-like as that of Bonaparte's Gull.

Sabine's forages mostly by swimming and snatching prey from the surface of the water while at sea, and it feeds in shallow pools at breeding sites by stirring up aquatic invertebrates by stomping the substrate with its feet (see Sabine's Gull 1). It does not respond to chum as readily as kittiwakes on pelagic birding trips. It also hovers and plucks prey from the surface. When foraging on beaches, Sabine's walks nimbly.

In migration, birds resting on the water gather in tight (typically small) clusters. Sabine's is fairly tame while on the water, allowing close approach by boats before flushing. On West Coast pelagic trips, Sabine's Gulls are usually seen in small groups. In the interior, single birds are the norm, and these may mix with Bonaparte's Gulls.

STATUS AND DISTRIBUTION Localized Arctic breeder. Fairly common during migration in fall, primarily in offshore northern to central Pacific coastal North American waters; very rare along East Coast in fall. Winter records are extremely rare in North America, with only a few instances of birds remaining until January. Subadult (1st winter) birds typically remain in southern waters until their 2nd year.

This handsome, mostly pelagic gull breeds in Arctic and subarctic regions but winters in tropical seas off western

SABINE'S GULL 1 Adult breeding. This small, smart-looking, Arctic-breeding gull with a deep charcoal hood going blacker at the collar and front of the face is unique. A delicate yellow-tipped black bill and red orbital ring add to the bird's distinctiveness. Bold white spots are present on the outer primary wing tips. Sabine's Gull occurs in pelagic waters away from breeding areas, but some storm-blown birds are occasionally seen along coastlines. During fall migration, Sabine's are regularly found at interior western lakes, and they have been documented in every one of the lower forty-eight states. Alaska, June

SABINE'S GULL 2 Adult breeding. *Left* photo shows Sabine's in its classic tundra breeding setting, with a deep charcoal and black hood, gray back, and black outer wings with bold white primary tips. The mostly breeding adult in flight shows the bold black, white, and gray upper wing pattern, and the head is completing its molt to breeding plumage in May. Note the small head of Sabine's Gull in flight, and the forked tail with broad, round corners. Alaska, June (*left*); Madeira, May (*right*)

South America and southern Africa. In North America, it breeds in coastal tundra of western Alaska, the North Slope, and islands of the Canadian Arctic Archipelago, which are far from most human population centers. It also breeds in northern and central Greenland.

There are numerous records of Sabine's Gulls in the North American interior, mostly in fall, and regular records in the Great Plains and Great Basin regions (*Gulls of the Americas*, Howell and Dunn, 2007). Fall migration is from late July through October; spring migration is from March through May (occasionally into June).

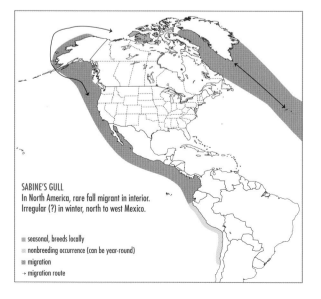

SABINE'S GULL
In North America, rare fall migrant in interior. Irregular (?) in winter, north to west Mexico.

▦ seasonal, breeds locally
▦ nonbreeding occurrence (can be year-round)
▦ migration
→ migration route

ADULT BREEDING Standing birds are slate gray above, with visible black outer wings that have bold white tips (back is darker gray than in Bonaparte's Gull), and white below with dark legs. *The idiosyncratic yellow-tipped dark bill is distinctive*, and the slightly forked tail is easy to see in flying birds when it is not fanned. At close range, the dark charcoal-gray hood transitions to black along the crisp lower border and on the forecrown, but the head appears totally black in dull light. By early fall, some adults are already transitioning to nonbreeding plumage, and some show a mottled head and blackish hind collar, appearing fully hooded at a distance, while others have attained nonbreeding condition by late September (see Sabine's Gull 4).

ADULT NONBREEDING The dark hood is now restricted to a shadowy rear cap and upper nape, with a black ear spot connected to the dark hood at the rear crown.

IMMATURE (juvenile) Juveniles are mousy grayish or brown above, with pale feather fringes and black markings near the tip of grayish-brown feathers. The crown and hind neck are similarly brownish, giving birds the appearance of wearing a shawl-like hood. By comparison, juvenile Black-legged Kittiwake appears white headed, with a contrasting narrow black collar and ear spot.

In flight, juvenile Sabine's Gull's strong upper wing pattern is like that of adults, but instead of gray inner wings, it shows brownish-gray ones with strong pale fringes, and the outer primaries are not jet black as in the adult, but blackish gray with paler gray shading on the interior. A white tail shows a

SABINE'S GULL 3 Sabine's Gull, adult on tundra nest. Sabine's Gull nests in high Arctic tundra in wet microhabitats. This species typically nests in small colonies, often near Arctic Terns, where the very aggressive terns help protect the Sabine's nests from ground and aerial predators, such as jaegers, larger gulls, and Arctic fox. Alaska, June

SABINE'S GULL 4 Adult nonbreeding. Sabine's is a stunning gull, even in nonbreeding plumage. Here it shows a partial blackish rear hood; an iconic black, white, and gray upper wing pattern; and a muted pale grayish underwing that barely shows the upper wing pattern. California, September

bold, relatively narrow black tip, which accentuates the unique forking. Note that kittiwakes have narrow, boomerang-shaped wings, while Sabine's wings are broader and more acutely angled (not curved) back.

SUBADULT (1st winter) You rarely see this plumage in North America, as most adults and juveniles depart North America in October for their South American winter locations off the Pacific coast of Peru and northern Chile. If you do see this plumage, the upper back is gray as in adults, but the wings are worn and brownish, with retained juvenile feathers. A dusky rear collar is present, with a thin slash extending toward the eye. The crown, face, and underparts are white.

SABINE'S GULL 5 Juveniles. Juvenile Sabine's Gulls have mostly brownish-gray upperparts; a dusky brownish to grayish head and upper breast sides; and whitish underparts. The more heavily marked, crisper-plumaged bird in the *right* photo was photographed on September 3, and the paler bird in the *left* photo, with a whitish face and larger, paler upperpart feathers, in mid-October. The pale feather edges and dark centers give the back a scaly appearance, especially on the *right* bird. Note the small head and petite all-black bill that lacks the yellow tip of older birds. On the flying bird, note the bold upper wing pattern and the black-trimmed, forked tail. Juvenile Black-legged Kittiwake and several other species also show an M-shaped upper wing pattern, but not the brownish-gray plumage or forked tail. While Sabine's Gull is smaller than kittiwakes, it has proportionally broader inner wings. New Jersey, October 18 (*left*); Connecticut, September 3 (*right*)

SUBADULT (1st summer)   Birds at this age mostly resemble adults but have mottled dark markings on a white head instead of a full dark gray hood. Subadult birds in 1st summer plumage are not commonly seen in North America, but one possible bird of this age was found by Marshall Iliff and photographed in New Jersey by Kevin. In *Gulls of the Americas* (Howell and Dunn, 2007), the bird in this photo was aged as either a late 1st year or retarded 2nd year (meaning that the plumage is not the typical advanced adultlike plumage of this age [2nd year] but instead may be a variable 1st summer plumage). Confusing stuff, but this is why we are just calling it a subadult, with a specific age not crucial to our ID.

SABINE'S GULL 6 Subadult, with Laughing Gull. This spring adultlike Sabine's is either an advanced 1st summer bird or a 2nd summer bird with less advanced plumage (*Gulls of the Americas*, Howell and Dunn, 2007). It has mostly adult plumage except for the spotted, dusky hood, which is typical of late 1st year birds. Compared to the adult breeding Laughing Gull in the *right* photo, Sabine's is noticeably smaller and more slender; shows a smaller black bill with a yellow tip; and has bolder white outer primary tips. Laughing Gull has a larger, drooping, reddish bill, a bigger head, and a bulkier body. The *left* photo shows how quickly Sabine's takes flight from a floating position. New Jersey, May

BLACK-LEGGED KITTIWAKE
Rissa tridactyla

SIZE **16–18 inches long** WINGSPAN **36.5–47 inches**

A true "sea" gull. (PD)

BLACK-LEGGED KITTIWAKE
Rare to casual in interior North
America, mainly late fall.

▪ seasonal, breeds locally
▫ nonbreeding occurrence (can be year-round)
▪ migration

PROFILE A small marine gull (larger than Bonaparte's). *Overall compact, with a squarish head, short legs, and a small, pointy, slender bill* with a down-turned gape (visible line at base of bill juncture) that gives birds the suggestion of a frown. Large dark eyes on a blank face impart a gentle expression.

In flight it shows a somewhat compact and tubular body *with long, narrow, boomerang-shaped wings* and a tail that is narrow and long. The bird's nimbleness in flight coupled with its wing shape and quick, stiff wing beats suggests a swift, bulky tern. On land it appears short legged, with an upright

BLACK-LEGGED KITTIWAKE 1 Adults breeding, at nest ledge. This medium-sized, long-winged gull is seen mainly at sea outside of the nesting season, but it is sometimes visible from land. It has a relatively short, stubby bill with a drooping, pointed tip; short legs; and a bright red mouth lining. The name is a phonetic rendering of the bird's call, which is given loudly and continuously near the breeding cliffs. It appears as though someone forgot to bring home the fish. Alaska, May

BLACK-LEGGED KITTIWAKE 2 Adults breeding. Overall a very dapper gull with a prominent, projecting head and boomerang-shaped wings that have crisply defined "dipped-in-ink" wing tips. Stiff wing beats impart the suggestion of a bulky tern to flying birds, and this species can fly swiftly, even into a headwind. Note the black legs, which help separate this species from Red-legged Kittiwake. Alaska, May

BLACK-LEGGED KITTIWAKE 3 Feeding flock. Black-legged Kittiwakes often gather in large feeding flocks when sardines and other favorite foods are concentrated in one area. Unlike most gulls, kittiwakes may dive headfirst into the water in pursuit of fish, whereas most gulls plop to the surface and then plunge their heads beneath the water to grab fish and other food sources. Note the two much larger immature Glaucous-winged Gulls in the flock and the diving adult kittiwake. Alaska, May

BLACK-LEGGED KITTIWAKE 4 Nesting colony. Kittiwakes typically nest in large, noisy colonies, where their nests are often very close together on precarious cliff edges. A study of the birds clustered on the cliff shows where the prime real estate is located. When disturbed, especially by Bald Eagles, the kittiwakes fly around the nest colony in noisy flocks. Note the two-toned upper wing pattern on flying birds, which is particularly apparent at a distance. Can you pick out the larger Glaucous-winged Gull in the *right* photo? Alaska, May

posture. Unlike most gulls, *kittiwakes will dive headfirst into the water to secure prey*, in the manner of terns.

STATUS AND DISTRIBUTION   Black-legged Kittiwake is an Arctic and subarctic cliff-nesting breeder, commonly seen in appropriate habitats onshore near nest islands in Alaska and the Gulf of Saint Lawrence. Population numbers are increasing in some areas, and many birds now nest in Homer, Alaska, on the girders of small bridges connecting the Homer Spit to marina docking locations because of saturation on nearby breeding islands. It is fairly common in winter well offshore on both coasts.

Black-legged Kittiwakes are uncommonly seen on land, except on breeding cliffs and adjacent shorelines in Arctic and subarctic regions and on coastlines where tired birds come to rest on sandy beaches or rocky shorelines, especially on the Pacific coast. Offshore they commonly gather where other marine birds are foraging, most notably Northern Fulmars and alcids. Most land-based observations in the Atlantic are storm or wind related, but migration in the northwestern Pacific region allows occasional viewing from shore in fall. Black-legged Kittiwakes winter along both coasts, often very far from shore.

BLACK-LEGGED KITTIWAKE 5 Adult breeding. Black-legged Kittiwake is a bird of mainly marine environs, especially in northern regions. This image shows a two-toned upper wing; a grayish-white underwing with a paler outer section; and dipped-in-ink triangular black wing tips. The contrast of the upper wing with the paler outer half becomes more pronounced as distance increases, and the underside of the wing shows a translucent patch in the outer flight feathers. Alaska, May

BLACK-LEGGED KITTIWAKE 6 Adult breeding. This image shows the down-turned gape line behind a pointy, bright yellow bill, which imparts a dour expression to adults, but the dark eye against a plain white head gives the bird a gentle expression. Alaska, May

ADULT BREEDING Birds are very plain, showing a white head and underparts and gray upperparts that are slightly darker than those of adult Herring Gull. *In flight, upper wings show two tones of gray, darker on the inner wing and paler on the outer wing*, with a small, crisply defined, triangular black wing tip. Translucence appears on the outer primaries on the underwings, which are pale gray with whitish primaries and secondary (inner wing) wing tips (see Black-legged Kittiwake 5).

ADULT NONBREEDING Similar to breeding adult but shows a pale gray nape and dark ear patch. Atlantic breeding birds show a black collar that connects to the ear patch

(see Black-legged Kittiwake 7, *right* photo). The plain, all-yellow bill with a decurved upper tip is distinctive and considerably longer than the yellow, snub bill of Red-legged Kittiwake.

IMMATURE (combines juvenile and 1st winter) Mostly grayish back; white head and underparts with a prominent black ear patch; broad, black hind collar; black diagonal bar on inner wings; black outer primary tips; and black terminal tail band. Bill is black but develops a pale base by late winter. A wide black diagonal bar on the upper wing combines with black outer flight feathers to form a distinct "M" pattern on the upper wing of flying birds. Legs are pinkish.

BLACK-LEGGED KITTIWAKE 7 Fresh juvenile with adult (*left*); nonbreeding adult (*right*). The *left* photo shows a very fresh-plumaged juvenile flying with an adult and probably begging for food as well. Note the strong black markings on the nape and the strong contrast of the black-and-white wing pattern. The *right* photo shows a nonbreeding adult with black and gray nape markings, which are typical of birds (subspecies *R. t. pollicaris*) from the northern Pacific region, with Atlantic birds having only a gray nape. Alaska, early September, (*left*); Pacific coast, early January (*right*)

BLACK-LEGGED KITTIWAKE 8 Immature (1st winter) Black-legged Kittiwakes. Immature birds in their 1st winter show a grayish upper back; a dark ear spot; a broad black collar that wears to a dull gray in advanced immatures (*right* photo); and a black-banded tail. Note the mostly black bill on the *left* bird compared to the black bill with a yellow base on the more advanced immature (*right*). The bold M-shaped upper wing pattern is shared by several other species, including Bonaparte's, Little, Sabine's, and Black-headed Gulls, but these lack the kittiwake's black collar. Alaska, early May (*left*); Alaska, May (*right*)

SUBADULT (1st summer) Like nonbreeding adult but shows reduced black to brownish spotting on upper wing from juvenile plumage and a dark tip on the mostly yellow bill; legs are dull pink.

BLACK-LEGGED KITTIWAKE 9 Adult breeding, with fish. The fish-rich waters of Alaska ensure high breeding success, and this kittiwake is repeatedly grabbing small fish from the water's surface. Alaska, May

RED-LEGGED KITTIWAKE
Rissa brevirostris

SIZE **15.5–17 inches long**   WINGSPAN **33–36 inches**

This is the snub-billed kittiwake telling you that you really are far from land. (PD)

PROFILE   Like Black-legged Kittiwake but *stockier and more pigeon-like, with a slightly smaller, rounder head and a distinctly shorter bill*. In all plumages, it shows slate-gray upperparts (slightly darker than in Black-legged Kittiwake and about the same shade as in adult Sabine's Gull). In flight, Red-legged shows more white on the trailing edge of the wing than Black-legged (again recalling the larger Sabine's Gull). Short reddish legs and a stubby yellow bill help distinguish Red-legged.

RED-LEGGED KITTIWAKE 1 Adult breeding. This species is found only in very limited habitats on remote islands in the Bering Sea, and its winter range is incompletely known. It is a small to medium gull with a relatively short, stubby bill; short red legs; and longish wings. Upperparts are dark slaty gray, with black outer primaries that have very small white tips. The big eye in a blank face gives this species a gentle expression. The bigger head with steeper forecrown and larger eyes compared to Black-legged help this species to find food on the water's surface while foraging at night, when it is most active. Alaska, early August

In flight, Red-legged appears slimmer and longer winged than Black-legged Kittiwake, and a stubby bill and steep forehead impart a distinct pug-faced look. Red-legged forages aloft over open water (often in the company of Black-legged Kittiwake), dropping to the surface to feed and sometimes plunging into the water. It often feeds at night, where its very large eyes allow for added light gathering, which aids in finding fish near the surface.

STATUS AND DISTRIBUTION   An uncommon, somewhat nocturnal, mostly solitary, and very geographically restricted marine gull, breeding on islands in the Bering Sea.

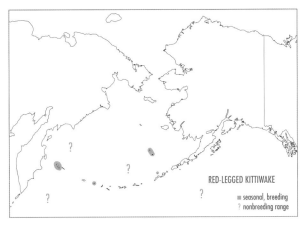

RED-LEGGED KITTIWAKE

■ seasonal, breeding
? nonbreeding range

RED-LEGGED KITTIWAKE 2 Breeding adults; Black-legged Kittiwake, breeding adult. This photo array shows an adult Red-legged Kittiwake (*left*) brandishing its namesake trait. Another adult Red-legged (*center*) shows a short, stubby bill and darker upperparts compared to the larger, longer-billed, paler-winged adult Black-legged Kittiwake (*right*). Red-legged Kittiwake never shows black legs; juveniles (not shown) have pink to orange legs. The bulky head and no-necked look impart a pugnacious look to this species. Alaska, July (*left* and *center*); Alaska, May (*right*)

In winter it is limited to the deeper waters of the North Pacific. Because of its very restricted range, there is a very low incidence of vagrancy, and its nocturnal feeding habits seriously limit your chances of encountering this bird away from its North Pacific environment.

ADULT BREEDING Shows a gleaming white head, dark eye, *and short yellow bill*. The dark eye gives birds a gentle expression.

ADULT NONBREEDING Similar to summer adult but shows a dark scar-shaped ear patch. The yellow bill takes on a greenish cast that is very eye-catching. Because of the darker upper wing and gray-shaded underwing, the contrast with the black triangular outer wing tips is less pronounced on Red-legged Kittiwake than on Black-legged Kittiwake.

IMMATURE (juvenile/1st winter) Similar to adult but shows a prominent hind collar, plus an ear patch that may give the impression of a double collar. The short bill is black, and the tail is all white, showing no black tip as in immature Black-legged Kittiwake and Sabine's Gull.

In flight, upper wings show a black, gray, and white pattern reminiscent of that of several other species (most notably Sabine's Gull and Black-legged Kittiwake), but black is limited mostly to the outer wing, so a complete bold black "M" configuration on the upper wing is lacking on immature Red-legged. Underwing shows a broad, white trailing edge that contrasts with the darker underside of the outer wing. Pinkish legs become orange to dull red by the 1st summer.

SUBADULT (1st winter) Similar to immature but with black-tipped, greenish-yellow bill and orange to reddish legs.

HEERMANN'S GULL *Larus heermanni*

SIZE **18–20 inches long** WINGSPAN **50–52 inches**

Also known as "false jaeger." (PD)

HEERMANN'S GULL

■ resident, breeds locally
▨ nonbreeding occurrence (can be year-round)

PROFILE A distinctive, dark-bodied, medium-sized gull about the size of Ring-billed Gull. Birds show a long-winged, angled back profile with wings almost touching the sand when birds walk or stand. Breeding adults, with their bright white head and bright red bill contrasting with an all-gray body, stand out among the more blandly patterned gulls and terns lounging on California and other Pacific coast beaches. Highly gregarious, the birds typically cluster in tight monotypic flocks.

When foraging on the beach, they space themselves within the wave zone, typically standing in the water. *A very aerial gull, Heermann's is often the first gull off the beach to pursue another gull approaching with fish.* While generally jaeger shaped, Heermann's is longer billed and lacks the distinctive white patches on the underside of the wings that are typical of Parasitic and Pomarine Jaegers. Some Heermann's, however, may show white patches on the upper wing, so use caution with these birds.

STATUS AND DISTRIBUTION Regular to common on Pacific beaches and nearshore waters to southern Canada from June to November. This species breeds in the Gulf of California, Mexico, but some nonbreeders are present on West Coast beaches year-round. Postbreeding birds

HEERMANN'S GULL 1 Adult breeding. This gull is as striking as it is unique. Its overall dark body, black legs, white head, and red lipstick–colored bill distinguish this West Coast beach denizen from all other North American gulls. This medium-sized gull breeds in northwestern Mexico and disperses north along the Pacific coast to southern Canada after breeding. California, February

reaching coastal British Columbia typically do so in July and August, and they return south in fall and winter. This uniquely plumaged gull is primarily coastal and is typically seen on Pacific beaches, harbors, and bays or foraging over kelp beds offshore, where it pursues other birds to steal food.

ADULT BREEDING (includes some advanced 3rd year birds) The combination of a gleaming white head and all-charcoal-gray body is unique. A bill the color of red lipstick with a small black tip is striking, bordering on garish.

ADULT NONBREEDING Similar to breeding adult, but head is heavily dusky with whitish flecks, and red bill is less striking and may have a more extensive dark tip. Chest may also be paler on some birds, especially 3rd year individuals.

IMMATURE (includes juvenile, 1st winter and 1st summer) *Uniformly dark chocolate brown, which is unique among gulls* (other immature gulls show paler underparts or have more contrastingly patterned upperparts). Slightly darker head contrasts with long, thin, pale, dark-tipped pink bill. Long legs are all dark. Juveniles show strong white-fringed

HEERMANN'S GULL 2   Adult breeding. This photo shows the long but broad-based wings of this species. A bright white head contrasting with an all-dark body and upper wings is unique among North American gulls. Note that a few aberrant individuals may show a white patch in the outer wings. California, February

HEERMANN'S GULL 3   Nonbreeding adults. Nonbreeding adult and mostly adult Heermann's Gulls show a heavily mottled hood that contrasts with the pale to dusky-gray chest and dark gray back. The reddish bill with a black tip is present throughout the year. Slightly larger than Ring-billed Gull, the broad-winged, long-faced Heermann's Gull is a common denizen of West Coast beaches. The *left* bird may be a 3rd summer because of the larger black bill tip and nonuniform upperparts, but aging can be difficult with some adultlike Heermann's Gulls. Note the white trailing edge on the dark wings and the white-tipped black tail on the flying bird. California, November (*left*); Washington, October (*right*)

wing and upperpart feathers. Very dark postjuvenile upper back feathers contrast strongly with worn juvenile wing coverts by late fall. (See Heermann's Gull 4, *left* photo.) Except for its longer, pale bill, immature Heermann's Gull might be confused only with a dark Parasitic or Pomarine Jaeger or Sooty Shearwater while flying offshore.

SUBADULT (2nd winter) Similar to immature but now overall sooty brown, as opposed to chocolate brown, and lacking worn wing coverts of 1st winter birds; bill reddish orange with a strong black tip versus pink based on 1st winter birds.

HEERMANN'S GULL 4 Juvenile and immature (1st winter). The *right* photo shows a fresh-plumaged juvenile Heermann's Gull with long but broad wings; neatly arranged white-fringed upperpart feathers; and a long, narrow, pale, dark-tipped bill. The overall dark brown plumage and penchant for pursuing other gulls and seabirds for cached food often lead to confusion with jaegers. The *left* bird is an immature in 1st winter plumage that is mostly dark overall but has worn juvenile wing coverts and tertials to break up the uniformity. A pale dusky bill differs from the 2nd winter's brighter bill. California, November (*left*); California, August (*right*)

HEERMANN'S GULL 5 Immatures (2nd winter). Uniformly dark plumage without worn wing coverts in combination with a narrow reddish-orange bill and dark legs help to age these birds and distinguish this exclusive West Coast species. The *right* bird is more worn and browner at this later date (February) than the fresh-plumaged bird (*left*) in November, and the reddish-orange bill with the demarcated black tip helps separate these birds from 1st winter ones that have a paler bill with a dark tip. California, November (*left*); California, February (*right*)

HERRING GULL,
adult

GRAY-BACKED WHITE-HEADED GULLS

HERRING GULL
CALIFORNIA GULL
RING-BILLED GULL
MEW GULL
ICELAND GULL
GLAUCOUS GULL
GLAUCOUS-WINGED GULL

HERRING GULL *Larus argentatus*

SIZE **22–26 inches long** WINGSPAN **47–59 inches**

It's the large, silver gray–backed gull with the six-pack holder around its neck, a testimony to its slim head and a token of its proclivities for landfill trolling and Dumpster diving. (PD)

PROFILE This large, somewhat awkwardly proportioned gull has such variation in its size, structure, and plumage that it is arguably one of the more confusing gulls in the world. Some are short winged and stocky in shape, with wings that extend just slightly past the tail, which gives them a compact overall profile. Others are more slender and tapered to the rear and have long wings that extend well past the folded tail, which gives them a profile somewhat similar to that of Lesser Black-backed Gull (see Intro 15). *A long, relatively slender bill contributes to a front face structure that suggests pulled taffy, and a head that may appear too small and thin for the body on some birds. The gape line behind the bill may curve slightly downward, but it is typically straighter than the more strongly down-curved gape on California Gull.*

Longish pink legs are set midspan on the body, and the head is either rounded or flat topped and devoid of bumps or peaks. The bill on some individuals droops at the tip, which, in combination with the noticeable gonydeal bulge (expansion of the lower bill just inside the tip) and hooked tip, *suggests a "church key" can opener.*

HERRING GULL 1 Adult breeding. Many individuals show a mostly round, comparatively smallish head; a long, narrow, mostly straight bill shaped like a beer can opener; shortish wings that extend slightly to moderately beyond the tail; and long legs set at midspan, which enhance the overall sense of compactness. Adults have a pale gray back; black outer primaries with small to large white tips; long pink legs; a yellow bill with a red spot near the tip; and a white head. Bright yellow eyes and a straightish to slightly down-turned yellow to red gape line (thin bare skin behind the rear bill juncture) give birds a menacing appearance. Walking with a waddling sailor's gait, these birds cover ground quickly. New Jersey, May

HERRING GULL 2 Immatures. These two Herring Gulls show similar plumage but are noticeably different in body size, structure, and bill size. Note the bigger, deeper, flatter head on the *right* bird (2nd winter), as well as the much larger bill and the incoming pale gray feathers (back and flanks). The *left* bird (1st winter) has a smaller, rounder head; smaller, thinner bill; and more streamlined body shape. However, both birds have the tapered snout of Herring Gull; overall brownish-gray plumage with fairly heavy streaks on the head and underparts; and a fairly slender, straight bill, which are all features of Herring Gull. Note the Sanderling in the foreground for size comparison. New Jersey, early April

HERRING GULL 3 Herring Gull with Ring-billed Gulls. An immature (2nd winter) Herring Gull is shown swimming with smaller, more petite-billed adult Ring-billed Gulls. Note the Herring's much larger size and long, pinkish-yellow bill with a dark tip compared to the more slender, tapered profile; smaller head; thinner neck; and more delicate, bright yellow bill with a dark ring inside a pale tip of the Ring-billed Gulls. New Jersey, March

HERRING GULL 4 Immatures to adults. This early April photo shows a mix of 1st and 2nd winter Herring Gulls, with one adult at *right*. The three birds with uniform brown, patterned wings; dark eyes; and ill-defined pink-based bills with large black tips are 1st winter birds, while the three birds with distinctly gray backs; somewhat messy wing panels with some gray feathers; and strong pink bills with black tips are 2nd winter birds. These birds also have pale dusky to yellowish eyes, which are hard to see in this small photo. The bird at *far upper right* is harder to age, but the dark eye; dusky head and underparts; and upper back and wing covert patterns suggest a 1st winter bird. Note the overall compactness but comparatively lean bodies and mostly long, straight bills on these birds, which are traits of Herring Gull. Large groups of Herring Gulls often include multiple ages. New Jersey, early April

HERRING GULL 5 Feeding frenzy. After a fishing vessel dumped its bycatch near the jetty tip in Barnegat, New Jersey, these Herring Gulls of all ages appeared instantly to fight frantically for the scraps. There are multiple ages here, but they are all Herring Gulls, since no Ring-billed Gull wants to be part of a Herring Gull food fight. The very small, brown, dainty, slender-winged, small-billed 1st winter Herring Gulls at *upper left* suggest small females, but nothing definite. New Jersey, February

Plumage is also highly variable in Herring Gull, with *some warm and brownish in immature plumage, while others are grayish and cold in overall appearance.*

Highly aquatic, *Herring Gull often forages in shallow water and tide pools.* It finds food by flying over potential food-bearing habitat and then lands to fetch and consume the catch. It is quickly drawn to concentrations of feeding gulls, where it steals food from other birds. Herring Gull walks with a rolling sailor's gait but swims readily and well, often preferring to forage while swimming rather than wading, and it is regularly seen floating on the water. Herring Gull often roosts in large, compact flocks with other large gulls.

STATUS AND DISTRIBUTION The most widespread large gull with pink legs in North America. It is common in the eastern United States but less common in some central and most western areas. Along the Atlantic coast, it is typically the most numerous large gull, but on the Pacific coast,

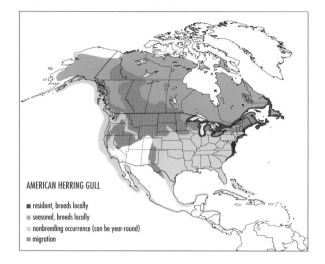

AMERICAN HERRING GULL

■ resident, breeds locally
■ seasonal, breeds locally
■ nonbreeding occurrence (can be year-round)
■ migration

Herring Gull is uncommon and usually outnumbered by Western and Glaucous-winged Gulls. It is fairly common inland on large bodies of water, especially in the eastern half of the United States, and may gather in large numbers at landfills or fish-processing plants; ten thousand were estimated at a garbage dump site in a recent inland Pennsylvania Christmas count (2017). Migratory Herring Gulls breed widely across the upper tier of North America, from Alaska east to Newfoundland and Nova Scotia. Resident Herring Gulls breed from Newfoundland and Nova Scotia to the Great Lakes, and southward along coastal Atlantic areas to North Carolina. Winter range is vast and widespread, but a large region of the southwestern United States lacks this species.

ADULT BREEDING (combines adult and some 3rd summer subadults) Has a pale, silvery-gray back, white underparts, black outer primary tips with small to large white spots, dull pink legs, and a yellow bill with a red spot near the tip (some individuals may show a black spot inside a small, pale tip in the early stages of adult plumage that may suggest the dark-ringed bill of an adult Ring-billed Gull).

HERRING GULL 6 Herring Gulls with other gulls, a fairly typical East Coast beach scene. Present in this photo are seven Herring Gulls (five adults and advanced subadults, including two sleeping at *right*, and two immatures, one preening at *right*, and one partial bird at *extreme left*) and one immature (*rear center*) and two adult Great Black-backed Gulls. Adults, 2nd winters, and one 1st winter Ring-billed Gull clustered in *front* are staying away from the big guys. Second winter Ring-billeds are similar to adults in plumage but have greenish-yellow bills and legs compared to the yellow ones of adults, and they lack white spots on the outer primary wing tips. Comparing common species like this helps with single-species sightings in the future. New Jersey, March

white mirrors on outer two primaries

HERRING GULL 7 Adults. Adult Herring Gulls in flight appear well balanced, with the head and tail projecting about an equal distance from the body. Wings are neither broad nor slender. Limited (Atlantic breeding) to more extensive (western breeding) black primary wing tips contrast markedly with the otherwise pale underparts, and the white mirrors inside the tips of the outer two primaries are traits of eastern birds, with western birds mostly showing a white mirror only on the outer primary. Note the menacing skeletal-faced look to the *center* bird, which shows the coarse, lavish streaking of a nonbreeding adult. This streaking can be very dense or relatively sparse, as in the bird at *right*. New Jersey, May (*left*); New Jersey, January (*center*); New Jersey, March (*right*)

HERRING GULL 8 Immature (juvenile) composite. Juvenile Herring Gulls have a distinctive dark brown plumage that is held for several months (July–September). The overall dark brown shading wears to a paler brownish to grayish color by midfall, when crisp, pale feather edges wear off, and the upper back feathers are replaced by grayish ones with dark interior markings. Note the black bill with the variable pinkish base; slender, nonchesty appearance, and long-snouted look to the face. New Jersey, July (*left*); New Jersey, August (*center*); New York, early September (*right*)

ADULT NONBREEDING In winter, head and neck are lavishly overlaid with coarse, dark, blotchy, grayish-brown streaking that looks like it was applied with a putty knife, making birds look dirty headed, hooded, or disheveled. *Bright yellow eyes appear hard and mean.*

IMMATURE (juvenile) In the East, juvenile Herring Gulls stand out as the darkest gull on the beach. Fresh juveniles (mid-July to August) can be completely dark brown, with buff fringes and internal markings on the upperpart feathers. By September, more white feathers are visible on the head, and the buff upperpart fringes have worn to whitish. Pink legs; a straight, mostly dark bill (sometimes with varying amounts of pink at the base); and black outer flight feathers that contrast with the brown plumage complete the picture of this common gull.

IMMATURE (includes 1st and some 2nd winter birds) Mostly uniformly brownish to grayish brown above and below with evenly apportioned patterning or spangling on upperparts. Some birds can show a colder, grayish-brown overall plumage. Older immature birds become increasingly disheveled looking, showing worn and paler patches of plumage, particularly about the head. The bill shows varying amounts of diffuse to defined pink at the base by midwinter, but some birds may have a mostly black bill until spring. Pink at the bill base of mid- to

HERRING GULL 9 Herring and Great Black-backed Gulls, immatures (juveniles). These two photos show the similarity in plumage of fresh juvenile Herring and Great Black-backed Gulls. Note, however, the bulkier overall proportions of Great Black-backed (*right*), with its huskier chest; bigger head; heavier bill with a strong bulging tip; and thicker legs. Different plumage features include a whiter head and chest in Great Black-backed and larger, pale spots on the wing panel (wing coverts) and back feathers. While Great Black-backed is often much larger, a small Great Black-backed (like this bird with a relatively small bill and slender body for this species) can be about the same size as a large Herring Gull, so use the distinguishing physical features as well as the supportive plumage details for a sure ID of extreme-sized birds of both species. New Jersey, August (*left*); New York, early September (*right*)

HERRING GULL 10 1st year immature composite. This photo array shows a variety of plumages for Herring Gull in its 1st year. The *upper left* photo shows a juvenile bird (New Jersey, September) whose upper back feathers are plainer than those of younger juveniles because of wear and sun bleaching. The *upper middle* photo (Florida, November) shows a grayish-brown immature (1st winter) bird with a paler overall appearance that might suggest a more northerly interior-breeding bird that could show a colder, grayer overall plumage than Atlantic birds. The *upper right* photo (Florida, January) shows replacement of most juvenile upper back feathers, but the overall appearance is still close to that of a juvenile bird. The *lower right* photo (New Jersey, February) shows a very cool gray overall plumage that reflects the wide variation in shading of immature Herring Gulls. The very small bill, petite round head, and long wings suggest a female, but determining the sex of a single bird in the field is problematic because of the wide variation between males and females. The *lower middle* photo shows a bird (New Jersey, early April) that is whiter overall, especially the head and upper breast, and has a bill with some diffuse pinkish color, and fully replaced upper back feathers that are pale gray, some with dark centers. The *lower left* photo (New Jersey, July) shows a particularly dark individual with extensive worn plumage, especially the very worn, pointed wings (primaries). Note the overall uniformity in plumage for all these birds, tonal differences notwithstanding.

greater wing coverts with dark inner shading

HERRING GULL 11 Immature (1st winter). All photos show a balanced overall physical profile; a fairly slender, not bulky or chesty body; a medium to long, slender bill; and a pulled-taffy (tapered-snout) look to the front of the head. The bill is mostly black, but the inner bill shows various diffuse pink color. Some 1st winter Herring Gulls, however, can show a pink bill with a black tip (mainly central and western North American breeders). Note the densely barred dark rump of the *right* bird, which is white on Great Black-backed and lighter on Lesser Black-backed Gulls. The inner primary window (see *right* photo) shows distinctly grayish feathers with small black markings, which break up the uniformity of dark flight feathers on the wing; this differs from the uniform dark shading of the flight feathers on 1st winter Lesser Black-backed Gull (see Lesser Black-backed Gull 11, *right* photo, page 172; Lesser Black-backed Gull 12, *center* photo) and from the darker gray inner primaries with more extensive, elongated black markings on 1st winter California Gull (see California Gull 12, p. 102). New Jersey (all photos), November (*left*); December (*center*); March (*right*)

HERRING GULL 12 Herring Gulls with Lesser and Great Black-backed Gulls (all immatures). A picture is worth a thousand words! Immature (1st winter) Lesser Black-backed Gull (*front center*) and immature Great Black-backed Gull (*rear center*) are flanked by immature Herring Gulls (1st winter, *right*; 2nd winter, *left*). Note the 1st year Herring Gull's overall uniformity, including the brownish head and neatly arranged wing panel compared to the 2nd winter's whiter head and upper chest; grayish upper back; pale eye; and gray-infused feathered wing panel. Both Black-backed Gulls show a paler head and underparts than either Herring Gull. Also note the smaller size and trim proportions of the Lesser Black-backed (including the petite bill) compared to the bulky, chesty, heavy-billed proportions of the Great Black-backed. New Jersey, early April

late 1st winter birds is typically ill defined on birds from Atlantic breeding areas of the eastern United States, while Herring Gulls that breed in central and more western areas can show strong pinkish bills with demarcated black tips from early winter onward, similar to 2nd winter Herring Gulls (see Intro 18, *right* bird, p. 25). These birds may also show a whiter head and upper breast by spring (see Herring Gull 15, *left* bird).

Underparts are mostly uniformly grayish brown or show blurry, brown, bruise-like spotting. *If you are on the East Coast and see a large, mostly all-dark brown gull with unstreaked underparts, STOP; you are looking at a Herring Gull.* On the West Coast, the commoner, more robust, and heavier-billed Western Gull and paler Glaucous-winged Gull are likelier candidates.

Except for juveniles, the head is slightly paler than the body. Some 1st winter birds acquire grayish upper back feathers by spring, but these usually have dark internal markings and differ from the adultlike, pale gray feathers on many 2nd winter and subadult birds. *First winter birds have strongly patterned, warm-toned wing coverts, which differ from the darker-centered ones on Lesser Black-backed Gulls, but these feathers may wear or bleach by spring to show no patterning.*

Second winter immatures often acquire some silvery-gray adult feathers on their back that are unmarked as the winter progresses, and this helps distinguish them from 1st winter birds. Some 2nd winter birds appear very similar in plumage to 1st year birds, but they typically show a less neatly arranged wing panel with fine light and dark vermiculation on the lower part (greater wing coverts) compared to overall darker greater wing coverts with larger dark spots and areas of dark shading on the inner section of the greater wing covert feathers on 1st winter birds (see Herring Gull 10 and 13). *Second winter birds that appear similar to 1st winter birds usually show pale to dusky eyes, which allows you to age them as 2nd winter individuals.*

HERRING GULL 13   Older immatures (2nd winter). This photo array shows variation in plumage, bare parts, and eye color in immature (2nd year) Herring Gulls from August to the following April. A field mark that identifies Herring Gull in its 2nd year is a pale, straw-colored eye, though a small number of Herring Gulls can show a dusky eye from their 1st summer through 2nd winter. Photos that show what appear to be dark eyes on 2nd year Herring Gulls are often a result of poor lighting, shadows, or a bad angle, and these are usually dusky eyes. At the *upper left* is a freshly molted early 2nd winter bird (New Jersey, August) with feathers very similar to those of 1st year birds but with differences in internal feather markings (fine vermiculation) on the greater wing coverts (no, don't quit now; you really don't need to learn this if you don't care to); more-rounded wing tips; and a strongly demarcated pink bill. *Upper center* bird (New Jersey, September) is similar to *upper left* bird but slightly more worn, with a few new grayer feathers molting in on the back. *Upper right* bird (Florida, January) has acquired gray adultlike feathers on the upper back and whiter feathers on the head and underparts but still has a pale dusky eye. *Lower right* bird (Florida, January) is similar to *upper right* bird and was photographed on the same day. It has a cleaner white overall appearance and bulkier structure than the previous bird, and a pale eye that identifies it as a 2nd winter bird or older. *Lower center* bird (New Jersey, February) shows the more heavily streaked look of younger birds, but with scattered pale gray upper back feathers and a strongly demarcated pink bill with a black band, and a pale tip more typical of more advanced birds. *Lower left* bird (New Jersey, early April) is more advanced, with extensive gray upper back feathers, distinct pale eyes, and adultlike body plumage.

HERRING GULL 14 Immature (2nd winter). This photo array shows a variety of plumages for immature Herring Gull in its 2nd year. The bird in the *left* photo (New Jersey, December) appears quite similar to a 1st winter bird, but the pale bases to the outer tail feathers identify it as a 2nd year bird. The *center* bird (Texas, March) shows the grayer inner primaries and pale eye of a 2nd winter bird, with a 1st winter bird showing a dark eye and inner primaries that are not as clean gray as this. The bird in the *right* photo (New Jersey, February) differs from the other two birds with its adultlike gray upper back feathers and pale straw-colored eyes, all features of 2nd winter birds. With all these complicated details, it is perfectly fine to just call them immature Herring Gulls.

Worn summer immatures: In summer, it is possible for immatures to show pale, very worn, sun-bleached heads, especially in southern areas where the sun is more intense (see Herring Gull 15, *left* bird). These very worn individuals may even have mostly whitish or buffy bodies that suggest immature Iceland or Glaucous Gull. In summer, white-headed, brown-bodied birds are regularly encountered, so don't let this plumage fool you.

SUBADULT (includes some 2nd and all 3rd winter birds) Extremely variable. Some 2nd winter birds show a silvery-gray back similar to that of adults; worn, brown wing panels with pale gray feathers on the lower part (midwinter to summer); and the dark tail bands of immatures, but these tails now show white at the base. Underparts and neck on 2nd winter subadult birds are either heavily and coarsely streaked or spotted, or whitish with sparse streaks that contrast with a darker belly. Legs are pink, and the bill is pinkish to yellow, with a defined dark tip. Eye color on 2nd winter birds is typically pale yellow to dusky, with dusky eyes often appearing dark at a distance or in indirect light.

HERRING GULL 15 Herring and Great Black-backed Gulls, immatures. A very sun-bleached, immature late 1st winter Herring Gull (*left*) is shown with an immature late 1st winter Great Black-backed Gull. Never mind the plumage. Look at the Great Black-backed's superior size, girth, and chestiness, with a squarish head and heavier bill with a bulging lower tip compared to Herring Gull's rounder head and slender bill. Also apparent is Great Black-backed's longer, sturdier legs. Whitish, bleached plumage on Herring Gull is probably an effect of it spending the winter in Florida, where the sun's rays are stronger. Note the Great Black-backed's piano key–like wing coverts compared to the Herring's more unkempt, worn ones. Florida, April

HERRING GULL 16 Subadults. This subadult Herring Gull sampler shows birds with more advanced gray, adultlike upperparts, but with immature feathers in the wings and residual spotting on the chest. Birds of these age classes typically look unkempt. *Upper left* bird is a 2nd winter subadult (New Jersey, March) in somewhat advanced plumage for this age, showing a gray upper back but only a few gray feathers in the wing panel (wing coverts). All other birds are 3rd year subadults that show considerably more gray feathers in the wing panel (*center*, *upper right*) or mostly gray upperparts with just a small number of older, worn feathers interspersed. The *lower left* bird appears similar to a breeding adult with its yellow bill and red spot, but it has a small number of retained brownish feathers in the wing panel and no white spots on the outer primary wing tips. The dusky eye of the *lower left* and *center* birds is a result of shadows, a bad camera angle, or very low light conditions where the black pupil expands to cover much of the eye. All birds except the *upper left* were photographed in New Jersey in July.

HERRING GULL 17 Subadults. These three subadult Herring Gulls represent a late 2nd winter bird (*left*) and two 2nd summer to 3rd winter birds in worn summer plumage. The *left* bird (New Jersey, early April) shows a grayish back, four muted gray inner primary feathers, and some gray upper wing feathers (upper wing coverts). A white rump is consistent with a 2nd winter and older Herring Gull. The *center* bird (New Jersey, July) shows more adultlike gray inner primaries with white tips, which ages it as a 2nd summer bird transitioning to 3rd winter. The *right* bird (New Jersey, July) shows a good number of gray feathers on the back and wings; a number of adult primary feathers (one with a black tip and white spot); and head streaking of a nonbreeding adult. While aging gulls seems complicated to many birders, it is perfectly fine to just call all these birds subadults and leave it at that.

HERRING GULL 18 Subadults. These two near adults (3rd summer) show all-gray upperparts, a yellow to mostly yellow bill, and pale eyes. The red spot on the *right* bird's bill is like that of an adult, while the orange to red spot and black lines on the paler yellow bill of the *left* bird point to a less mature bird of the same age. Note the paler, straw-colored eye on the *right* bird, as well as less spotting on the head and breast, which is typical of maturer subadults. New Jersey, July

Birds in their 3rd winter typically show mostly gray upperparts that lack the brownish-gray wing covert feathers of 2nd winter subadults. Scattered retained, brownish wing feathers are usually seen near the lower wing coverts or near the tertials. The pinkish to yellow bill usually has a strong black spot near the tip and sometimes shows a red spot next to the dark spot, as in California Gull. More advanced subadult birds may have a full yellow bill with a red spot, as in adults, but some worn, retained feathers are usually visible on the upperparts or wing (see Herring Gull 16).

Note that in winter, the head and neck of subadults are often very heavily streaked, as in winter adults, making birds appear particularly shabby or unkempt. These subadults are typically the most unkempt-looking birds on the beach.

HYBRIDS Herring Gull sometimes mates with gulls of other species, creating a hybrid condition that may resemble either adult or portions of both. Gulls that it regularly hybridizes with include Glaucous-winged and Glaucous Gulls, and less frequently Lesser Black-backed Gull.

HERRING GULL 19 Herring Gull × Lesser Black-backed hybrid, adult. You're right, the back shading is much too dark for adult Herring Gull, whose back and wings would be only slightly darker than those of the adult Ring-billed Gull in the *rear*. Size and shape are perfect for Herring Gull, with a rounded crown; a pulled-taffy, tapered-snout look to the frontal face; a narrow yellow bill with a bulge near the tip on the lower bill and a strongly hooked tip; bright yellow eyes; and short wing projection past the tail. The yellow legs and charcoal-shaded back are typical of an adult Lesser Black-backed Gull, but the orange orbital ring around the eye is not red, as in Lesser Black-backed, but it is also not yellow, as in Herring Gull. It is orange, which is usually the case with hybrids of these two species. Yes, you are looking at a Herring Gull × Lesser Black-backed Gull hybrid. The overall compact structure with short wings and a very long bill with a hooked tip immediately drew Kevin's attention when he saw this bird in Daytona Beach, Florida, in January.

HERRING GULL 20 Herring Gull × Glaucous-winged Gull hybrid, adult. An adult Herring Gull with a dusky eye and thin reddish eye ring? Not likely. Thayer's, perhaps? No, the bill looks too robust for this; the underwing pattern on the far wing is wrong (Herring Gull has a black, not pale gray, outer primary inside the white mirror); and the legs are too pale pink. It's another hybrid, a Herring Gull × Glaucous-winged Gull, which is fairly common in southern Alaska's Kenai Peninsula. The dusky eye is consistent with that of Glaucous-winged, but the wing tips are too dark for this species, which suggests Herring Gull genes. The bill also seems to fit Glaucous-winged better. Alaska, May

CALIFORNIA GULL *Larus californicus*

SIZE **18–23 inches long**   WINGSPAN **48–55 inches**

It's a Herring Gull drawn by El Greco with a Mormon cricket in its mouth. (PD)

PROFILE A lean and appealingly proportioned gull, *between Herring Gull and Ring-billed Gull in size,* with a small, round head and long wings. The long, straight, narrow bill is shaped like a popsicle stick and at a distance appears somewhat blunt. On adults, red and black marks near the tip of the yellow bill resemble those of some subadult Herring Gulls, but *the red and black marks at the tip of the bill are particularly conspicuous on California Gull.*

Back shading on California is medium gray in tone. On standing birds, shortish legs are set well forward and folded wings are often angled down, with tips nearly touching the ground. Therefore, standing birds may appear to slump or slouch.

CALIFORNIA GULL 1 Adult breeding. A medium to medium-large gull with relatively long wings. It is a handsome, pleasingly proportioned gull with a relatively small, round head and a long, narrow, bright yellow bill with a black and red spot near the tip in adults. California ranges between Ring-billed and Herring Gull in size, with males at the larger end of the scale. Note the dusky (brownish-yellow) eye and *gray upper back that is darker than that of Herring or Ring-billed Gull,* which both have sharp yellow eyes as adults. Unique among large gulls is the strongly down-turned gape (line behind the rear bill juncture) on California Gulls of all ages. Herring Gull may have a slightly down-turned gape, but nothing like California's more obvious one. California, February

CALIFORNIA GULL 2 California Gulls and Western Gulls, nonbreeding. Adult nonbreeding California Gulls (*left*) show the often dense streaking on the back of the head and lower neck that contrasts with a whitish face and forecrown, but some birds may be more uniformly streaked on the head in winter as well. Note their smaller size and overall more diminutive features compared to those of the larger nonbreeding Western Gulls (*right*), including a smaller head and bill and more streamlined body shape. California, November

California Gull shows a number of plumage variations in its first year, and birds of the same age may exhibit three distinctly different plumage appearances at the same time in early winter, which can cause confusion.

Very arguably, this is the true "western gull." Habitats include beaches and nearshore waters, marshes, meadows, landfills, rivers, and cities and towns. It forages on a number of vertebrates and invertebrates, most notably grasshoppers.

This specialization earned the species a special place in the hearts of Mormon settlers, who honored it with a statue in Salt Lake City's Temple Square in grateful recognition of the bird's gastronomic solution to a crop-devastating plague of crickets that greeted settlers in 1848, a year after their arrival on the shores of the Great Salt Lake. It uses a number of feeding strategies and is adept at snatching prey in the air; it also runs along lakeshores with its head down, inhaling brine flies.

CALIFORNIA GULL 3 Immatures (1st winter); subadult (late 1st spring *right*). Note the long, narrow, straight, pink bills with black tips on the *left* two birds, which are typical in the 1st winter. Both photos were taken on the same day in early February. Pale faces are also present in this plumage. The *right* photo shows a subadult in its 1st spring with a yellowish bill, pale bluish-green legs, and a recently acquired gray back that reflects the darker shading of adult California Gull. This bird is aged as a late 1st year bird because of the worn, retained primaries and tertials, which appear to be old juvenile feathers, but we call it a subadult because of the gray, adultlike upper back. California, February (*left* and *center*); Utah, May (*right*)

CALIFORNIA GULL 4 Adult breeding. California Gulls rely for food on the millions of brine flies that are present on inland salt lakes in Utah during the breeding season. This bird is racing along the lakeshore inhaling brine flies. Adult Ring-billed Gull, which is slightly to noticeably smaller than California, shows no red on a smaller bill and has pale eyes. The overall more robust Herring Gull shows pink legs and typically shorter wings projecting past the tail. Great Salt Lake, Utah, July

CALIFORNIA GULL 5 California and Ring-billed Gulls, adults nonbreeding. Immediately apparent is California Gull's larger size and darker upperparts. With further study, you'll note California Gull's dark eye (yellow in Ring-billed), red-and-black-marked bill, and collared hind neck with a whitish face. Ring-billeds are showing either winter plumage with dense head and neck streaking or the cleaner white head and neck of more advanced birds that are attaining breeding condition in early February. Also note the larger head and bill on the California, and the bolder white primary tips on the black wings. Oregon, early February

In mixed flocks, this species clusters in species-specific groups that are typically off to one side of larger gull species. It often roosts with Ring-billed and Mew Gulls when members of its own species are absent or few in number (see California Gull 5).

CALIFORNIA GULL 6 California Gull and Mew Gull, nonbreeding adults. It is easy to spot the obvious differences in these two species, and direct comparison illustrates the marked variation between these denizens of the Pacific coast winter beach. About the only things they have in common are dusky eyes, a gray back, and greenish-yellow legs, with California being larger, showing bulkier structural features, and having a longer, heavier bill with black and red markings near the tip compared to Mew's slender, all-yellow bill. California also has a bigger head with a whiter face and crown (variable) and heavily streaked collar. Mew shows a paler gray back and smudgy gray head that typically is not as distinctly streaked as in California Gull. The darkness of the dusky cheek on this nonbreeding Mew Gull is not typically this apparent, with some birds being more lightly streaked. California Gull's red and black bill markings and limited dark streaking, which is concentrated on the nape (rear neck), rule out Herring and Thayer's Gull, which also show pink legs. Big Sur, California, November

STATUS AND DISTRIBUTION Common on inland lakes and ponds in the western United States and Canada, and along Pacific coast beaches, in nearshore waters and some adjacent inland areas, especially central California. Some birds can be found in these areas year-round.

CALIFORNIA GULL 7 Adult breeding. Relatively heavy body structure with longish, somewhat narrow wings. White mirrors (white patches inside the wing tips on the outer two primary flight feathers) are fairly extensive on subadult and adult California Gull. Longer outer wing feathers reflect molt replacement of inner wing feathers on the breeding grounds in May. Note the dusky eye, prominent red and black marks on the long, slender yellow bill, and yellowish-green feet. Utah, May

California Gulls breed at western inland locations (excluding the Southwest and most of California) in the United States and west-central Canada. In migration, they can be seen throughout much of the West. They also winter widely along coastal areas in Mexico, including the Gulf of California.

In summer, California Gull is very much a bird of the interior, and it is common as a breeder and postbreeder on salt lakes and prairie sloughs in the Great Basin and northern prairies. In winter, many birds move to coastal and near-coastal regions from southern British Columbia to southern Mexico, and some birds remain inland. In winter, large numbers commute from the Pacific coast to interior valleys every day, where they may be the commonest gull (*Gulls of the Americas*, Howell and Dunn, 2007).

ADULT BREEDING AND NONBREEDING (combines 3rd winter and adult) Like a smaller, trimmer Herring Gull except for slightly darker gray upperparts, yellowish-green legs, and a *dusky eye* (bright yellow in adult Herring and Ring-billed Gulls). Red and black marks near the tip of the adult's slender yellow bill are particularly obvious (note: red may be absent in 3rd winter birds, whose bill then somewhat resembles that of adult Ring-billed, whose black ring is just inside the yellow bill tip).

Yellow legs are often more greenish tinged than adult Ring-billed Gull's yellow legs, and some 3rd winter California Gulls still show the idiosyncratic bluish legs that are typical of 2nd winter or subadult birds (see California Gull 14, *left* bird). In winter, streaking on the head is often heaviest on the hind neck, imparting a collared appearance. Third winter birds mostly resemble adults but have scattered brownish feathers on the wings, some flight feathers, and rear upper back (tertials) (see California Gull 14). More advanced late 3rd winter birds may closely resemble adults but may lack or show reduced white outer primary tips and show brownish feathers in the wings.

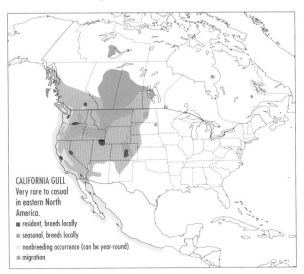

CALIFORNIA GULL
Very rare to casual in eastern North America.
■ resident, breeds locally
▦ seasonal, breeds locally
▫ nonbreeding occurrence (can be year-round)
▦ migration

CALIFORNIA GULL 8 Adults nonbreeding. *Note how streaking imparts a collared look to the head and neck*, with the streaking on Herring Gull typically being more uniformly apportioned on the head and neck. On Ring-billed Gull, the streaking is finer and typically sparser, but some birds will show heavy streaking. *The California Gull on the right shows classic yellow-green legs, which are yellow on Ring-billed Gull and pink on Herring.* The narrow, straight bill without a deeply hooked tip on these individuals is typical of this species, as are the dark eyes and the pronounced red, black, and yellow tip to the bill. California, February (*left*); California, November (*right*)

CALIFORNIA GULL 9 Juvenile plumage. This plumage is often present for a relatively short time after hatching, and by fall it changes to immature (1st winter) plumage, shown in California Gull 3 (*left* photo). However, some birds may retain this juvenile plumage into early winter. Juvenile Western Gull is similar, but it is larger and bulkier overall and has a heavier bill with a bulging tip. Note the uniformity of the brownish plumage and the straight, slender, blackish bill with a pinkish base, and the dark brown feather centers on the upper back with bold white fringes. California, August

CALIFORNIA GULL 10 Adult (*left*) and fresh juvenile. A worn breeding California Gull (*left*) is accompanied by a recently hatched juvenile, which shows the overall very dark juvenile plumage of this species (see California Gull 9 for an older, slightly paler juvenile). Utah, July

IMMATURE (combines juvenile and 1st winter) Fresh juvenile California Gull (mid-July to late August) differs from 1st winter-plumaged birds by its heavily brown-streaked head, neck, and underparts, and dark brown upperpart feathers with bold white edges. Bill is mostly black, with variable pink on the lower base (see California Gull 9). The plumage of very dark juveniles closely resembles that of fresh juvenile Western Gull, but California is smaller and more slender bodied, with longer wings and a smaller, straighter bill that lacks the bulging tip of Western (see Western Gull 8, p. 148).

From late August to October, California Gull begins to show whiter feathers on the head, neck, and chest, with the

CALIFORNIA GULL 11 Immature (1st winter, *left*); Herring Gull immature (2nd winter, *right*). Apparent is Herring Gull's larger size; heavier bill; longer, pink legs; paler gray feathers on the upper back; and very pale eye, which California Gull doesn't typically show at any age. Note the longer primaries of California Gull compared to the shorter, broader primaries of Herring Gull, which contribute to Herring's stockier appearance. Immature California also shows a whiter face and upper breast on average compared to some Herring Gulls, with the heavy streaking on the nape giving the bird a collared appearance, and shorter, grayish legs. Connecticut, March

CALIFORNIA GULL 12 Immatures (1st winter) *left* and *center*; immature/subadult (late 1st spring) *right*. This array shows California Gull through its 1st year. The *left* and *center* birds show fairly typical 1st winter plumage with mostly mottled brown upperparts, dark primaries with dusky gray inner webs, and a pale head that contrasts with a heavily streaked rear neck and brown upper back. The tail is all dark, and a wide dark trailing edge to the wings is visible. The worn 1st spring bird (*right*) has a variable gray upper back (not seen); worn brown upper wings from juvenile plumage with a few gray feathers; a yellowish bill with a dark tip; and a whitish head and underparts with sparse spotting, except for the heavy streaks on the rear neck. All birds show long, tapered wings. First winter Ring-billed Gull's bill would be smaller, and it would have an all-gray back. Herring Gull's can opener–shaped bill would often be larger and more conspicuously hooked, and the inner primary window (see photo) would be more conspicuously paler gray compared to the rest of the trailing edge of the upper wing (see Herring Gull 11, p. 91). The bills on some 1st winter Herring Gulls, particularly Atlantic coast birds, show only small amounts of diffuse pink at the base, which differs greatly from 1st winter California's strong pink bill with a black tip, but some Herring Gulls are similar. California, February (*left* and *center*); Utah, May (*right*)

new postjuvenile upper back feathers showing a mix of gray, white, and brown shading. Note that some California Gulls may retain juvenile plumage into early winter.

By the 1st winter, the long, thin, mostly dark bill (of juveniles) turns pink with a dark tip, like that of Ring-billed Gull, whose black ring may cover the entire tip at this age. *Face, head, and throat show a good number of white feathers by midwinter, with the head becoming mostly whitish by the 1st summer.* Legs are dull pink, sometimes with a bluish tinge on the upper leg. First winter birds usually show a heavy, almost greasy collar at the back of the neck. There are often scattered gray feathers molting in on the back by mid- to late winter (see California Gull 11, *left* bird). First summer California Gulls show a white head and underparts, a gray upper back, and worn wing coverts and flight feathers, resulting in a messy overall appearance (see California Gull 12, *right* bird).

Confusion with immature Herring Gulls, which have dark eyes in their 1st winter and may show pale dusky eyes in their 2nd winter, is possible. Note, however, Herring Gull's larger overall size; stouter bill; shorter wing projection past the tail; pinker legs; and paler gray back feathers (mostly 2nd winter). California Gull in 1st winter often shows a grayish to greenish upper leg (tibia) that is lacking on the pink legs of immature Herring Gull; a shorter tibia than Herring; and

typically a pronounced down-turned gape (line behind the bill), which is usually straighter in Herring (see California Gull 11).

SUBADULT (2nd winter) Extremely variable during this age class, with some birds showing almost completely gray upperparts; others showing scattered gray back feathers; and some having mostly brownish-gray upperparts that somewhat resemble those of 1st year birds, at least early in the season. May be similar to some gray-backed subadult/2nd winter Herring and late 1st winter Ring-billed at this same developmental stage but with the darker gray back of adult California and mostly brownish-gray wings that show mostly brownish greater wing coverts. Underparts are typically very dirty or disheveled looking. Standout features are the dusky eye *and the unique bluish or gray-green legs* (but some individuals can show pinkish legs at this age also). Herring Gull at this stage shows pink legs, a pink-based bill, and usually a pale eye, and greater wing coverts that lack the mostly brownish shading of California. In winter, the head and especially the hind neck of California are very heavily spotted or streaked.

SUBADULT (3rd winter) By its 3rd winter, California Gull appears quite similar to adults but usually shows some brownish

gray median wing coverts

CALIFORNIA GULL 13 Subadult/adult in flight. This photo array shows California Gull in its 2nd winter plumage (*left*), which has mostly immature feathers except for the upper back, where there are adultlike gray feathers, and incoming gray feathers on the upper wing panel (median wing coverts). The *center* bird is a 3rd year subadult with mostly adult plumage except for the dark tail band and splotches of older, dark feathers on the wings. The *right* bird is an adult in breeding plumage. California, February (*left*); Utah, May (*center* and *right*)

CALIFORNIA GULL 14 Possible adult breeding (*right*); subadult 3rd summer (*left*). This photo shows a good comparison of mostly adult breeding plumage (*right*) and 3rd year subadult plumage. Differences include worn flight feathers; heavy nonbreeding streaking on the head and neck; dark tail; and scattered worn feathers on the back and wings on the subadult (*left*). Subadult's legs still show traces of unique bluish color, while adults have mostly yellowish-green legs. Reduced white in the primary wing tips; slight dark head spotting; and a brownish cast to the feathers in the lower wing panel (greater wing coverts) may point to a mostly breeding-plumaged 3rd summer bird, which is similar to a full adult. Utah, May

wing feathers and a dull yellow bill with a black spot near the tip that may have a small adjacent red spot. Many 3rd summer birds retain fairly heavy spotting on the head and nape and don't acquire the clean white head of adults, but some

3rd summer birds mostly resemble breeding adults in plumage and have a yellow bill with red and black spots near the tip, but often show reduced white outer primary tips and some pale brown feathering in the wing.

RING-BILLED GULL *Larus delawarensis*

SIZE **17.5–20 inches long**   WINGSPAN **45–53 inches**

It's the medium-sized, pale silver gray–backed gull standing in the parking lot with the sesame-seed bun in its mouth. (PD)

PROFILE   This active, dapper, medium-sized, and plump-breasted gull *is pleasingly proportioned and nimble footed.* It is probably the most widely known gull in North America because of its widespread occurrence across most of the continent in summer and winter.

Longish legs and quick, mincing steps differ from Herring Gull's waddle-and-stride style of walking. The well-defined narrow black ring near the tip of adult Ring-billed's yellow bill (and the absence of a red spot) is very useful for identification, but the namesake dark ring of adult Ring-billed is also found on 3rd winter Herring and California Gulls, whose larger size and respective pinkish or greenish legs help distinguish them.

The bill on subadult Ring-billed (1st winter) is also very eye-catching (pink to pinkish yellow), with a crisply defined dark tip. The silvery-gray back of subadults and adults is slightly paler than that of Herring Gull and distinctly paler than that of the larger, similar gray-backed adult California Gull and slightly smaller Mew Gull.

Ring-billed is slightly larger than Mew Gull, with which it may associate. It resembles a small Herring Gull, from which adults are distinguished by their yellow legs (dull pink in adult Herring) and slender physical profile. *Overall more plump breasted than Herring Gull, Ring-billed also has a rounder head and an acutely sloping forehead that terminates at the base of the bird's short, straight, somewhat blunt pencil stub of a bill* (be aware that some males have quite a long bill, with a decurved tip on the upper bill; see Ring-billed Gull 14, *lower left photo*).

Highly terrestrial, Ring-billed forages afoot in an array of habitats, including those generally avoided by other gulls. On seacoasts, Ring-billed forages actively in the wave zone, but also on the dry high beach, a habitat shunned by many gulls for feeding (but not roosting). Ring-billed is disinclined to forage offshore, the habitat favored by Herring Gull and other larger gulls, perhaps because its smaller size makes it vulnerable to kleptoparasitism (in which food acquired by one species [Ring-billed] is taken by another species). But Ring-billed does forage on mudflats, where its nimble biped tendencies give it an advantage. While it uses elevated perches (like parking lot light fixtures) to spot food, this species locates most of its food on foot, not by aerial cruising, as is common in Herring Gull. In winter, foraging birds are usually solitary or well spaced.

RING-BILLED GULL 1   Adults breeding. This medium-sized, pleasingly proportioned gull is one of the most widespread and common gulls in North America. It is like a petite Herring Gull, but one with yellow rather than pink legs as an adult; a round head with a steep, sloping forehead; and a short pencil stub of a bill. A crisp black ring just inside the pale bill tip is obvious in adults. This gull excels at biped locomotion, walking with quick, mincing steps. Pictured here are two habitats often frequented by foraging Ring-billed: the coastal wave zone and the upper beach, which is a habitat rarely targeted for foraging by other gulls. The pale gray upper back is slightly paler than in adult Herring Gull and much paler than in California Gull. Note the reduced, worn, white primary wing-tip spots on the *right* bird in midsummer, and the dark iris resulting from very low light after sunset. Florida, March (*left*); New Jersey, July (*right*)

RING-BILLED GULL 2 Adults with two other species. Two adult Ring-billed Gulls (the large birds) are shown standing on a Delaware Bay mudflat with two adult nonbreeding Bonaparte's Gulls (*front left* and *right*) and three nonbreeding Forster's Terns (*rear*). While not a large gull, Ring-billed is considerably bigger than these other two species. Ring-billed is often more comfortable standing with these smaller species than with larger gulls. The streaking on some nonbreeding Ring-billeds may impart a masked appearance, as in the front bird. New Jersey, March

RING-BILLED GULL 3 Adults. In flight, Ring-billed shows balanced proportions with equally projecting head and tail, and wings that are relatively long and tapered. The outer two black primaries show bold white mirrors just inside the tip. Nonbreeding birds show a streaked head and nape, which may be coarse and heavy (*right*) and somewhat similar to the less elegantly shaped Herring Gull, or more typically neat, sparse, and fine, as on the *left* bird. Florida, January (*left*); New Jersey, February (*right*)

RING-BILLED GULL 4 Ring-billed Gull with Royal Tern. While you are unlikely to confuse Ring-billed Gull (*right*) with Royal Tern, you may be surprised by the similarity in size. This 1st winter Ring-billed shows a typical black-tipped pinkish bill and worn, sun-bleached wing panel (wing coverts). Note the steep, sloping forehead and short, slender bill on Ring-billed. Florida, March

RING-BILLED GULL 5 Ring-billed and Herring Gulls, adults nonbreeding. This Ring-billed appears especially small compared to the near-adult Herring Gull (*left*), which has a very large bill, flat crown, and bulky, compact body often found in large males, but it is better to just call it a very large Herring Gull. Ring-billed shows yellow legs versus pink on Herring and has a smaller head; more slender overall profile with a plump breast; tapered rear body; proportionally longer wings; and a much smaller bill. Note the touch of red on Herring Gull's bill, which Ring-billed never shows. New Jersey, December

RING-BILLED GULL 6 Subadult, 1st winter, with subadult Great Black-backed Gull (*right*). A worn 1st winter Ring-billed Gull is keeping a respectful distance from this much larger subadult Great Black-backed Gull on a Florida beach. Note how small the Ring-billed is compared to this Great Black-backed Gull, and the pink cast and well-defined dark tip to the bill of Ring-billed. Florida, March

STATUS AND DISTRIBUTION Ring-billed is arguably the most common gull in North America, where it can be seen in all forty-eight contiguous US states, all lower Canadian provinces, and south in winter to southern Central America. Breeding range is widespread across the upper tier of the United States and lower Canadian provinces, and winter range includes Atlantic and Pacific US coastal regions and much of the interior United States where water remains open, at least for most of the year. Ring-billed is the common gull in parts of Mexico and Central America, as well as on some Caribbean Islands.

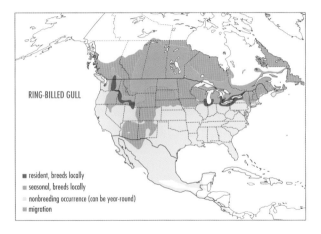

RING-BILLED GULL

■ resident, breeds locally
■ seasonal, breeds locally
□ nonbreeding occurrence (can be year-round)
■ migration

Ring-billed frequents an array of habitats, including inland lakes and water courses, parking lots, parks, golf courses, fast-food restaurants, plowed fields, and seacoasts. While it may join mixed gull flocks, where it often situates itself on the periphery, Ring-billed more typically gathers in homogeneous groups ranging in size from two to five birds to many hundreds in prime wintering areas, such as the tilled agricultural land near the Salton Sea of California. Across much of interior North America, this species is the default white-headed gull.

ADULT (combines adult and 2nd winter) The silvery-gray back is slightly paler than in adult Herring Gull and distinctly paler than in the larger California Gull and smaller Mew Gull. *The bright yellow bill with a crisply defined black ring in combination with bright yellow legs and eyes distinguishes it* (although 2nd winter birds retain the dusky eyes of younger birds and often show a greenish bill with a small yellow tip, greenish legs, and a bold black ring near the bill tip) (see Ring-billed Gull 9). In winter, birds show a strong to lightly speckled and/or streaked head, neck, and upper breast that appear more sparsely and neatly patterned than the dark, coarse, heavy streaking of Herring Gull and California Gull, and streaks, spots, and smudgy brownish-gray shading of Mew Gull.

RING-BILLED GULL 7 Ring-billed and Bonaparte's Gulls, adults nonbreeding. While Ring-billed is a medium-sized gull, it looks very large and imposing next to a diminutive Bonaparte's Gull. Bonaparte's regularly forages adjacent to Ring-billed in shallow waters in winter to take advantage of the food that is stirred up by Ring-billed's feet. No aggression from the larger Ring-billed occurs, as it accepts its smaller cousin without protest. Ring-billed tends to walk while foraging, while Bonaparte's swims. This Ring-billed is shaped much like one of the larger white-headed gulls, and its very long, heavy bill and bulky body structure are on the large end of its scale. Florida, January

RING-BILLED GULL 8 Ring-billed Gull with Lesser Scaup. Ring-billed Gulls, like this subadult (1st winter), habitually poach food from diving ducks like Lesser Scaup. They wait until the duck dives for its food and then rush in to grab any scraps that might escape the duck's bill when it surfaces. Ring-billed's round head, with the sloping forehead and dark-tipped dull yellow bill of a subadult, is shown here. Florida, January

RING-BILLED GULL 9 Ring-billed Gull, subadult (2nd winter). Second winter Ring-billed appears very similar to adults, but it has greenish legs and bill versus yellow in adults, and it may show a brownish tinge on the lower wing panel (greater wing coverts). The bill has a yellow tip, as in adults, and there is typically fine streaking on the head and nape in nonbreeding birds, but the fine spotting on the breast is similar to juvenile feathers, even though these are new 2nd winter feathers. Black outer primaries lack the white tips of adults as well. Florida, January

RING-BILLED GULL 10 Adults nonbreeding. Nonbreeding adults may be lightly streaked on the head and nape or more faintly streaked, like the bird at *right*, which has already started its early body molt to breeding plumage in late January. Both birds show a classic black ring on a yellow bill, yellow legs, and pale yellow eyes. Upperpart shading on the *right* bird appears dark, as in a California Gull, but this is a result of very low light after sunset. California would also have dusky eyes and a red spot to go with the black ring on the bill. New Jersey, October (*left*); Florida, late January (*right*)

RING-BILLED GULL 11   Fresh juveniles (immatures). This fresh juvenile plumage (*left* and *center*) shows neatly arranged wing coverts and dark-centered upperpart feathers with crisp white edges. This complete juvenile plumage is usually seen for only a short time in July and August, after which Ring-billed molts in (replaces) large numbers of adultlike feathers on the upper back. Some juveniles, however, retain juvenile plumage into very late fall, but this is not typical of this species. Juvenile Ring-billeds are mostly brownish gray with strongly marked upperpart feathers and underpart scalloping, and black outer primaries. A very small pink bill has a smudgy black tip. The flight photo (*center*) shows long, tapered wings and a rounded tail with a broad, dark band and a narrow, pale tip. The bills of young Ring-billeds are typically smaller than those of adult birds, and the *right* bird shows a particularly small bill that recalls Mew Gull. However, juvenile Mew Gull has a less distinctly streaked head with more smudgy brownish shading; a shorter, thicker neck; a mostly dark bill; and a slight, pale rear collar on the back of the head. The *right* bird is quite similar to juvenile Mew Gull, however, and requires close examination to separate it. Rhode Island, late July (*left* and *center*); New York, early August (*right*)

RING-BILLED GULL 12   This Ring-billed Gull caught a Needle Fish, but could not swallow it due to the long, pointed bill that probably would have gotten stuck in its throat, with dire consequences. It then dropped the fish near some White Pelicans, who also were afraid to swallow it. Florida, March

IMMATURE (juvenile)   Mostly overall brownish gray, with body coarsely spotted or patterned, and head finely streaked with brown markings. Upperpart feathers are dark brown in the center with strong white fringes, similar to the upperparts of juvenile Mew Gull, which differs by having a grayish-brown wash to the head and neck with diffuse gray streaks. Similar to juvenile California Gull (see California Gull 9, p. 100), but note the more petite bill and more neatly patterned upperparts on Ring-billed. While most juvenile Ring-billed Gulls molt into 1st winter plumage by early fall, some may retain their juvenile plumage until late fall or early winter.

SUBADULT (combines 1st winter and 1st summer)   Shows pale gray back similar to that of adults, but with white fringing and some dark interior spotting in fall; brownish to blackish primaries; and brown, patterned wing coverts of juvenile birds that are retained throughout the 1st year. Most closely resembles a miniature subadult (2nd year) Herring Gull, with the gray upper back of an adult and brownish wing coverts. In this age class, *note subadult Ring-billed's smaller, pinkish bill with the crisply defined black tip* and the pink to yellowish legs (bluish in comparably plumaged subadult [2nd winter] California Gull; dull pink in Herring Gull). First winter birds often retain light to heavy juvenile brown spots on the breast and flanks until midwinter, and occasionally until spring.

RING-BILLED GULL 13 Subadult (1st winter). Subadult (1st winter) Ring-billed Gulls show evenly balanced proportions; contrasting upper and underwing patterns; a grayish upper back; a broad black band on the tail; and a small pink bill with a black tip. Note contrasting gray inner primaries (inner primary window), which are not feathers replaced in the 1st winter but just grayer feathers from juvenile plumage. Florida, January

RING-BILLED GULL 14 Subadult (1st winter). We refer to this age group as subadult (1st winter) because of the adultlike, pale gray upper back feathers, which typically occur in larger white-headed gulls in their 2nd or 3rd winters. First winter Ring-billed Gull shows gray upper back feathers somewhat similar to those of adults but retains brownish juvenile feathers on the wing panel (wing coverts) and tertials. Note the pale fringes on the fresh gray upper back feathers (*upper left*) in November, and the dark chevron markings on the postjuvenile gray back feathers of the *upper right* bird (Florida, January). Also note the classic pale pink bill with the crisp black tip of early 1st year birds, with the more advanced bird in April (*lower left*) starting to show a slight yellow cast on the bill and tip, as in adults. Juvenile head streaking and body spotting may be heavy until midwinter (*lower right*), after which it attains a more uniform overall whitish appearance. Florida, November (*upper left*); Florida, January (*upper right* and *lower right*); Florida, April (*lower left*)

MEW GULL *Larus canus*

SIZE **16.2–19 inches long**   WINGSPAN **39–47 inches**

It's the smallish, silver-backed gull with my ham sandwich in its mouth (refer to introduction, p. 15). (PD)

PROFILE Mew Gull is *a medium-small, nimble, somewhat elegant gull* with a refreshingly uncomplicated plumage pattern. Physical profile is horizontal, somewhat tern-like, with a short neck, round head, and petite bill. Ring-billed and California Gulls have longer, blunter, and more classically hook-tipped bills.

As our smallest "white-headed gull," Mew Gull is most commonly confused with the larger Ring-billed Gull but is more delicately proportioned, with a rounder head and a more *slender, pointy, thrush-like bill*. Dusky eyes on Mew Gull impart a gentle expression (although some individuals have paler, amber-colored eyes). Darker primaries extend well beyond the tail and are often slightly elevated. Observers may find structural commonality between this species and kittiwakes (mostly pelagic gulls).

Mew Gulls are very social and are often seen loafing on beaches or foraging together. They use several foraging techniques: fluttering low and slow over water with their head turned down and legs dangling; sitting high on the water and swimming buoyantly while turning in the manner of a feeding phalarope; or swimming hard against the current, snapping up edibles as they pass. Loafing birds tend to cluster, sometimes near Ring-billed and California Gulls, but in general they avoid larger species. On land they forage by walking and sometimes catch insects in flight.

MEW GULL 1 Adult breeding. This classic adult breeding Mew Gull shows an unmarked yellow bill, yellowish legs, and a dusky eye with a red orbital ring. Call is a high, petulant-sounding *yip* that is breathier and more squealing than that of Ring-billed. This adult is defending its subarctic nest territory by standing on a tall conifer and warning other gulls to steer clear. Alaska, May

MEW GULL 2 Adults breeding. A mated pair of Mew Gulls sitting on ice floes in their subarctic breeding range is a familiar sight. These delicate birds are fairly common local breeders in subarctic regions of Alaska and Canada, and their dainty profiles with dusky eyes in blank faces make them all the more appealing. Note their round heads and high-profile crown, dull yellow legs, and petite, thrush-like, unmarked yellow bills. Alaska, May

MEW GULL 3 Comparison to Ring-billed Gull, adults. Adult Mew Gulls *left*; Ring-billed Gulls *right*. On Mew Gulls note the rounder head, somewhat plumper body, darker upperparts, dusky eye, and petite, unmarked, thrush-like yellow bill. Ring-billed shows a longer-bodied profile; longer legs; a longer, thicker bill with a dark ring near the tip; a pale yellow eye; and more exposed black on the outer primaries, which is best seen on flying birds. More extensive white tips on the black outer primaries of the Mew Gulls are evident here. Note the broad white outer portion of the tertials (rear upper back feathers) on Mew versus the very limited white tertial markings on Ring-billed, which is a field mark that can be useful in separating distant flying birds. The dark eye imparts a gentle expression to Mew Gull, whereas Ring-billed's yellow eye imparts a sly impression. Alaska, May (*left*); Florida, March (*right*)

MEW GULL 4 Mew Gull and Ring-billed Gull, comparison of subadult/1st winter birds. Note Mew Gull's (*left*) rounder head, more petite bill with a black tip, and overall less contrasting plumage. Mew also has a shorter neck and a more compact body and wing profile. Some gray feathers are beginning to show on the upper back of Mew Gull, whereas Ring-billed's upper back at this date is mostly gray. Ring-billed's larger, brighter pink, dark-tipped bill stands out compared to the dull grayish-pink bill base of Mew Gull. California, December (*left*); Florida, January (*right*)

MEW GULL 5 Adults on nest with forced copulation. These adult breeding birds show round heads, petite, unmarked yellow bills, and dusky eyes. Wait, one of these has pale eyes! OK, some Mew Gulls show pale gray eyes. Note the grayish outer two primaries with two large white mirrors just inside the tip, which are larger than those on Ring-billed Gull. This copulation on the nest was the wish of only the male; the female sitting on the eggs wanted no part of this behavior at this stage of nesting. Alaska, May

STATUS AND DISTRIBUTION Common far-northern breeder from Alaska east to upper western Canada, and a common winter visitor along the West Coast from Washington south to the upper Baja California coastline, but rare elsewhere. Mew Gull occurs year-round in lower coastal Alaska.

In winter, Mew is usually found in nearshore ocean waters, often foraging over kelp beds, and it occurs inland in several locations where it follows large rivers. It also frequents inlet estuaries, sewage outflows, and treatment facilities. Inland it visits short-grass pastures, plowed fields, and sewage treatment ponds, but less typically landfills. Mew Gull also inhabits cities and towns, such as Anchorage, Alaska, where it sits on buildings and forages for scraps of human food in streets and parks. While this species feeds primarily on natural food sources in winter, it occasionally mobs humans for handouts near breeding sites in Alaskan cities when people foolishly take out a few morsels of food to feed the cute gulls nearby.

ADULT (combines adult and 2nd winter) Gray wings and back are conspicuously darker than on adult Ring-billed Gull. The petite yellow to yellow-green bill may show a faint dark tip or ring in the 2nd winter, but it is otherwise plain. Black primaries show small to large white spots at the tip, and the outer two primaries have two bold white rectangular patches (mirrors) just inside the tip, best seen in flying birds or those with raised wings (see Mew Gull 5). Legs are yellow to greenish yellow. Nonbreeding Mew Gull has a whitish head with a smudgy gray wash that contains fine streaks on the crown

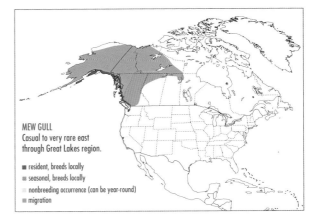

MEW GULL
Casual to very rare east
through Great Lakes region.

■ resident, breeds locally
▨ seasonal, breeds locally
 nonbreeding occurrence (can be year-round)
▨ migration

and cheek, but it can also show heavy streaking on the head as well. The rear neck and upper breast can also show smudgy gray spots and heavy streaks. Head and neck of adult California Gull are very coarsely streaked in winter (see California Gull 8, p. 100). The dusky to pale grayish eye of adult Mew Gull is duller than Ring-billed's pale yellow eye.

IMMATURE (juvenile plumage) Fairly uniformly grayish brown above and below, with a paler face and throat and a pale line of feathering behind the cheek. Upperparts are strongly fringed with gray edges, and the under tail is heavily barred. Except for its dark brownish-black outer wings and tail, the bird is characterized by a smooth, bland, gray-brown uniformity. The bill is mostly black with a pale pink lower base

MEW GULL 6 Mated pair at nest site. These Mew Gulls are shown in their typical subarctic microhabitat. Call is a petulant-sounding *yip*. Note the dusky eye on the *right* bird, which reflects variation in eye color. Alaska, May

large white mirrors
on outer two black
primaries

MEW GULL 7 Adults. These two breeding and one nonbreeding (*right*) Mew Gulls show limited black on the primaries but two large white bars (mirrors) within the extensive black of the outer two primaries. Their flight profile is somewhere between that of Ring-billed Gull and Black-legged Kittiwake, with buoyant, fluid wing beats that appear effortless. Medium-gray upper wings and back; whitish underwings; a white wedge-shaped tail; and a broad white trailing edge to much of the wings complete the plumage profile. Breeding adults have a clean white head, neck, and underparts, while nonbreeding adults show gray spotting and smudging on the head, neck, and breast, with a grayish-streaked cap and cheek spot. A shadow of a dark ring just inside the tip is found on nonbreeding adults. Note the extensive black shading and large size of the white mirrors on the outer two primaries, which are present on all large gulls but are typically smaller on most other gulls compared to Mew Gull. Alaska, May (*left* and *center*); California, January (*right*)

in young juveniles, but it appears grayish to pinkish with a dark tip by midfall, when grayish upper back feathers may start to appear. Some birds retain their juvenile plumage until late fall. *Its small size, petite bill, and plumage uniformity distinguish it,* especially when it is standing among more contrastingly patterned gull species. In flight, the mostly brownish-black

lower tail is very conspicuous, as is the heavy barring on the upper tail coverts. Ring-billed Gull's whiter tail shows a terminal band that is narrow and black.

SUBADULT (1st winter)   Still retains a sense of the uniform grayish to brownish plumage but shows a gray upper

MEW GULL 8 Immatures (1st winter). Except for the dark outer upper wing and tail, 1st winter Mew Gull shows an overall grayish-brown plumage with pale feather edges that lack strong contrast. Underwing is mostly whitish or pale gray and shows little to no dark shading on the outer wing and primary wing tips. These younger immatures have not yet replaced their juvenile upper back feathers with gray adultlike feathers, and thus they appear uniformly grayish-brown above, unlike most Ring-billed Gulls at a similar time of year. First winter Ring-billed's upperparts show a strong contrast between retained juvenile wing coverts and the fresh gray upper back, and their upper wings are boldly patterned with much contrast. Note Mew Gull's petite bill, which is dull pink with an ill-defined black tip, not bright pink at the base with a strong black tip, as in 1st winter Ring-billed. California, December

MEW GULL 9 Subadults. A late 1st winter subadult Mew Gull (*left*) has lost much of the typical gray spotting and smudging on the head of 1st winter birds due to wear and sun bleaching, and the underparts are also appreciably whiter, with only a smattering of gray spots. The underwings are typical of 1st winter birds, but the upper wings show whitish feathers on the wing panel, which could be a result of bleaching and wear. The bill is yellowish, with a black tip. The *right* bird is a 2nd winter bird that has a mix of darker gray adultlike feathers and paler gray 2nd winter ones, including some with a brownish cast. Note the black spots on the tail and the lack of white primary wing tips. The white mirrors in the outer two primaries are also smaller than in adults. Alaska, May (*left*); California, January (*right*)

MEW GULL 10 Immature 1st winter and subadult 2nd winter. A late 2nd winter Mew Gull (*left*) shows gray versus black outer primaries in adults; a yellowish bill with a shadowy dark tip; and dark gray spots on the tail tip. The late 1st winter Mew Gull (*right*) has mostly retained juvenile plumage except for the smudgy grayish upper back and whiter head and underparts. Bills on juveniles and 1st winter birds have black tips, as in Ring-billed Gulls, while 2nd winters can have either a black tip or a muted gray tip, as in the *left* bird in spring. Note the unusually long bill and overall larger physical proportions on the *right* bird, which suggest a male and are more similar to those of Ring-billed, compared to the typical delicate bill and smaller proportions on the *left* bird. Both show the long, tapered wings of this species. Alaska, May

back somewhat similar to that of adults, which contrasts with the brown, patterned juvenile wing panel. Mew Gull is overall less contrastingly patterned than subadult Ring-billed Gull. The pale pink to grayish bill shows a crisply defined black tip. Underparts are brownish and smudged with a slightly paler breast. So despite their ongoing molt, 1st winter birds on the whole retain their neat, uniform plumage. Subadult Ring-billed in comparison shows mostly white underparts with neat brown scalloping and a much whiter upper tail.

(2nd winter) Mew Gull at this age often shows remnant dark spots on the tail tip from immature plumage; reduced white spots on the wing tips; a mix of gray and brownish feathers on the wing; a darkish bill tip; and a brownish cast to the inner wing (see Mew Gull 10).

ICELAND GULL *Larus glaucoides,*
includes subspecies *kumlieni* and *thayeri*

SIZE of ssp. *kumlieni*: 19–24 inches long
WINGSPAN 49–57 inches SIZE of ssp. *thayeri*:
19.7–25 inches long   WINGSPAN 54–58 inches

It's the smallish, plumpish-bodied, round-headed, petite-billed, short-legged, uniformly pale gull nestled amid the collage of contrastingly patterned Herring Gulls clustered on the beach. (PD)

PROFILE   This medium-large, pleasingly proportioned gull *is smaller, plumper breasted, and shorter legged than Herring Gull, and typically distinctly smaller and less bulky than the similarly plumaged Glaucous Gull,* from which Iceland may be distinguished by its longer wings that extend well beyond the tail of standing birds (generally a bill length beyond the tail). In adult birds, primaries range from white or light gray to charcoal gray, and to black in Thayer's Gull, a subspecies of Iceland Gull.

Iceland's bill ranges from *petite and bullet shaped* to fairly long, with a decurved tip on larger birds. The bill is *mostly dark*

ICELAND GULL 1 Adult, mostly breeding plumage. Iceland Gull has a round head; gentle expression; very pale silver-gray back; short pink legs; and a short, slender, bullet-shaped bill. Even by Iceland Gull standards, this adult is particularly plumpish and petite billed. These pallid gulls resemble immature Glaucous Gulls in all plumages except for the grayish wing tips found on many adults of the Kumlien's subspecies. While dark gray to blackish primaries (exposed outer wing tips) are more typical in Thayer's Gull, the yellow eye, the tiny yellow bill, and the pale gray back are consistent with the Kumlien's subspecies of Iceland Gull. Note that the wing tips extend more than a bill length beyond the tail, which gives Iceland a long, tapered rear body impression. This helps separate it from Glaucous Gull, which has a stockier, more compact overall profile and wings that extend just past the tail (see Iceland Gull 3). New York, March

ICELAND GULL 2 Adult plumage. Adult showing ice-blue upperparts and white wing tips that eliminate all but similarly plumaged Glaucous Gull. But note Iceland's round head, petite bill, and wings that extend well past the tail tip. While difficult to assess here, Iceland's smaller size was apparent in the field. This plumage is similar to that of the nominate Iceland Gull (*L. g. glaucoides*) that breeds in Greenland and winters in Iceland and northern Europe, but it is not presently possible to identify this bird with certainty to nominate Iceland Gull or Kumlien's subspecies. Massachusetts, February

ICELAND GULL 3 Iceland and Glaucous Gulls, immatures/1st winter (digitized photo). This shows the smaller size, rounder head, and longer-winged profile of Iceland compared to the larger size of Glaucous and its bigger, oval-shaped head, bulkier chest, and relatively short wings that extend slightly past the tail. Note Iceland's more centrally positioned eye, which is set forward on Glaucous because of the wider rear head. Overall white plumage flecked with gray or buff spotting is typical of both species. Particularly apparent is Glaucous Gull's heavy, pink bill with a well-defined dark tip compared to Iceland's dull pink–based bill with a poorly defined dark tip. Connecticut, April (both birds)

on immature/1st winter birds, but some birds can show a pinkish to yellowish bill with an ill-defined black tip at this age. Immature Glaucous Gull's larger bill is richer pink and has a more sharply demarcated dark tip compared to that of immature Iceland. A round head, short neck, and shortish legs impart a plumpish, pigeon-like impression to many Iceland Gulls (an attribute never applied to the bulky, barrel-chested Glaucous Gull). In winter, the head of adult Iceland shows limited to no streaking, except for the Thayer's subspecies, which can show a heavily streaked head and neck. In a mixed flock with Herring Gulls, Iceland's (Kumlien's) smaller size and plain, pale, uniform plumage stand out.

Thayer's subspecies of Iceland Gull (*thayeri*) averages intermediate in size and structure between large Kumlien's Iceland Gull and small Herring Gull, but its adult plumage is much closer to that of Herring Gull with respect to the gray shading of its upperparts and black wing tips. While many adult Thayer's have dark eyes, some birds on the Pacific coast have pale to dusky eyes, so this field mark is not absolute. Rather than including extensive ID criteria for the Thayer's subspecies here, we ask that you please refer to captions in the Thayer's subspecies section of Iceland Gull at the end of this account for characteristics that distinguish it from Kumlien's Iceland Gull and Herring Gull.

STATUS AND DISTRIBUTION The Iceland Gull you are most likely to encounter in eastern North America is the subspecies *kumlieni*, which is casually known to birders as Kumlien's Gull. It is a low northeastern Canadian Arctic breeder, and because of its geographically restricted range, it is uncommon wherever it occurs. The nominate Iceland Gull, which breeds in Greenland and winters in Europe, may occur in North America, but separation is problematic.

Kumlien's Iceland Gull winters mainly in the Atlantic waters of Canada, but it is now a regular but uncommon

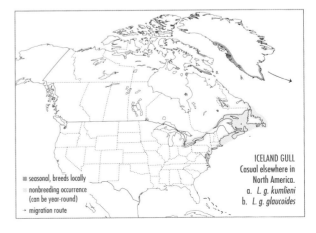

ICELAND GULL
Casual elsewhere in
North America.
a. *L. g. kumlieni*
b. *L. g. glaucoides*

■ seasonal, breeds locally
■ nonbreeding occurrence
(can be year-round)
+ migration route

ICELAND GULL 4 Iceland Gull (Thayer's subspecies), immature. This bird shows the round head, petite dark bill with a pink base, and plump-chested structure of Iceland Gull, but the patterned grayish-brown plumage, brown primaries with frosty edges, and brown-centered tertials point to the Thayer's subspecies of Iceland. Florida, January

ICELAND GULL 5 Iceland and Herring Gulls; immature 1st winter (*left*); adult nonbreeding (*right*). This classic uniformly pale immature (1st winter) Iceland Gull shows a plump body; long wings; and petite bill compared to the overall larger, more robust Herring Gull, which has a longer, heavier bill and longer legs. Immature Glaucous Gull, which also shares Iceland's pale wing tips and overall whitish plumage, would be slightly to noticeably larger than Herring Gull. The pink-based bill on this bird is seen in some immature/1st winter Iceland Gulls. New Jersey, January

wintering gull in coastal New England south to New Jersey and Pennsylvania, and in inland areas connected by waterways, especially garbage dumps. It also winters along the Saint Lawrence River to the Great Lakes. It is very uncommon to rare south to Florida and the panhandle Gulf states. The Thayer's subspecies of Iceland breeds in high Arctic Canada in various locations and winters primarily along the Pacific coast from northern British Columbia south to Mexico. Smaller numbers winter around the lower Great Lakes and in a small number of inland locations. *Inland records of Iceland Gull are usually of the Thayer's subspecies.*

Thayer's has been regularly found in winter in small numbers in recent years from Florida to Texas and along the Atlantic coastline. In the western Canadian Arctic Archipelago and along the West Coast, individuals (subadults and adults) with darker, even blackish, primaries dominate and

ICELAND GULL 6 Immature with other species. This immature (1st winter) Iceland Gull (Kumlien's subspecies) shows the typical creamy white, uniformly pale overall plumage with dusky mottled belly; black bill; dull pink legs; and dusky primaries with white highlights. This is a large, bulky Iceland Gull with a heavy bill for that species, but Thayer's is eliminated by tertial patterns. Other gulls include near-adult (*rear center*) and immature (*left rear*) Herring Gulls and nonbreeding Laughing Gulls for size comparisons. Florida, January

were until 2017 considered a separate species, "Thayer's Gull." Except for their slightly smaller size and less robust bill, these Thayer's Gulls with dark wing tips might be mistaken for adult Herring Gulls (see Quiz 28, p. 197). *Some smaller Herring Gulls of all ages may closely resemble larger Thayer's Gulls, however, so extreme care must be taken with these birds. A careful assessment of their body and bill shape, and the presence of a dark eye and deep pink legs, help to separate these birds.*

ADULT (combines adult and 3rd winter) Except for the white head and neck, upperparts on Kumlien's are ice blue to pale gray, and some birds have an upper back as pale as that of adult Glaucous. Others, typically West Coast Thayer's subspecies, show an upper back as dark as or darker than that of adult Herring Gull. Wings of eastern North American Iceland Gulls typically show pale gray to charcoal primaries, but individuals with pure white primaries are occasionally seen.

ICELAND GULL 7 Iceland Gull (Thayer's subspecies, *front*) in worn immature late 1st winter plumage. This Thayer's in late 1st winter plumage shows bleached, worn, white feathers, especially the older wing feathers (wing coverts) and tertials; the deep pink legs of this subspecies; and a smaller, more slender bill compared to the immature Herring Gull behind it. Herring Gulls in worn, bleached 1st summer plumage can occasionally appear similar to this Thayer's, but with darker primaries, as in the rear Herring Gull. This bird shows a physical profile similar to that of Herring Gull, including the pulled-taffy look to its face and the flat crown, so extreme care is necessary in identifying this bird in the field. New Jersey, June

The petite to medium-sized bill is all yellow, with a red spot on the lower bill near the tip in adults, and yellow green with a dark ring like that of Ring-billed Gull near the tip in the 3rd winter. The bill of adult Glaucous Gull is much larger and is a rich yellow, with a red spot on the lower bill near the tip. In winter, nonbreeding adult Iceland shows fine streaking on the head that can be denser on some birds. Some nonbreeding Thayer's Gulls are so heavily streaked that they appear hooded. Eyes are pale on Kumlien's but dark on most Thayer's, with some showing pale to dusky eyes. Legs are deep pink on Iceland Gull.

ICELAND GULL 8 Adults. These mostly breeding adults show the characteristic ice-blue upperparts and gray-tipped outer primaries that are seen on the Kumlien's subspecies. Wings are typically long and tapered near the tip, except on some larger birds (see Iceland Gull 11). Note the round head, petite yellow bill, gentle expression, and wing tips that extend well beyond the tail of the swimming bird. In flight, broad-based wings add to the bulky-chested profile of this species. New York, February

ICELAND GULL 9 Thayer's subspecies (*left*) and probable (by range) Kumlien's subspecies (*right*), adults nonbreeding. The nonbreeding Thayer's (*left*) shows slightly heavier streaking than the adult nonbreeding Kumlien's (*right*), but this is just normal variation. The presumed Kumlien's shows an icy blue-gray upper back; long wings that project well past the tail; and pale yellow eyes, which differ from the pale to dusky eyes and darker gray back of this West Coast Thayer's. Thayer's has black primary wing tips with bold white spots, while this Kumlien's has pure white primary wing tips, which are very similar to those of the nominate Iceland Gull (*L. g. glaucoides*), from which it can't be separated in the field. Note how similar the overall structural proportions are. Closer inspection shows a slightly smaller head and bill; a thinner neck; and a slightly more slender body on Kumlien's, which are differences between these subspecies, but these differences could also be the result of variation within each subspecies. California, November (*left*); Massachusetts, February (*right*)

ICELAND GULL 10 Immatures (probable Kumlien's subspecies). These two immature (1st winter) Iceland Gulls show the characteristic off-white plumage and leg color of 1st winter birds but apparent differences in the overall structure, head shape, and bill size. There is considerable variation in size and structure among gulls, but the *left* bird is especially large and bulky for Iceland Gull, which suggests a male, but nothing certain. Iceland Gulls have a plumpish body (especially the breast); a short, thin, black bill (pink with a defined black tip in immature [1st winter] Glaucous); and wings that extend well beyond the tail. The *right* bird is a textbook juvenile 1st winter Iceland right down to the gentle expression, while the *left* bird is on the large side for Kumlien's. Florida, January (*left*); Connecticut, April (*right*)

ICELAND GULL 11 Immature (1st winter). This upper wing shot shows the eye-catching, overall pale whitish-gray plumage with pale brownish spots; mostly white flight feathers; and broad wings that impart a sense of stockiness to this species in flight. White primaries (outer flight feathers) exclude all immature gulls except Glaucous, which this bird might suggest because of the two-toned pink-based bill that Iceland occasionally shows in the 1st winter. However, Glaucous has a heavier bill than this bird, and a deeper pink one as well. New York, April

IMMATURE (includes juvenile to 1st winter and some 2nd winter) For the most part, a uniformly pale grayish to whitish gull, with fine buffy to brownish spotting on the up-perparts. Juvenile birds are browner overall. Underparts on 1st winter birds are typically brownish gray with diffuse dark spots and a whiter throat and head. A small to medium, all-dark bill is common in 1st winter birds, as are dark eyes, but some birds show a distinct pink bill with a dark tip in the 1st winter. Projecting wing tips may have the same shading as the upper back, which ranges from buff to grayish to gray brown. Thayer's subspecies shows *contrastingly darker brown wing tips with frosty edges* and tertials that are mostly brownish with pale barring near the tip.

secondaries (inner flight feathers)

primaries (outer flight feathers)

ICELAND GULL 12   Subadults. These subadult (2nd winter) Iceland Gulls show some pale gray adultlike upper back feathers but immature wing, body, and flight feathers and a pinkish to yellow bill with a dark tip. The *left* bird shows the grayish-marked white primaries of Kumlien's Iceland Gull. The *right* bird's all-white primaries are also possible at this age, though sun bleaching may have played a part in these very white wings. Note the round head, gentle expression, and pale eyes of 2nd year birds. New York, March (*left*); California, April (*right*)

ICELAND GULL 13   Immature, comparison with Great Black-backed Gull adult. Classic immature (1st winter) Iceland Gull (same bird as in Iceland Gull 5) showing uniformly pale plumage shared only by immature Glaucous Gull, which would be close to the size of this adult Great Black-backed. Comparisons like this help you remember the general size of single birds in future sightings. New Jersey, January

ICELAND GULL 14 Worn immature. These photos show an extremely worn, sun-bleached immature (1st winter) Iceland Gull brandishing a damaged leg, which probably kept the bird in St. Augustine, Florida, for the summer. The flying bird shows how the flight feathers have been reduced to just shafts with remnants of feathering. This is not a Glaucous Gull because of the thin bill with an ill-defined pinkish base and the very long, projecting wings past the tail. Despite the stark white plumage, this bird retains the classic gentle expression of Iceland. Ivory Gull is ruled out by the pale pink–based bill with a dark tip (dark bill with a pale tip on Ivory) and pink legs (black on Ivory), and leucistic Herring Gull by the very small size of this bird compared to the Herring Gulls that were nearby (not pictured here). This is not an albino gull because of the darker underwing coverts and dusky belly and undertail markings that were not bleached by sun exposure. Florida, May

SUBADULT (2nd winter) Second winter birds show the mostly white head and scattered pale gray upper back feathers of adults but also show brownish, strongly patterned wing panels similar to those of 1st winter birds, which typically become heavily bleached whitish by late winter (see Iceland Gull 12, *right* photo). The bill is pale pinkish to dull yellow, with a strong black tip (but nowhere near as bright as immature Glaucous Gull's bright pink bill with a black tip). Subadult Iceland's eye is dull yellow, or dark to dusky in some Thayer's.

ICELAND GULL *Thayer's subspecies,*
Larus glaucoides thayeri

The implications of all your present field guides notwithstanding, there is no such species as Thayer's Gull anymore. (PD)

PROFILE   Thayer's is now a subspecies of Iceland Gull. In 2017, Thayer's Gull and Iceland Gull were lumped; that is, they were determined by the American Ornithological Society to constitute a single species whose variation ranges from birds with pale wing tips in the East to birds with blackish wing tips breeding on the islands of the western Canadian Arctic Archipelago and wintering mostly along the West Coast

ICELAND GULL 15   Adult breeding. This adult Thayer's (subspecies of Iceland Gull) shows some Iceland proportions, including a slender bill and wing tips that project well past the tail, although the bill is typically larger than that of many Kumlien's Iceland Gulls. The round head with a steep forehead; the smallish, straight bill; the dark eye with a deep red orbital ring; and the extensive white mirror on the underside of the outer primary on the far wing would eliminate Herring Gull, whose upper back shading and black wing tips are similar to those of Thayer's. The deep pink legs also differ from those of Herring. Churchill, Manitoba, June

ICELAND GULL 16   Adult nonbreeding. In flight, this adult Thayer's shows the classic broad-winged stockiness of Iceland, but the blackish primary tips and outer primary pattern with large white mirrors distinguish this bird as Thayer's. Larger Glaucous-winged would have a longer, heavier bill and no black on the wing tips. Note the pale dusky eyes of this West Coast bird, which are not that unusual for Thayer's Gulls of that region. California, February

and Great Lakes, constituting a clinal variation within a single species group, "Iceland Gull." However, because of the long-standing ID challenges with this former species, we are treating it separately in the Iceland Gull photo section.

Thayer's was considered a subspecies of Herring Gull until 1963, when it was given full species status. It can closely resemble Herring Gull at all ages, so coverage is important to separate it as Iceland Gull from Herring Gull. Captions for Thayer's Gull photos show how it differs from other species and subspecies, including Herring Gull and Kumlien's Iceland Gull.

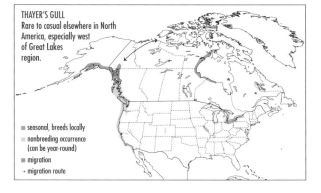

THAYER'S GULL
Rare to casual elsewhere in North America, especially west of Great Lakes region.

■ seasonal, breeds locally
  nonbreeding occurrence
  (can be year-round)
■ migration
→ migration route

ICELAND GULL 17 Adult nonbreeding. This adult nonbreeding Thayer's shows the classic Iceland features of a round head, petite bill, and gentle expression. Projecting primary wing tips are black, which is typical of Thayer's, and the white tips to these primaries are often distinctly larger than those of adult Herring Gull. The dusky eye with a thin red orbital ring (bolder in breeding birds) is also fine for Thayer's. California, November

ICELAND GULL 18 Kumlien's and Thayer's subspecies, immature/1st winter. These photos show a larger immature 1st winter Kumlien's Iceland Gull (*left*) and a similar-aged Thayer's Iceland Gull (*right*). In fact, both birds were photographed on the same day and on the same beach in Florida. Note how the large, bulky Kumlien's subspecies shows structural features and bill size and shape similar to those of this Thayer's compared to the small Kumlien's in Iceland Gull 19. Thayer's differs from Kumlien's Iceland Gull in several plumage details, most notably the browner primaries with frosty edges and brownish tertials with white markings near the tip versus whitish tertials with thin brown bars in Kumlien's. Florida, January

ICELAND GULL 19 Kumlien's (*left*) and Thayer's subspecies (*right*), immature/1st winter. This photo array was put together when these were separate species (early 2017). Differences are mainly in plumage, with the brownish, frosty-edged primaries of Thayer's differing from the white primaries of Iceland (note, however, that some darker Kumlien's Iceland Gulls can show pale brown primaries). Careful review of tertial patterns, secondary flight feathers (not shown), and tail patterns, which were used to separate these two "species" for many years, is no longer important for some birders since the birds are now both Iceland Gulls. The brownish tertials with some white barring near the tip on Thayer's differ from the whitish tertials with thin brown bars on the probable Kumlien's subspecies of Iceland (*left*). Connecticut, April (*left*); Florida, January (*right*)

ICELAND GULL 20 Thayer's subspecies, Kumlien's subspecies, and Herring Gulls, immatures/1st winter. This photo is worth its weight in gold, but it meant more to some birders when these were separate species. It shows a direct comparison of 1st winter Thayer's (*front left*); 1st winter presumed Kumlien's (*right*); and 1st winter Herring (directly *behind* Thayer's) Gulls. First winter Thayer's Gulls may resemble Herring Gulls in general structure and overall plumage shading, but note the paler brown primaries with frosty edges, the smaller bill, the frostier appearance of the upper back feathers, and the overall smaller proportions on Thayer's. The Kumlien's Iceland Gull shows typical overall pale plumage with very long, whitish primaries, a small dark bill, a rounded head, a plump breast, and dusky-spotted underparts. Kudos to Julian Hough of Connecticut for capturing this unique photo. Connecticut, December

ICELAND GULL 21 Thayer's subspecies and Herring Gull, immatures/1st winter. Here is a very illustrative comparison of 1st winter Thayer's Gull on the *right* and 1st winter Herring Gull on the *left*. First notice the smaller size, more petite bill, and overall paler, frostier upperparts plumage of Thayer's. The blackish primaries of Herring versus the brownish primaries with frosty edges of Thayer's are also shown. Florida, January

GLAUCOUS GULL *Larus hyperboreus*

SIZE **21.5–29 inches long** WINGSPAN **55–63 inches**

It's the very large, barrel-chested, overall pallid gull with the robust bill, the Great White Gull. (PD)

PROFILE *This large, robust-bodied gull typically shows overall pale plumage and white wing tips that project less than a bill's length beyond the tail,* giving the bird a more compact profile that the longer-winged but similarly plumaged Iceland Gull does not suggest. First year birds show dusky markings on the lower chest and belly and dark gray streaks on the head.

Glaucous is typically conspicuously larger than the array of Herring Gulls standing around it (see Glaucous Gull 3), and it usually appears much larger than any Iceland Gull that might be mixed in the crowd. Glaucous Gull also has a longer, heavier bill. Its large head often makes it appear beady-eyed. Because of plumage similarities with Iceland Gull, *a careful assessment of size, structure, and bill size and color is very helpful in separating these two "white-winged gulls."*

STATUS AND DISTRIBUTION Glaucous Gull is a fairly common high Arctic breeder from Alaska to Greenland, but it is uncommon to rare south of Canada. Winter range includes southern coastal Alaska south to the northwestern Pacific region of the United States, the Great Lakes region, and Atlantic regions from Greenland south to North Carolina, with some birds regularly appearing at the Great Lakes and many miles inland from coastal regions. Uncommon to rare south to California, Florida, and Texas, including adjacent Gulf coast states. In the northern areas, it may winter at sea, but in the United States and coastal Canada, Glaucous joins other gulls in places of food abundance (for example, dumps, fisheries, and coastal beaches).

GLAUCOUS GULL 1 Adults breeding, Alaskan breeding subspecies *barrovianus*. This large gull of northern regions, which overlaps with Great Black-backed Gull in size, is distinguished by its barrel-chested proportions; long, heavy bill; and relatively short wings. Females may be slightly to noticeably smaller than males, and this mated pair includes a larger male with a bigger bill in the *rear*. Individuals often appear compact in body shape, an impression heightened by pale primaries that project only modestly beyond the tail. The head is not as round as that of the smaller Iceland Gull (especially in the larger eastern subspecies), although some very small Glaucous Gulls may appear close in size to a large Iceland Gull. Note the adult's pure white, unmarked wing tips, a trait shared only by some adult Iceland Gulls. Upper back shading varies but is typically paler than that of Herring Gull. Alaska, June

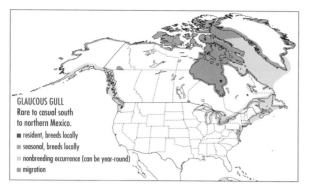

GLAUCOUS GULL
Rare to casual south
to northern Mexico.

■ resident, breeds locally
■ seasonal, breeds locally
■ nonbreeding occurrence (can be year-round)
■ migration

GLAUCOUS GULL 2 Glaucous and Iceland Gulls, 1st winter immatures—"another picture worth a thousand words." While the plumage on these two "white-winged gulls" is very similar, Glaucous (*rear*) is larger and has a longer, heavier bill with strong demarcation between the pink inner bill and the black tip; a bigger head; and longer, thicker, pink legs. Iceland has a smaller, thinner bill with diffuse pink on the base; a smaller, rounder head; and proportionally longer wings that extend farther beyond the tail. Note how the larger head of Glaucous often makes it appear more beady-eyed. This is a digitized photo from two separate images. Connecticut, February

GLAUCOUS GULL 3 Immature (1st winter) with Herring Gulls (2nd winter). Glaucous Gull's larger size, more robust proportions, bigger head, and overall paleness draw your eye to the Glaucous Gull in this pack. A long, pink, sharply demarcated, bicolored bill and white primaries showing only modest projection past the tail confirm your suspicion. This bulky, large-billed Glaucous belongs to the eastern North American subspecies (presumed by range), which is on average larger and has bigger physical proportions and a longer, heavier bill than the Alaskan-breeding subspecies. New Jersey, January

GLAUCOUS GULL 4 Adult breeding. This typically pale individual shows the long neck, pale eyes, barrel-shaped chest, and long, mostly straight bill that characterize this species. Its ghostlike plumage makes it conspicuous against the tundra landscape. Alaska, June

older, longer outer primaries

recently replaced inner primaries and secondaries

GLAUCOUS GULL 5 Adult breeding. This photo shows the long, broad-based wings of this species, with its white primaries (outer flight feathers) and uniform pale underwing. Overall paleness gives birds a "ghostly" appearance. The longer, older, outer primaries are a result of this adult molting (replacing) its inner flight feathers (secondaries and inner primaries) while on the breeding grounds in Arctic Alaska. These shorter, still-growing inner wing feathers don't portray the broad inner wings typically seen in this species. Note again the long, heavy, yellow bill with the red spot near the tip. Alaska, June

ADULTS (combines adult and 3rd winter) Exceedingly pale, icy gray above, with white primaries, white head, and bright white underparts setting off long, thick, pink legs and a bright yellow bill with a red spot near the tip. By early in the 3rd winter, birds have a yellowish bill and eyes and pale gray upper back feathers. Third winter birds somewhat resemble adults, but they often have a brownish cast to the lower wing coverts, sparse brown spots on the underparts, and a pinkish to yellow bill with a black spot near the tip. In winter, sparse grayish-brown streaking, spotting, or flecking may be limited to the rear crown, giving birds a capped appearance. Heavier, blotchy spots are located on the neck and upper breast of nonbreeding birds of the subspecies of adult Glaucous that breeds in Alaska (*L. h. barrovianus*), which can give these birds a hooded appearance.

IMMATURES (combines juvenile, 1st winter, and some 2nd winter) First winter birds are whitish overall, with sparse to heavy brownish spotting on the upperparts and fairly heavy diffuse brownish markings on the belly and lower breast. The upper breast, neck, and nape are typically whiter in contrast. Flight feathers are white, and upper wings are spotted with brownish gray. *In all immature plumages, the large bubble-gum-pink, dark-tipped bill stands out.* Note that a severely sun-bleached immature Herring Gull may be confused with immature Glaucous Gull, but Herring Gull's bill will be thinner, mostly dark or dull pink based, and less robust.

GLAUCOUS GULL 6 Immature (1st winter). This eastern North American subspecies (*L. h. pallidissimus*, presumed by range) is showing the uniformly pale whitish to buff-colored plumage with white wing tips and the dusky wash to the underparts of 1st winter birds. A long pink bill with a strongly demarcated black tip stands out on immatures, with the pink covering two-thirds of the bill. The pink on smaller-billed 1st winter Iceland Gull is restricted to the base or totally absent. New Jersey, January

GLAUCOUS GULL 7 Immatures. A small 1st winter immature with smallish (but stout) bill (*left*) shows the white, translucent flight feathers; dusky spotting on the underparts; finely streaked head; lightly barred tail; and dark eye typical of this age group. A 2nd winter immature (*right*) shows the cleaner white underparts, head, and wings; pale eye; and brighter pink bill of this age group. Note the broad wings on this individual. New York, March

GLAUCOUS GULL 8 Subadults. These photos show a 2nd summer Glaucous Gull (Alaska-breeding subspecies, *L. h. barrovianus, left*) and a 2nd (or maybe 3rd) summer eastern subspecies (*right*), which averages larger, bulkier, and heavier billed in comparison (though variation within the species, including sex, may also be responsible for the differences shown here). The petite, small-billed 2nd summer bird has acquired pale gray back feathers and some gray wing coverts, and it shows the typical pink legs and yellow-based bill of older 2nd year birds. The *right* bird shows similar plumage but seems to have more gray wing coverts. Aging this bird is not straightforward (at least for us), so you can safely call it a subadult. Note again the short primary projection past the tail and the long, straight bill. Alaska, June (*left*); Churchill, Manitoba, June (*right*)

SUBADULT (2nd winter) Shows the partial pale gray upper back of an adult, although some birds may show a whitish upper back with brown spots and gray feathers on the lower part of the upper back in their 2nd winter. Wing coverts may show a line of adultlike gray feathers within a mostly white wing (see Glaucous Gull 8). Flight feathers are mostly white, and upper wings are white with muted brown spots. Underparts are mostly white (paler than in 1st winter), with scattered, diffuse grayish-brown spots. A long, heavy, dark-tipped, pink bill is still evident and may show a pale tip.

GLAUCOUS GULL 9 Immature 1st winter with other gulls. The largest, all-white gull in the *center* is an immature 1st winter Glaucous Gull. Using this bird as a size guideline, try to identify the other gulls in the photo. Answers are in the appendix, p. 206. Hint: There are three other gull species, and three different age groups for one of the species. Florida, January

GLAUCOUS-WINGED GULL
Larus glaucescens

SIZE **22–26 inches long**   WINGSPAN **54–59 inches**

It's the large, silver-backed gull with the sockeye salmon scrap in its mouth, while the balance of the fish remains firmly wedged in the jaws of the grizzly bear. (PD)

PROFILE   *A large, stocky to slender gull* with medium-gray upperparts, pink legs, and short primary projection past the tail. *Glaucous-winged is variable in size and structure;* some birds show a large, bulky body like that of Glaucous Gull, while others are more slender, like small Herring Gulls. Head shape ranges from domed to flat topped, and the bill can be long and robust or smallish and slender.

Glaucous-winged is somewhat the same size and general shape as the dark-backed Western Gull (though some Glaucous-winged can be longer bodied). It shares with Western a fairly long bill (though typically straighter and more slender) and a preference for beach habitat. The two species commonly associate with each other, and where ranges overlap, they interbreed freely. Glaucous-winged is the only large, gray-backed gull with gray wing tips. (The wing tips of Herring Gull, which occurs in its range along the North American Pacific coast and Alaska, are black.) Older immatures and adults are distinctive with their pale gray wing tips, which are roughly the same shading as their upperparts.

GLAUCOUS-WINGED GULL 1 Adults breeding. This mated pair shows pale gray overall plumage with wing tips about the same shading as the upperparts; large yellow bill with a bulbous tip and a red spot near the tip; and dusky eyes with a red orbital ring. Bold white spots occur on the outer wing tips, and legs are a rich pink. Note the larger size of the male (*right*), which also has a larger head and a much heavier bill (note that some males may show smaller and more slender bills, with much variation possible). These differences between sexes are more easily noted in mated pairs like this and can be verified by copulation. Alaska, May

In all plumages, pure birds are distinguished from most other large, white-headed gulls by the general bland uniformity of their pale plumage, which lacks a pronounced contrast between upperparts and primaries. Compare to the darker primaries of Herring and Thayer's subspecies of Iceland Gull and the paler primaries of Glaucous Gull.

Over water, Glaucous-winged may pluck food from the surface or plunge into the water from a floating position or from low-level flight. It often drops hard-shelled prey (clams and crabs) onto hard surfaces to crack the hard exterior and allow easier access to the food inside. Outside the breeding season, Glaucous-winged roosts and interacts with other large gulls, most commonly Western Gull and, in Alaska, Herring Gull.

STATUS AND DISTRIBUTION Common to very common. While many birds remain throughout the year in northern breeding areas from near-coastal northern Oregon to Alaska, others move south to the West Coast of the United States and Baja California, Mexico, for the winter months,

GLAUCOUS-WINGED GULL 2 Adult chasing immature Bald Eagle. "None too pleased to share it." In Alaska, where both these species nest close to each other, Glaucous-winged often chases the larger predator out of its breeding territory. Although it is smaller and has less potent built-in weaponry, it gets the upper hand by flying above the eagle and attacking it from behind. Alaska, May

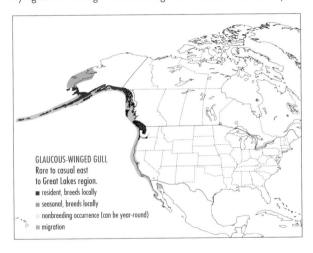

GLAUCOUS-WINGED GULL
Rare to casual east
to Great Lakes region.
■ resident, breeds locally
■ seasonal, breeds locally
  nonbreeding occurrence (can be year-round)
■ migration

GLAUCOUS-WINGED GULL 3 Subadult with sea otter. Glaucous-wingeds are opportunistic feeders and often poach food from other birds and mammals. This cagey bird is waiting for the otter to spin around to clean its chest from the scraps of the sea urchins it is eating. The gull will then swim in and pick up the floating scraps. Biologists call this an asymptotic relationship, where only one species benefits from the interaction, although the otter seems to be enjoying the bulk of the food without any help from the gull. Alaska, May

including the Gulf of California. By April, most wintering migratory birds have departed north for breeding zones.

Almost wholly coastal, Glaucous-winged favors bays, inlets, harbors, beaches, mudflats, and in winter, offshore waters where fishing vessels operate. It is also increasingly common in coastal cities, parks, and landfills. This species is almost never encountered far from coastal regions. It also frequents locations where bears feed on salmon and is a regular poacher where Bald Eagles feed on discarded halibut and salmon carcasses.

ADULT (combines 3rd winter and adult) Adults show silvery-gray upperparts that are darker than those of Glaucous Gull, *with grayish outer primary tips about the same shade as the upperparts or slightly darker.* In winter, the head, neck, and sides of the breast of nonbreeding birds are lightly to heavily streaked and washed with brown, giving more heavily marked birds a strong, hooded appearance. Most adults have dusky eyes and a bright yellow bill with a red spot near the tip; the 3rd winter bill shows a dark band inside the very small, pale tip.

IMMATURE (combines juvenile and 1st winter) Juveniles are uniformly grayish brown, with contrasting brownish markings on wing covert feathers and grayish-brown markings on the interior of upper back feathers. The 1st winter bird in Glaucous-winged Gull 6 (*left* photo) shows juvenile plumage that is somewhat paler than that of earlier-season birds

because of sun bleaching and feather wear by late November. The flying bird in the same composite photo shows a similar plumage with neatly arranged juvenile feathers on the wings. The lower wing panel (greater wing coverts) on some 1st winter birds shows some muted gray shading that contrasts with the rest of the strongly marked wing and is unique among large gray-backed gulls.

Mid-1st winter Iceland Gull (Kumlien's ssp.) differs from 1st winter Glaucous-winged by its whitish-gray upper back feathers with darker gray internal markings that match the rest of the upperparts compared to the mostly solid darker gray feathers of Glaucous-winged Gull in later 1st winter (see Iceland Gull 10, p. 123). Another difference is the pale gray tertials with grayish-brown barring in Kumlien's versus the mostly gray tertials with limited barring near the tips in Glaucous-winged. The head is whitish with strong gray-brown streaks on 1st winter Glaucous-winged.

First winter birds appear similar to the ones in Glaucous-winged Gull 6, with uniformly pale gray-brown plumage and grayish primaries about the same shading as the body. However, birds in late winter and spring display older feathers that have become bleached white, and these combined with newer, darker feathers create an unkempt, blotchy appearance to the plumage (see Glaucous-winged Gull 7). By the 1st summer, much bleaching has occurred, and the still mostly all-black-billed birds appear patchy, piebald, or all whitish. Juvenile and 1st winter immatures have all-black bills.

GLAUCOUS-WINGED GULL 4 Adult breeding. Note the silver-gray back that is darker than in Glaucous Gull but paler than in adult Herring Gull. In overhead flight (*center*), wings are whitish to gray, with translucent pale outer flight feathers that show only limited dusky outer primary shading with white tips. The pale gray shading on the outer primaries on the upper wing of the flying bird (*right*) is consistent with this species, with the light charcoal primaries of the floating bird (*left*) near the dark end of the curve for a pure Glaucous-winged. Alaska, May

GLAUCOUS-WINGED GULL 5 Glaucous-winged Gulls poaching scraps from Bald Eagle feeding frenzy. On Kenai Peninsula beaches, when fishermen discard the carcasses of halibut and salmon after cleaning them, Bald Eagles appear in large numbers to feed on them. Glaucous-winged Gulls often fearlessly enter the fray and grab pieces of fish. Note the immature late 1st winter Glaucous-winged in the middle of the pack with sun-bleached white plumage, black bill, dark eye, and pale wing tips that match the back. These large eagles could easily kill one of the gulls and eat it, but they are fully absorbed in fighting for tastier fish scraps and disregard the numerous gulls in their midst. Alaska, May

secondaries
(skirt)

greater wing
coverts (lower
wing panel)

GLAUCOUS-WINGED GULL 6 Immature (1st winter). These photos show a relatively robust black bill and the overall pale uniformity of plumage in 1st winter Glaucous-winged that ranges from pale grayish brown to pale brown, with a whitish background in lighter birds. Note that the primaries are the same shading as the back (compared to contrastingly white in Glaucous Gull and blacker in Herring Gull). Also note the grayer lower wing panel (greater wing coverts), which is a unique trait on this species compared to other large gray-backed gulls of the same age. The plain feathers beneath this panel are the secondary flight feathers, which form a "skirt" below the wing panel, a trait most often associated with large Pacific gulls (Cameron Cox, personal comment). Immature Glaucous Gull differs by having a bold pink bill with a defined dark tip and white primaries. California, November (*left*); California, January (*right*)

GLAUCOUS-WINGED GULL 7
Immature (late 1st winter). By late 1st winter, plumage is appreciably whiter overall, with flight feathers and tail translucent white and a whiter background to the head, upperparts, and underparts. Underwings and belly still show strong dark mottling, since the sun does not bleach these areas and they don't wear as much as the upperparts, tail, and wings. Bill remains mostly dark, except for some pale areas near the base. Similarly plumaged 1st winter Glaucous Gull has a strong pink bill with a demarcated black tip. Alaska, May

SUBADULT (2nd winter) Mostly overall pale grayish to dirty brown with pale gray upper back (of adult) or dingy grayish back feathers that are darker than adult ones. Primaries are the same gray-brown color as the body and lower wing panel. Underparts are smudgy gray or whitish in birds with more advanced plumage. The long bill can be mostly dark with diffuse pink or distinctly bicolored, with a pinkish pale base and a dark tip that recall Glaucous Gull, which would show contrastingly paler wing tips; a longer, deeper bill; and a pale eye, not dark like that of Glaucous-winged.

recently
replaced shorter
secondaries

GLAUCOUS-WINGED GULL 8 Immature/subadult (2nd winter). By late in the 2nd winter, Glaucous-winged typically shows a mix of mostly immature feathers and cleaner pale gray upper back feathers, which are similar to those of adults. The *left* swimming bird exhibits irregular pink color on the bill with a dark tip, which is also characteristic of this age. The *right* bird in flight shows the typical uniform pale wings of this age group, with the bicolored bill and active molt replacement of shorter inner flight feathers (secondaries) pointing to a 2nd year bird, versus a 1st winter, which would have uniform length flight feathers. Alaska, May

secondaries

secondaries

inner
primaries

GLAUCOUS-WINGED GULL 9 Subadults (2nd and 3rd late winter). These photos show a dorsal view of 2nd and 3rd winter Glaucous-winged Gulls. The 2nd winter bird (*left*) has gray back feathers, similar to those of adults, but the rest of the plumage is similar to that of immatures. Note the irregular pink color to the bill and the black tip, and the mostly uniform whitish to pale brownish-gray upper wing feathers and brownish tail, typical of 2nd year immature birds. The *right* bird in late 3rd winter plumage has a gray back and upper wing coverts (feathers on inner forewing) and adultlike secondaries (rear inner wing) and inner primaries (inner part of outer wing), which show bold white spots at the tip. A yellow bill with a red spot is also typical of older subadult and adult birds. Alaska, May for both photos

GLAUCOUS-WINGED GULL 10 Adults breeding. These large, stocky, West Coast to Alaska gulls are variable in size, physical proportions, and occasionally plumage. They have a large, stout bill with a bulbous tip, except for some birds that show a more slender, straighter bill, as in the *right* bird in the photo. Wings extend slightly past the tail, and the head may look flat topped on some individuals. They show a darker upper back than Glaucous Gull, which is silver gray as opposed to icy gray, and grayer primaries than those of Glaucous, which are typically the same shading as the upper back (as evidenced by the *left* bird). Note that the blackish primaries on the *right* bird are darker than is typical for this species and outside the range for a pure Glaucous-winged Gull, which strongly points to Herring Gull genes at this Alaskan location. Why not a pure Herring Gull? Dusky eyes with a red orbital ring versus bold yellow eyes with a yellow orbital ring on Herring. Near Homer, Alaska, May

GLAUCOUS-WINGED GULL 11
Glaucous-winged × Western Gull hybrid. In Washington, hybrids of these two species are commonly seen. This bird shows the stocky, bulky body structure and heavy bill with bulbous tip of Western Gull, but it has a medium gray rather than charcoal back, and a dusky rather than darkish eye, as in Western Gull. The medium gray shading of the upperparts is much darker than that of Glaucous-winged, and exposed blackish primaries are much too dark for Glaucous-winged. The pale under primary on the far wing is also paler than that of adult Western Gull. Northern Oregon, June

GLAUCOUS-WINGED GULL 12
Hybrid Glaucous-winged × Herring Gull adult. This bird is showing a somewhat pale eye rather than a dark eye, and grayish-black rather than black outer flight feathers (primaries) with small white tips, as would be the case in a pure Herring Gull, pointing to a hybrid between these two species. The outer primaries are too dark for any pure Glaucous-winged Gull but contain too much gray shading for Herring Gull. This hybrid condition is commonly noted in southern Alaska on the Kenai Peninsula, where this photo was taken. Alaska, May

GLAUCOUS-WINGED GULL 13 Adult breeding, with immature Bald Eagle and Northwestern Crow. A classic profile of this species showing pale gray upperparts and matching primaries with white tips; a clean white head and underparts; a large, mostly straight, yellow bill with a red spot near the tip; a bulky body with a tapered rear end; rich pink legs; and a dusky eye with a red orbital ring. This large gull shows no fear of this large predator when sneaking in to poach a scrap of fish. Note the white "skirt" of secondary tips under the wing coverts. A Northwestern Crow gives you an idea of the size of this gull, even though it appears small next to the very large eagle. Alaska, May

LESSER BLACK-BACKED GULL,
1st winter

LARGE DARK-BACKED GULLS

WESTERN GULL *Larus occidentalis*

SIZE **21–26 inches long**   WINGSPAN **53–55 inches**

It's the large, dark-backed gull standing on a piling at Monterey Pier waiting for the fishing boats to unload their catch, or for a tourist to drop a corn dog. (PD)

PROFILE   A large gull with an overall stocky, robust profile, Western Gull is about the same size as Herring and Glaucous-winged Gulls, but adults show a darker, charcoal-gray back. The large head supports a *stout, bulbous-tipped bill* (smaller and straighter on some birds) and a *curious bump or peak on the head* (just above the eye, or sometimes above the nape)

WESTERN GULL 1 Adult breeding. A large, sturdy, West Coast gull; essentially *the* dark-backed gull of the West Coast. This heavily built, broad-winged gull is more robust than Herring Gull and has a thicker, more bulbous-tipped bill. Some birds, however, can have a relatively slender bill. Westerns can show a flattish crown or a more rounded crown that has a bump over the eye. This breeding adult shows typical dark upperparts (noticeably darker than those of Herring Gull) and a protruding "skirt" (secondary wing tips) on the lower part of the folded wing on perched birds (see photo). Adult Western also has a bright yellow bill with a red spot near the tip, and pink legs. Eyes may be mostly dusky, as in the bird pictured, or yellowish, with these birds more closely resembling Yellow-footed Gull. This individual's bill, while long and heavy, is not as bulbous tipped as that of some other Westerns. Upperpart shading varies somewhat between northern and southern subspecies (paler gray in more northern birds). La Jolla, California, February

greater wing coverts

tips of secondary flight
feathers (skirt)

WESTERN GULL 2 Adult nonbreeding. This nonbreeding adult from Monterey County shows intermediate gray upperpart shading and very reduced spotting on the head and neck, which sometimes occurs in this species. California, November

WESTERN GULL 3 Western and Ring-billed Gulls, adults. A crisp breeding-plumaged Western Gull (*right*) is much larger and bulkier than the slender, long-winged nonbreeding Ring-billed Gull. Western's back is darker gray, and the much heavier bill is yellow with a red tip, versus yellow with a black inner ring as on Ring-billed. The pink legs and dusky eye of Western also differ from the yellow legs and eyes of Ring-billed. Seeing two very differently shaped gulls together helps you remember the different physical features of each species. La Jolla, California, February

black outer primaries

gray inner primaries

WESTERN GULL 4 Adult nonbreeding, with hybrid Western × Glaucous-winged Gull (*left*). Western Gull interbreeds regularly with Glaucous-winged, and the hybrid offspring may resemble the physical profile of either species, but they normally don't have all the typical plumage field marks. The *left* bird has the upperparts shading (though maybe slightly darker than average) and heavy nonbreeding streaking of Glaucous-winged, but the bulky body structure and large head and bill are more typical of Western. The pale eye and black wing tips are typical of Western, not Glaucous-winged, but the underwing pattern on the far wing with pale highlights is closer to Glaucous-winged. This pale-backed bird might be mistaken for a Herring Gull but for the pale primary underwing, pale to dusky eye (Herring has a bright, straw-colored eye), heavier bill, gray inner primaries, and darker gray upperparts compared to Herring's slightly paler gray ones. Monterey, California, November

WESTERN GULL 5 Western Gulls with Brown Pelican. Western Gulls are large gulls, but they are dwarfed by this adult Brown Pelican. Nevertheless, gulls go where the food is, and these two immatures (1st winter, *middle* and *left*) and subadult (*right rear*) hear the dinner bell. They hope to retrieve scraps that escape the pelican's bill while it feeds but are keeping a safe distance for the time being. La Jolla, California, February

that makes the head of Western Gull more convex (rounded) than the overall thinner head and drawn-out face of Herring Gull. The bill of Western typically appears thicker, shorter, and more bulbous tipped compared to Glaucous-winged's longer, straighter bill, with the exception of some smaller Westerns that have slender bills. Standing birds with neck retracted often appear to slouch. When birds are standing, wing tips extend well beyond the tail and are often elevated, leaving a slight gap between wings and tail.

Western mixes freely with other gulls, especially Glaucous-winged, and is often found where humans concentrate. It feeds primarily by scavenging over ocean waters for marine invertebrates. Its large size and bulky profile result in dominance over most gulls in its range. A Western Gull standing atop some elevated point on an ocean pier is a typical and iconic image. In the wave zone, it typically forages alone.

Two subspecies exist in Western Gull, with subspecies *occidentalis* occurring in northern California and farther north, and subspecies *wymani* occurring in southern California and farther south. Southern-breeding birds have a slightly darker back than northern ones, but recognition of this shading difference requires a good amount of study and exposure to both, and birds in the broad overlap zone show intermediate gray shading.

STATUS AND DISTRIBUTION A common and highly coastal West Coast gull, *the default dark-backed gull of the West Coast.* Breeding range is from the central Washington State coastal zone south to the coastal zone of the central Baja California Peninsula, Mexico. Winter range includes the breeding range and smaller areas north to the Canadian border and south to the southern tip of Baja, as well as the northern Gulf of California.

In winter on California beaches, Western is typically the most numerous gull species. If you are standing on a California beach and you are looking at a large, dark-backed gull, STOP; you are most likely looking at an adult or 3rd winter Western Gull. Western Gull also frequents landfills, harbors, lakes, and rivers. No other large, charcoal gray–backed gull typically occurs within its range along the Pacific coast.

WESTERN GULL 6 Adult courtship display. Note the bright yellow, heavy bill and deep pink legs and feet of adult Western Gull. Courtship behavior includes sensitive posturing involving head and neck contact. La Jolla, California, February

ADULT (combines 3rd winter and adult) This is a slam-dunk ID. Completely charcoal-gray upperparts make adult Western the darkest-backed gull on the coastal Pacific beaches where it occurs. Similarly dark Slaty-backed Gull is too rare for serious consideration, but if you think you have one, adults will have slightly darker upperparts and a less bulbous-tipped bill than Western. In winter, *adult Western shows little streaking on the head and neck, unlike the heavy streaking on adult Slaty-backed Gull.*

The very similar Yellow-footed Gull is geographically restricted (for now) to southern California's Salton Sea region; shows bright yellow legs, not pink as on Western; and has a thicker bill on average. A small number of Yellow-footed Gulls have been sighted on the California coast in recent years, however.

IMMATURE (includes juvenile and 1st winter) Immature Western is overall cold grayish brown and colder toned, darker, and more coarsely patterned above than immature Herring or Glaucous-winged Gull. Western also has contrastingly blackish-brown primaries. Juveniles are a deep brownish-gray

WESTERN GULL
Casual north to southeastern Alaska, south to western Mexico and the interior west.
■ resident, breeds locally
▨ nonbreeding occurrence (can be year-round)

WESTERN GULL 7 Adult breeding. Western Gull shows a heavy-bodied flight profile with long, broad wings that bulge slightly on the inner half. Upper wings of adult Western Gulls show extensive blackish outer primaries. White mirrors are located inside the tips of the two outer primaries (as on most large gulls), with small to moderate white spotting on the tips of the outer primaries and a bold white trailing edge on the rest of the wing. White spotting is greatly reduced or absent on 3rd winter subadults. La Jolla, California, February

WESTERN GULL 8 Juvenile plumage. Wow, here are a few tough ID photos! These very young juvenile Western Gulls show typical overall dark brown plumage with strong white feather edges on the upperparts and wings. This plumage is typically seen until late summer, and by early fall, the upper back feathers are replaced with more muted gray and brown ones. The young bird at *left* shows some pink on the lower inner bill. Upperpart feathers of the flying bird are crisp and neatly arranged, which is typical of juvenile birds. This plumage suggests an immature Heermann's Gull, which is smaller and has more slender wings. Immature Western is typically the darkest gull on the beach, along with immature Heermann's Gull. California, August (*left*); California, September (*right*)

WESTERN GULL 9 Immature (1st winter). These photos show Western Gull in early 1st winter plumage. Birds at this time of year still have their juvenile feathers, but these have worn slightly, resulting in a paler overall appearance compared to the birds in Western Gull 8. The *left* bird (September) is slightly paler than the flying juvenile in Western Gull 8 on the upper wing, head, and neck, but the dark flight feathers and mostly dark lower wing panel (greater wing coverts) are consistent with this species. The *right* bird in November still has a full complement of juvenile feathers, but pale feathering on the head, upper back, and breast is more apparent now that the dark edges have worn off. The *right* photo shows an immature (1st winter) Western Gull with very dark lower underpart feathers, a grayish-brown head and neck interspersed with whitish feathers, and very dark wing coverts with crisp, white fringes. The slender bill with a reduced bulging tip is just variation in bill size and shape in this species. California, September (*left*); Monterey, California, November (*right*)

WESTERN GULL 10 Immature (1st winter). These immature 1st winter Western Gulls show overall dark brown to gray plumage, a black tail tip, and a long, heavy bill with a bulging tip. Gray upper back feathers with dark centers have replaced dark juvenile feathers in this area, although some birds may retain dark juvenile feathers until late fall or early winter. This heavily marked dark plumage is typical in 1st year birds of this species. Note the mostly dark bill with the pale base on the lower bill. Dull legs are beginning to show a pink cast in the *left* bird. La Jolla and San Diego, California, February

mostly dark greater wing coverts

light and dark barred greater wing coverts

WESTERN GULL 11 Western and California Gulls, immatures (1st winter). These two immature gulls appear similar at first glance, but several different physical and plumage features soon become apparent. Western Gull (*left*) has a noticeably heavier overall profile with a bigger head, broader wings, and a much thicker, dark bill with a bulbous tip compared to California Gull's more slender overall profile with thinner, tapered wings, a smaller head, and a thinner bill. The pale head, whiter underparts, and black-tipped pink bill of California Gull differ from the uniformly dark head, back, and body and mostly dark bill of Western. The mostly dark greater wing coverts with pale tips on Western differ from the dark and light barred ones of California Gull (see photos), and the upper wing appears darker overall on Western. San Diego, California, early February

WESTERN GULL 12 Subadults. These subadult (2nd winter) Western Gulls show a partial charcoal-gray upper back, brownish wings, a heavy, two-toned pink bill with a bulbous black tip, and mostly whitish underparts. Third year Western Gull would show more gray in the wings and upperparts (some almost adultlike), a strong yellow bill with a black tip, and a cleaner white head, neck, and underparts. California, February

WESTERN GULL 13 Subadult (3rd winter). This advanced subadult (3rd winter) shows nearly completely charcoal-gray upperparts and a dark-tipped bill with a yellow inner portion. Mostly dark gray upperparts, slightly paler eyes (variable), and a yellow-based bill with a strong black tip help to distinguish this bird from advanced 2nd winter individuals. Note the older brownish wing feathers and the lack of any white spots on the wing tips. This bird shows an extremely large, bulbous-tipped bill. Monterey, California, November

overall and show more contrasting dark upperparts with strong white fringes compared to 1st winter birds, which replace their upper back feathers with more muted ones, and which show more white feathers on the head, neck, and upper breast throughout the fall.

The bulbous-tipped black bill is distinctly more robust than in Herring Gull, and by late in the 1st winter there may be a pinkish cast to the inner lower bill, or a pinkish-based bill with a dark tip on more advanced individuals. Immature Slaty-backed has a smaller, slimmer, less bulbous-tipped bill, paler overall plumage, and a mostly blackish bill in winter. Immature Yellow-footed has brighter pink legs and a whiter belly with less streaking than immature Western. However, some birds of these two very similar species may be indistinguishable.

SUBADULT By the 2nd winter, telltale dark gray upper back feathers are evident, often with a brownish cast, and obvious browner immature feathers are shown mostly on the wings. The white head, neck, and sides of the breast are often lightly or moderately streaked brownish. The heavy pink bill has a dark tip. *Key here is the dark color of the back feathers,* darker than those of any other adult or subadult gull on the West Coast beach. Third winter birds appear quite similar to adults but show remnant worn brownish feathers on the wing coverts, and typically a yellow bill with a black tip, sometimes with a small red spot behind it on the lower bill. Some 3rd winter birds may appear similar to full adults.

YELLOW-FOOTED GULL *Larus livens*

SIZE **22–26 inches long** WINGSPAN **59–61 inches**

It's the large, heavy-billed, dark-backed, white-headed gull on the shores of the Salton Sea with the tilapia in its mouth. (PD)

PROFILE *Essentially a Western Gull with a very long, bulbous-tipped, heavy bill*, with yellow legs and feet (adult and subadult), which are pink in adult Western Gull. Yellow-footed was formerly considered a subspecies of Western Gull, which is coastal and not presently found regularly at the inland Salton Sea, as is Yellow-footed. Molt is more advanced in Yellow-footed compared to Western, with 2nd year birds showing plumage that is somewhat similar to that of adults, other than the color of bare parts.

STATUS AND DISTRIBUTION While endemic as a breeding species to the Gulf of California, it occurs as a post-breeding visitor north to the Salton Sea of extreme southern California. It first appears in late May, and hundreds may be present by July and August before birds retreat south again in the fall, although some nonbreeding individuals are generally present year-round. It is also a very rare visitor north to southern California and Los Angeles County, where it occurs with Western Gulls (*Gulls of the Americas*, Howell and Dunn, 2007).

YELLOW-FOOTED GULL 1 Adult breeding. Quick, you are on the shores of the Salton Sea in August (yes, you can almost smell the rotting fish). You see this large, dark-backed, Western-type gull with bright yellow legs. Whatizit? If you said anything but adult Yellow-footed Gull, it's possible that bird-watching is not the avocation for you. It is similar to Western Gull, but it averages a larger, heavier bill with a strong upward angle near the lower tip, a paler eye, a heavy body structure, and long, broad wings. Adult plumage is usually reached by its 3rd year, making it more advanced than Western and Glaucous-winged Gulls, to which it is closely related. Yellow legs are shown in all ages except immature 1st year and some early 2nd winter birds, which have pinkish legs. This bird is a breeding adult, with a yellow bill that has a red spot on the lower mandible near the tip, and a pale eye with a thin red orbital ring. Upperparts are medium to dark gray, and primary wing tips are contrastingly black with bold white spots. Salton Sea, California, August

YELLOW-FOOTED GULL 2 Mostly adult nonbreeding. This bird shows dark gray upperparts, black primary wing tips with white spots, a faintly streaked white head, and its namesake yellow legs. Most adult Western Gulls show pale pink legs and are modestly smaller billed. And they wouldn't be in the Salton Sea (or they should not be?). This bird may be a 3rd winter individual because of the black markings on the bill, but otherwise it resembles an adult. The light spotting on the head is typical of nonbreeding Yellow-footed, which does not acquire any heavy spotting in nonbreeding birds. Salton Sea, California, September

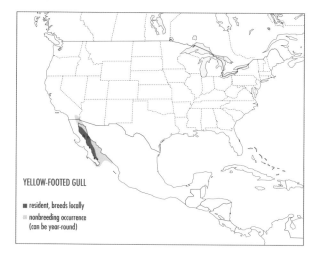

YELLOW-FOOTED GULL

■ resident, breeds locally
■ nonbreeding occurrence (can be year-round)

ADULT (combines 2nd winter and adult) Adults have dark gray upperparts that may be slightly darker than the slate-gray upperparts of some Western Gulls, but overlap occurs. *A very large, swollen bill averages longer and stouter than in Western,* and there is a red spot on the lower bill near the tip. Black outer primaries have slight to bold white tips, and legs are yellow versus pink in Western Gull. *Third year birds basically show adult plumage,* with a dark upper back, a yellow bill with a red spot, and yellow legs. Second winter birds have pinkish to yellow legs, a dark gray upper back with worn wing panels, similar to 3rd winter plumage on other large, dark-backed gulls, and a pink to yellowish bill with a dark tip.

YELLOW-FOOTED GULL 3 Adult nonbreeding. This worn adult nonbreeding Yellow-footed Gull shows mud-covered yellow legs and a bright yellow bill with a red spot near the tip. It looks as if it got caught in a washing machine, with messy feathers and an unkempt appearance, but maybe it just bathed in the highly saline waters of the Salton Sea and is trying to dry out. Either way, it will not win any beauty contest awards. Legs lack the brighter yellow of breeding birds. Salton Sea, California, November

IMMATURE (includes juvenile to 1st winter) Very similar to immature Western with overall mottled grayish-brown plumage, *but underparts are paler, contrasting with a streaked upper breast*; many individuals are also paler headed than juvenile and immature 1st winter Western. Immatures in 1st winter may show a diffuse pinkish color on the base of the bill (see Yellow-footed Gull 4) or a mostly dark bill with pale pink on the base of the lower bill. The amount of pink to yellow on the base of the bill varies with individuals, but some birds may show yellowish color here by spring.

SUBADULT (some 1st summer and 2nd winter) A mostly dark gray upper back is present, but some birds have worn brown immature feathers in the wings. Others show mostly dark gray upperparts with few to varying numbers of brown feathers in the wing panel. Underparts are mostly white and unmarked, but sparse streaking may be present on the head, neck, and sides of the upper breast. Legs may be dull pink (usually in younger birds) or faintly to obviously yellow in older birds of this age group. Bill is usually pinkish in younger birds (June–early winter) and yellowish after that, but a pink to yellow bill may occur in all birds in this age group.

YELLOW-FOOTED GULL 4 Immatures (juveniles/early 1st winter). Western Gulls of the same age as these birds can be quite similar, so you need to note several distinguishing features. These immature, mostly juvenile-plumaged Yellow-footed Gulls show a large, bulbous-tipped black bill with a dull, pale base, and a pale belly (dark on juvenile and immature/1st winter Western). The contrasting dark face and pale hind neck also support Yellow-footed Gull, with Western having an overall brown head and nape. The flying bird shows a lightly marked white rump, which in juvenile/immature Western is heavily barred and darker. A few grayish 1st winter feathers are starting to molt in on the upper back (scapulars) of the *left* bird. The Salton Sea location supports the ID of Yellow-footed Gull, insofar as Yellow-footed is common here and Western is absent. However, Western Gull is increasing in the Gulf of California and could appear at the Salton Sea in the future. Salton Sea, California, August

YELLOW-FOOTED GULL 5 First summer subadult. This bird shows worn brown plumage with a grayish upper back; lavish streaking on the head, neck, and sides of the upper breast; a black-tipped pink bill; and pink legs. The darker gray upper back feathers contrast with the retained brownish-gray wing feathers. This plumage condition, combined with pink legs that lack any yellow tones, helps to age this bird as a 1st summer (slightly over one year old) that is transitioning to 2nd winter plumage. Note the very heavy bill and dusky eye of a younger bird. Salton Sea, California, August

YELLOW-FOOTED GULL 6 Subadult. This subadult (presumed 2nd summer transitioning to 3rd winter) Yellow-legged Gull shows pinkish-yellow feet but more extensive black in the outer primaries than Western Gull. The complete dark tail band ages this bird as a subadult, probably in its 2nd summer (slightly over two years old). An adult would have a completely white tail. Note the strong, broad, white trailing edge on the inner wing compared to the thin white edge on the rest of the inner wing, which shows recent replacement of the more adultlike inner wing feathers. Also note the black and red markings on the bill. Salton Sea, California, September

GREAT BLACK-BACKED GULL
Larus marinus

SIZE **25–31 inches long**   WINGSPAN **57–65 inches**

It's the large, robust, black-backed gull on the Atlantic beach, picking at the beached dogfish as an entourage of Herring Gulls and Laughing Gulls looks on, all the while keeping a respectful distance. (PD)

PROFILE   This very large, menacing-looking gull (it truly is the largest gull in the world) has a big, squarish or oval-shaped head and a heavy bill. *This barrel-chested gull is typically noticeably larger and always chestier than Herring Gull,* with a larger, broader head, thicker neck, and distinctly heavier bill. Dull pink legs are long, thick, and set at midspan, accentuating the bird's barrel-chested appearance.

Adults have a dark charcoal to black back and a white head, while immature birds are spangled or granite patterned with gray, white, and black upperparts and a white head. This contrasting pattern stands out among the brownish-gray immatures and gray-backed adult ranks of Herring Gulls.

Great Black-backed is a fairly sedentary gull, spending much of its time loafing on the beach, resting on the water, or standing atop an elevated post or light fixture. It walks somewhat reluctantly, with a waddling sailor's gait. This species generally dominates other gulls when food is available and frequently displaces other gulls from prime perches. It is often found with other large, white-headed Gulls, especially Herring Gulls. Much smaller Ring-billed Gulls go out of their way to avoid any interaction with this species.

A consummate kleptoparasite (stealer of another's food), Great Black-backed often robs cormorants, other gulls, and seabirds of fish and other food items. This species is also

GREAT BLACK-BACKED GULL 1 Adult breeding. Great Black-backed Gull is typically the largest and huskiest gull on the Atlantic beachfront or Great Lakes shorelines, or anywhere else it is found, since it is the largest gull in the world. Long, thick, pinkish legs contribute to the barrel-chested bird's waddling sailor's gait. A large, oval or squarish head supports a thick, heavy bill, which makes this species appear formidable or menacing. Adults have a yellow bill with a red spot near the tip; a dark blackish back that is roughly the same shading (or slightly paler) as the outer primaries; a red orbital ring around a pale to dusky eye; and a clean white head and underparts in breeding birds. Nonbreeding adults show very minor, thin streaks on the head and neck. New Jersey, August

GREAT BLACK-BACKED GULL 2 Great Black-backed Gulls, three different ages. Adult Great Black-backed Gulls are shown in the *center*, with the larger, heavier-billed, bigger-headed bird on the *left* probably the male in this mated pair. The immature bird on the *left* with the black bill is in its 1st winter, while the similarly plumaged bird on the *right* is a 2nd winter bird because of the yellowish bill with a black spot near the tip, incoming blackish upper back feathers, and a strong pale tip to the bill. These formidable gulls own the beach and mudflats and, when foraging, are often avoided by other gulls. New Jersey, March

GREAT BLACK-BACKED GULL 3 Great Black-backed and Herring Gulls, immatures. Great Black-backed (*left*) is slightly to much larger than Herring Gull and shows a more piano-keyed appearance on the wing coverts on perched birds from late winter onward. Note the overall whiteness of this late 1st winter Great Black-backed compared to the dull brown uniform shading of this late 1st winter immature Herring Gull, whose wing panel (wing coverts) shows extreme wear and sun bleaching of the older juvenile feathers. Also note Great Black-backed's bulkier chest; overall neater, cleaner appearance; and heavier, mostly black bill compared to the pink-based bill and overall messy look of Herring Gull. Florida, April

GREAT BLACK-BACKED GULL 4 Great Black-backed Gull with two other species. Size alone separates this subadult (3rd winter) Great Black-backed Gull from the mostly adult-plumaged Lesser Black-backed Gull (*left*) and subadult 2nd winter Herring Gull (*2nd from right*). But if you are still uncertain, note Great Black-backed's heavier, deeply hooked bill; barrel-chested profile, and long, thick, pink legs. The Sanderling in front of the Great Black-backed allows you to see how large these gulls are. New Jersey, early April

GREAT BLACK-BACKED GULL 5 Great Black-backed Gulls fighting over food. This immature (1st winter) Great Black-backed is going to be hard pressed to get a morsel with these hungry adult birds dominating this moribund fish. Note the sparse streaking on the head of nonbreeding adults. New Jersey, December

GREAT BLACK-BACKED GULL 6 Immature Great Black-backed Gulls fighting. While Great Black-backed Gulls can be very aggressive and even kill their own kind, these two immatures (1st winter) are squabbling over food rather than attempting to consume each other. Fights like this usually end with the most aggressive bird asserting its dominance. New Jersey, December

highly predatory. It is known to harass diving birds, such as coots (which can't stay underwater very long), to exhaustion and then grasp the debilitated bird by the head, killing it outright or, failing that, drowning its victim. Kevin once saw an adult Great Black-backed kill and swallow whole a Northern Flicker that had been sitting exhausted on a beach in New York during fall migration.

STATUS AND DISTRIBUTION A fairly common gull that is typically found on Atlantic coast beaches, where it is a resident species, as well as on the Great Lakes, where it is also resident and increasing in numbers. Lesser numbers are found south to Florida (mostly on the Atlantic coast), where it is also increasing.

GREAT BLACK-BACKED GULL 7 Three age groups. A Great Black-backed Gull sampler: An immature (1st summer) *front left*, showing a granite-gray back, white head, and two-toned bill; a near adult at *left rear* with blackish upperparts, some browner feathers in the lower wing panel, and a bright yellow bill with a red spot near the tip; and subadults in their 3rd summer on the *right* showing mostly dark upperparts, worn wing feathers, a dark tail band, and a dark-tipped bill with a faint red spot. New Jersey, July

Great Black-backed breeds from southern Greenland and Newfoundland south through the Canadian Maritimes to North Carolina. It also breeds on the Great Lakes and along the Saint Lawrence River. Except for the smaller, more delicately proportioned Lesser Black-backed Gull and the much smaller Laughing Gull, this species is the only dark-backed gull likely to be found on the Atlantic coast of the northeastern United States south to Florida. It does not occur on the West Coast and is rare along the Gulf of Mexico.

Its winter range is expanding, with uncommon to rare occurrences in the West Indies and rare sightings on the Texas coast. Favored haunts include beaches, landfills, seafood processing locations, and docks. Great Black-backed's greater size and bulk will be immediately apparent in the presence of other gulls. This species may also be found far from shore in open marine environments.

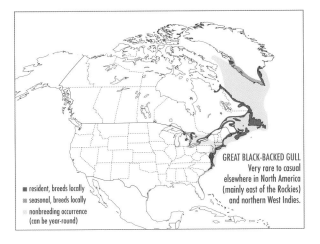

GREAT BLACK-BACKED GULL
Very rare to casual elsewhere in North America (mainly east of the Rockies) and northern West Indies.

- resident, breeds locally
- seasonal, breeds locally
- nonbreeding occurrence (can be year-round)

ADULT All-blackish upperparts contrast with a white head, neck, and underparts. In winter, some birds show a faint trace of grayish streaking on the head, while the head of Herring Gull and Lesser Black-backed Gull is heavily streaked. Long legs are dull pink (yellow in Lesser Black-backed Gull), and the bill is bright yellow with a red spot near the tip (dark

GREAT BLACK-BACKED GULL 8 Immature (1st winter). Superior size gives Great Black-backed the right of first refusal to all wave-borne fair. Note the overall whiteness of this species, especially on the head and underparts, though this is a particularly heavily marked bird; the black, brown, and white upperparts with the piano key–patterned wing coverts; the large black bill that adds to its large, finely streaked, whitish head; and the long, thick legs. A Sanderling is keeping a respectful distance, and the triggerfish is beyond caring. Great Black-backed is well known for its aggressive behavior and insatiable appetite. Florida, January

GREAT BLACK-BACKED GULL 9 Great Black-backed Gull with Laughing Gull. Adult Great Black-backed Gull simply dwarfs this adult breeding Laughing Gull. By seeing this very familiar Laughing Gull in direct comparison to Great Black-backed, you develop a lasting impression of the formidable size of Great Black-backed. Three of the shorebirds in the *rear* are Semipalmated Plovers. New Jersey, August

white mirror

white primary tip

GREAT BLACK-BACKED GULL 10 Adults. This species is a strong, majestic flier with slow, heavy wing beats. The bulky head projects well ahead of the long, broad wings, and its large bill is evident even at a great distance. Sparse streaking on the two birds in the *left* photo is typical of this species' nonbreeding plumage. The call is a low, hoarse, muffled *gowl*, which is gruffer and lower pitched than the call of Herring Gull. The outermost primary has a large, entirely white tip, which, when combined with a large white mirror (white spot or bar inside the tip of the outer two primary feathers) (*right* photo), creates a large amount of visible white on the dark outer wings (matched only by Slaty-backed Gull among the dark backed gulls). Note the broad, white trailing edge to the inner wing that narrows on the outer wing on the bird in the *right* photo. This often wears off by late summer to fall (see *left* bird in *left* photo). The underwing is white with dark gray to black outer flight feathers. New Jersey, October (*left*); February (*right*)

GREAT BLACK-BACKED GULL 11 Immature (juveniles). Young birds show the same bulky proportions as adults but exhibit a distinctly different plumage. The head and upper breast of young juveniles have a buff wash and more streaking than is present during the rest of the 1st year, and the underparts show heavier streaking or spotting than is typically present from fall to late winter (see *right* flight photo for comparison). Upper back feathers have strong brownish to black centers with white oval spots, while the wing coverts show a mix of black-and-white checkered feathers. First year birds have mostly dark bills until late winter, although juveniles may show some pink at the base. Underwings show uniformly dusky outer flight feathers and crisp black-and-white spotted underwing coverts. The lightly barred tail has a strong black band at the tip. Long, thick legs allow the bird to forage easily in the wave zone. New Jersey, August (*left*); New Jersey, early December (*right*)

GREAT BLACK-BACKED GULL 12 Fresh immature 1st and 2nd winter birds. First and 2nd year immature plumage is very similar in Great Black-backed Gull, but typical 2nd year birds (*right*) show distinct pink at the bill base, a different pattern to the upper back feathers that includes a whiter background, and a cleaner, whiter appearance on the head and underparts. Fresh juvenile/1st winter birds (*left*) have a mostly black bill, heavier streaks and spots on the head and breast, and darker centers on the feathers of the upper wing panel (lesser and median wing coverts). Fresh juveniles also show a warmish cast to the head and breast. Note the very short primaries (outer wing feathers) that are just molting in and still growing on the 2nd winter bird (*right*). The *left* bird is noticeably less robust and has a smaller head and bill compared to the *right* bird. New Jersey, late August

tipped in 3rd winter). In winter, the white head is always less streaked than in Lesser Black-backed Gull, and at a distance, birds appear fully white headed. *Some birds lack any obvious streaking on the head in winter. Primaries are only slightly darker than the back,* where the contrast between the black wing tips and the charcoal-gray back on the subspecies of Lesser Black-backed that occurs in North America is pronounced.

IMMATURE (combines juvenile, 1st winter, 1st summer, and some 2nd winter birds) Upperparts are coarsely but evenly spangled with gray, black, and white, *so bird's upperparts appear cut from coarsely patterned gray granite.* Checkered wing panels on juvenile and immature birds resemble piano keys with their alternating black-and-white patterns. Fresh juvenile birds can show a pale, diffuse pink wash to the bill base, but 1st winter birds have very large, heavy, black bills until late winter, when some irregular pink color may occur on the inner bill. Juveniles have variable fine streaking on the head and neck, which often thins out by late winter. Juveniles and 1st winter birds have coarse black streaks on the underparts and diffuse brownish spots on the flanks

and lower belly. Some 1st winter birds show distinct streaking and spotting into midwinter, including the head (see Great Black-backed Gull 8). Most juveniles are more heavily streaked on the crown, neck, and underparts compared to 1st winter birds and have a buff wash to the head and upper breast.

By spring, pink starts to appear at the bill base, and upper back feathers may show a grayer appearance. Underparts are mostly white by late winter but lavishly anointed with fine flecking or spotted streaks, heaviest along the sides of the breast; long legs are dull pink.

Second winter birds can appear very similar in plumage to 1st winter birds, but typically the upper back feathers show more pale gray interiors, and the dark bill has a varying amount of pink at the base. Some 2nd winter birds can show a fairly well-demarcated pinkish bill with a dark tip (see *center* photo of Great Black-backed Gull 15 for a January bird from Florida showing this pattern). While some birds retain their immature plumage until their 2nd summer, more advanced individuals may acquire dark, adultlike feathers on the upper back and a yellow-based bill with a dark tip.

GREAT BLACK-BACKED GULL 13 Immature (2nd winter) Great-blacked Back Gull with other species. This excellent comparison features immature (2nd winter) Herring Gull (*left*), immature (1st winter) Lesser Black-backed Gull (*center*), and immature (1st winter) Herring Gull (*right*). Can you pick out the Great Black-backed Gull? Distinguishing features include Great Black-backed's much larger size, heavier bill, bulkier proportions, and longer legs compared to the petite-billed and trimmer-bodied Lesser Black-backed. The plumage similarities with Lesser Black-backed are only feather deep, but Great Black-backed (*2nd from right*) has a cleaner, whiter head and paler wing panel compared to both 1st winter Lesser and Herring. New Jersey, early April

GREAT BLACK-BACKED GULL 14 Great Black-backed and Herring Gulls, immatures, and Black Skimmer. This is a good comparison of immature late 1st winter Herring Gull (*left*) and immature 1st winter Great Black-backed Gull. The head of immature Herring Gull at this time of year may be sun bleached as white as that of Great Black-backed, but note the differences in head size and shape, bill size, and leg thickness, as well as Great Black-backed's overall superior girth and barrel-chested appearance. Herring Gull's strong pink bill with a demarcated black tip differs greatly from 1st and 2nd winter Great Black-backed's bill, which is mostly black, sometimes with an ill-defined pink cast in late spring, and blackish with more defined pink on the inner bill in the 2nd winter. Thinner, more pointed outer primaries on this Great Black-backed age it as a 1st winter bird. Great Black-backed also has overall whiter underparts. Black Skimmer (*front*), an unmistakable and often familiar bird, allows you to gauge the size of both gull species. Florida, April

GREAT BLACK-BACKED GULL 15 Older immatures. These photos show a variety of different plumages for older immature birds in late 1st and 2nd winter. The obvious to diffuse pink color on the bill base and the pale bill tip are features of late 1st and 2nd year birds. Plumage can vary from clean, crisp feathers of black, brown, and white, as in the flying bird, to a mix of worn wing feathers and fresher upperparts, as in the almost one-year-old bird at the *left* in May, or a mix of different-aged feathers with a handful of solid dark upper back feathers, as in the late 2nd winter bird at the *right* in April. Standing birds have large, heavy bills, a chesty appearance, and long, thick legs. All three birds have a large whitish head, while many other large immature gulls show a brownish head (except the petite-billed Lesser Black-backed Gull and some sun-bleached gulls in late season). New Jersey, May (*left*); Florida, January (*center*); New Jersey, April (*right*)

SUBADULT (3rd winter) Somewhat resembles adult, with a mostly black upper back and occasionally dark wing panel feathers, but typically has brownish lower wing panel with scattered dark feathers and a pinkish to yellowish bill with a dark tip. Some advanced individuals may have a red spot on the lower bill just below the black spot inside a pale bill tip (see *right* photo of Great Black-backed Gull 16). Head and underparts are white, as in adult, but some birds retain fine streaks on the head and neck, and the dark eye may show a smudgy patch, giving birds a sleepy look.

GREAT BLACK-BACKED GULL 16 Subadults. These three subadult birds show a few of the variety of plumage conditions possible in the 3rd year. Most 3rd year birds show a yellowish bill, but the bird with fairly advanced plumage in the *center* photo, taken in early September, has a pinkish-yellow bill. Subadults typically show a black upper back and worn lower wing feathers. Bold, black markings near the bill tip are typical, but some advanced birds show a black and red tip, as in the bird on the *right* (early June), and a slightly paler eye with a red orbital ring. Note how long necked the birds can appear when they are alert. New Jersey (all); May (*left*); September (*center*); early June (*right*)

GREAT BLACK-BACKED GULL 17 Subadult. This subadult 3rd winter Great Black-backed shows robust proportions; broad wings; a heavy, black-tipped bill with a small red spot; a dusky tail band; and a hint of the dusky underwing pattern seen on adults. New Jersey, early April

LESSER BLACK-BACKED GULL
Larus fuscus

SIZE **20–24 inches long** WINGSPAN **46–59 inches**

Black-backed Gull "lite"—a slimmer, trimmer triathlete of a gull. (PD)

PROFILE *A medium-large, nicely proportioned, dark-backed gull that has a mostly slender body with a plump breast; a tapered rear end; and very long wings that extend noticeably past*

LESSER BLACK-BACKED GULL 1 Adults breeding (*left*) and nonbreeding (*right*). This medium-large, long-winged gull is an increasingly common visitor to North America, where flocks of up to several hundred birds are reliably seen in some locations. Shown are two adults with dark charcoal-gray upperparts, bright yellow legs, and a bill with a red spot near the tip. Streaking on the head and neck, which is typical of nonbreeding adults, is sometimes held into summer on subadult and less advanced adult birds. Note the punched-in-the-eye look (concentrated dark feathering around the eye) of nonbreeding birds, which is a signature trait often seen in this species. New Jersey, July (*left*); Florida, January (*right*)

LESSER BLACK-BACKED GULL 1 Subadults (3rd summer): differences in size, structure, and bill shape. There is much variation in the size, structural features, and bill length of Lesser Black-backed Gull. The bird at *left* has a bigger head; longer, heavier bill; and bulkier structural profile compared to the smaller-billed bird at *right*. Within a size range of roughly twenty to twenty-four inches, differences in extreme birds can be obvious, with males averaging larger. Some birds at this age still show pinkish-yellow legs, although most have yellow legs by the 3rd winter. The tricolored bill tip is typical in older subadults, as is streaking on the head and underparts, even in July. This streaking is similar to that of nonbreeding birds in winter but usually sparser overall. The inky-black, irregular markings on the bill are unique to this species, with no other large gull showing these markings in near adults. Note the pale eye on the *left* bird and the dusky eye on the *right* bird. Most subadult/adult Lessers have pale eyes, but some can show pale dusky eyes as well. New Jersey, July

LESSER BLACK-BACKED GULL 2 Lesser Black-backed (*center*), Herring (*left*), and Great Black-backed Gulls, immatures. Comparison photos like this are invaluable in comparing the different physical features and plumage of similar gulls. The immature (1st winter) Lesser Black-backed Gull (*center*) shows a mostly white, gray, and black plumage with a contrastingly white face and upper breast against a dusky belly and streaked crown and nape. The similar immature 1st winter Herring Gull (*left*) has a uniformly brownish-gray plumage, including the wing panel (wing coverts), which differs from Lesser's darker wing coverts. This Herring is especially small and has a very small bill and head and petite, slender body proportions, making it quite similar to Lesser Black-backed in profile. The head shape of these two birds is hard to compare because of the raised neck of the Herring, but it appears somewhat similar. The dark feathering around the eye of Lesser is always helpful for its ID. Immature Great Black-backed Gulls (*right* and *rear left*) are much larger and have a bigger head and bill and longer legs. The mostly white head and heavier bill of Great Black-backed are consistent features. A small Sanderling in front gives you an idea of how large these gulls are. New Jersey, early April

LESSER BLACK-BACKED GULL 3 Lesser Black-backed, Great Black-backed, and Herring Gulls. A picture worth a thousand words (again). Adult Lesser Black-backed Gull (*center*) is distinctly smaller than adult Great Black-backed Gull (*second from left*), and slightly smaller than the immature 1st winter Herring Gull *behind*. Note Lesser's long, lean profile, more petite bill, and slightly paler upperparts, not to mention the yellow legs, versus pink in Greater. This Great Black-backed is showing paler gray upperparts than usual, but this could be a result of the strong late afternoon lighting, which makes the back seem paler than the wing tips. Whatever the reason, these two black-backed gulls have similar plumage in this view, so beware of tricks that lighting can play. Flanking birds are immature Great Black-backed Gulls. New Jersey, early April

the folded tail. Long wings and long legs set forward give Lesser Black-backed a horizontal profile. A medium-length bill is somewhat slender and straight compared to Great Black-backed's larger, distinctly heavier bill, and some birds show a noticeable bulge near the slightly hooked tip. The smaller, rounder head and typically smaller, proportioned bill help distinguish immature Lesser Black-backed from immature Herring Gull, but some birds can closely resemble small Herring Gulls that have a similar head shape, a slender body, a comparable bill size and shape, and a long-winged profile (see Herring Gull 12, p. 91).

The adult looks somewhat like Great Black-backed Gull but is conspicuously smaller. It is overall trimmer, longer winged, and less robust than the barrel-chested Great Black-backed, which also shows a distinctly heavier bill. Another distinguishing feature is the paler charcoal-gray back of adult Lesser contrasting with the darker primaries (in the subspecies typically seen in North America) compared to adult Great Black-backed's more uniform and distinctly blacker back that is similar to the outer primary shading.

Lesser Black-backed Gull is usually slightly smaller than Herring Gull and typically plumper breasted, with a more tapered rear body (see Lesser Black-backed Gull 4). At a distance, compared to Herring Gull, Lesser Black-backed's trimmer profile is often evident.

An active forager, Lesser Black-backed is often found striding in the wave zone, often midleg deep in the surf. When loafing in mixed flocks, Lesser Black-backed is typically found on the periphery of the group or standing slightly apart, especially when in the company of Great Black-backed. Multiple Lesser Black-backed Gulls tend to cluster together, even when in mixed flocks.

STATUS AND DISTRIBUTION Previously uncommon to rare, but has increased dramatically in recent decades, especially along the Atlantic and Gulf coastlines and adjacent inland areas, and in some Great Lakes locations. Generally much less common than Great Black-backed Gull in appropriate range, but at times and in some southern coastal and near-inland locations, Lesser Black-backed outnumbers all

LESSER BLACK-BACKED GULL 4 Lesser Black-backed and Herring Gulls, immatures in summer. This excellent real-life comparison shows important physical differences between Lesser Black-backed (*left*) and Herring Gulls. Herring has a larger head with a pulled-taffy look to the front face; a bulkier, more compact body profile; a bigger bill with a stronger bulge near the tip; and thicker legs. Herring's plumage is also browner overall, while Lesser has a colder overall plumage with grayer feathering; noticeably longer wings; and a contrasting whiter face and upper breast. Note the dark eyes on both species, which are one-year-old 1st summer gulls. New Jersey, early July

LESSER BLACK-BACKED GULL 5 Third summer with adult Herring and Ring-billed Gulls. This great real-life comparison photo shows the physical and plumage differences of these three common gulls on the Atlantic coastline in summer. Herring Gull (*center*) is the largest of the three and has a noticeably longer, heavier bill; larger head; and bulkier overall body structure with moderate wing projection past the tail. Lesser Black-backed (*right*) shows a longer, more slender body profile with longer wings and a smaller, more uniformly straight bill compared to Herring. Adult Ring-billed (*left*) is the smallest of the three species and shows a smaller, more rounded head compared to the other two species. It also has shorter, yellow legs and a more evenly proportional body profile that more closely resembles that of Lesser Black-backed in its tapered rear body shape. New Jersey, August

LESSER BLACK-BACKED GULL
Very rare to casual elsewhere in North America, western Mexico, and the West Indies.

■ seasonal, breeds locally
■ nonbreeding occurrence (can be year-round)

other large gulls. On some southern New Jersey beaches in July and early August, Lesser Black-backed is the most common large gull, with numbers sometimes ranging from fifty to eighty birds (seen regularly by Kevin at Stone Harbor Point, New Jersey). Sightings also occur quite far inland, with scattered records documented even to the western states.

Breeding range was typically isolated to a small location in southern Greenland, but the large increase in wintering birds at many locations suggests there may be currently unknown breeding areas. One bird bred with a Herring Gull in Maine in 2007–2011, and one of the banded hybrid offspring was seen for a number of years at Daytona Beach, Florida, in winter. Other hybrids have been seen in recent years (see Hybrid 5, p. 191), with increased interbreeding likely with Herring Gulls.

Other locations where Lesser Black-backed occurs in large numbers include interior landfills, along eastern inland rivers, and on summer beaches. On Atlantic and Gulf coastal beaches, nonbreeding (immature and subadult) birds are often present year-round.

LESSER BLACK-BACKED GULL 6 Mostly adult nonbreeding, with adult Laughing Gull. While it is unlikely you will ever confuse Lesser Black-backed with breeding Laughing Gull, note the similarity in upperpart shading. Comparisons like this also allow you to become familiar with Lesser Black-backed's general size and shape. New Jersey, August

LESSER BLACK-BACKED GULL 7 Immature (*right*) and mostly adult. A mostly adult at *left* shows the classic lean, long-winged profile accompanied by bright yellow legs and a straight yellow bill with a red spot. Note the long, older outer primaries on this bird compared to the newly replaced fresh inner ones with the white tips. Aging this bird is not straightforward; we call it a mostly adult since it appears as such, but it could also be a 3rd summer bird. Immature (late 1st summer, *right*) shows the same profile and a few gray feathers present on the upper back but still has pink legs. New Jersey, early September

LESSER BLACK-BACKED GULL 8 Adult with Herring and Laughing Gulls. This photo shows an adult nonbreeding Lesser Black-backed (*center*) standing with two other common eastern US gulls. It is smaller overall and has a more slender profile compared to the adult Herring Gull (*left center*), with longer wings and shorter yellow versus pink legs. Note the plump breast of Lesser. Laughing Gulls are smaller still and have a small head with a peaked rear crown and shorter black legs. Note the similarity in the dark charcoal shading of the upperparts of Lesser and Laughing Gulls versus the pale gray upperparts of Herring. Florida, January

LESSER BLACK-BACKED GULL 9 Adult and subadult. A near-adult Lesser Black-backed Gull (*left*) showing a lean, long-winged profile; a uniform, straight bill; and black wing tips contrasting with charcoal-gray upperparts. Great Black-backed's darker upperparts are similar in shading to the wing tips. An adultlike (3rd winter) bird in flight shows yellow feet and legs and heavily streaked head, which Great Black-backed Gull never shows. This species has very long, tapered wings. Note again the punched-in-the-eye look in nonbreeding adults and subadults created by the dense, dark feathering around the eye. New Jersey, July (*left*); New Jersey, February (*right*)

ADULTS (combines adult and 3rd winter) The dark, charcoal-gray back is paler than adult Great Black-backed's blackish upperparts (adult Lesser Black-backed's upper back shading is almost identical to that of the much smaller adult Laughing Gull, with which Lesser Black-backed can hardly be confused). Black outer primaries on Lesser Black-backed are also conspicuously darker than the inner wings and back (unlike in adult Great Black-backed).

In winter, adult and subadult Lesser Black-backed Gulls typically show a heavily streaked head (adult Great-blacked Gulls are conspicuously white headed but at close range may show ultrafine streaking in winter). Some Lesser Black-backeds, however, can show a lightly streaked head in winter, and some summer subadults can have a very white head that shows only limited, fine streaking (see Lesser Black-backed Gull 15). Adult and subadult Great Black-backed never appear dirty headed, as is typical of winter adult Lesser Black-backed Gull. On some 3rd winter birds, a blackish to yellow bill often supports a distinctive and colorful amalgam of red, black, and yellow near the tip.

IMMATURES (juveniles to 1st winter) Juvenile Lesser Black-backed has a plumage that is not typically seen in most of the United States, except for Atlantic coastal areas, where it is uncommon from early fall onward. It is heavily streaked and spotted with brown on the head, neck, and underparts, with *dark brown feathering concentrated around the eye and cheek.* Upperparts are dark brown with bold white fringes, giving the upperparts a strongly contrasting appearance (see Lesser Black-backed Gull 10). These strongly contrasting upper back feathers are replaced in early fall by more muted grayish-brown ones, and the bold white fringes on the wing panel are reduced by feather wear by early winter. A whitish face and upper breast with sparse streaking contrast with a darker belly and fairly heavy rear head and face streaking in 1st winter birds.

LESSER BLACK-BACKED GULL 10 Fresh juvenile. This fresh juvenile plumage is rarely seen in most of the lower forty-eight states, but it is seen on a limited but regular basis from late September to November along the Atlantic coast. First winter birds appear later in fall with different, more muted upper back feathers. Upperparts are dark brown centered with crisp, white fringing, and the head and underparts are heavily marked brown with white feathering interspersed. Dense, dark feathering around the eye is present even in this young bird. Note the evenly shaped black bill that is smaller and slimmer than that of Great Black-backed, and less acutely hooked than that of some Herring Gulls, which may at this stage show diffuse pink at the base. Very long wings, a small head, and a trim body make Lesser Black-backed appear long and lean. Connecticut, October

LESSER BLACK-BACKED GULL 11 Immature 1st winter. This 1st winter Lesser Black-backed shows plumage somewhat similar to that of the juvenile bird in Lesser Black-backed Gull 10, but it has acquired plainer, more muted gray back feathers during its postjuvenile molt and shows more white background feathers on the head and underparts. This species has a plump, chesty appearance but a slender rear body profile with very long wings extending well beyond the tail. Note the all-dark trailing edge to the left wing in the *right* photo, which differs markedly from Herring Gull's paler inner primary window in 1st winter plumage (see *right* photo in Lesser Black-backed Gull 12). Also note Lesser's slim, all-black bill. Florida, January

A *punched-in-the-eye look* (shadowy feathered patch around the eye) is typical of immature and subadult birds in winter, and birds in summer often show a white head that lacks appreciable streaking (see Lesser Black-backed Gull 13, *right* photo). Immatures at a distance appear fairly dark above (cold grayish to blackish brown), with streaked underparts diminishing the contrast between upperparts and underparts, except for the paler head and upper breast, thus making distant birds appear overall dark bodied. The wing coverts on 1st winter birds are darker and more uniformly shaded than the strongly patterned wing panel on 1st winter and some 2nd winter Herring Gulls.

LESSER BLACK-BACKED GULL 12 Immature (1st winter). Immature Lesser Black-backed (*left* and *center*) appears small headed, slender bodied, and long winged and has a straight, slender bill. Note the lack of warmth in the gray, brown, white, and black plumage of this bird, which differs from the more uniform, often warmer brown plumage of a similar-aged Herring Gull. A whitish face and upper breast are commonly seen at this age, along with a slight punched-in-the-eye look. Dark brown underwing coverts with gray flight feathers, black outer primaries, long slender wings, and a blackish tail contrasting with the whitish rump are typical at this age. The *right* photo shows a similar-aged Herring Gull with pale inner primary flight feathers (inner primary window) that interrupt the uniform darkish feathers on the rear wing, which differs from the rear wing of Lesser Black-backed (see left wing on *center* photo and left wing on Lesser Black-backed Gull 11, *right* photo). Also note the brownish tail with a darker rump and paler wing coverts on Herring Gull. Florida, late January

As the winter progresses, 1st winter birds become increasingly pale breasted, thus heightening contrast between the dark back and the pale head and breast. This plumage differs from the more uniform brownish shading of immature Herring Gull, which typically shows little contrast between the brown body and the smudgy brown head and breast, except on some sun-bleached birds (see Herring Gull 15, p. 93). The colder-toned, darker upperparts of Lesser Black-backed also differ from the more uniform, warmer brownish to brownish-gray upperparts of immature Herring Gull, which often show little contrast to the underparts. Some immature Herrings, however, can be grayish overall, especially central- and western-breeding birds, but these are usually fairly uniform in shading (see Herring Gull 10, *lower right* bird, p. 90).

Immature Lesser Black-backed's upperparts are distinctly darker than the overall paler, granite-patterned, gray, white, and black upperparts of immature Great Black-blacked (see Lesser Black-backed Gull 13 and 14), and the head and underpart streaking is typically heavier as well. Bills are mostly dark in the 1st winter, but a pale pinkish spot is usually present at the base of the lower bill, which differs from the ill-defined pink cast to the lower bill on some Herring Gulls late in the 1st winter.

Note the mostly all-black bill of immature Lesser Black-backed compared to that of some immature 1st winter Herring Gulls, whose bills may begin to show an ill-defined pinkish base from early winter to spring, or a fully pink bill with a black tip (especially interior and western birds). When Lesser Black-backed is in the company of Herring Gulls, note its smaller size and longer-winged profile, with wing tips projecting well beyond the tail (see Lesser Black-backed Gull 4). One way to separate them from Herring Gulls in flight is to note the tail, which shows a distinct wide black band and a white base with fine to heavy black barring compared to the more evenly toned back, rump, and typically brownish tail of immature 1st winter Herring Gull. However, some 2nd winter immature Herring Gulls can show a white rump, so use caution with this field mark.

A good field mark to separate flying 1st winter Lesser Black-backed from Herring Gull is the continuous blackish trailing edge to the wings on Lesser Black-backed Gull (see *right* photo of Lesser Black-backed Gull 11), which differs on Herring Gull by having a handful of paler feathers just past the midpoint of the trailing edge of the wing on the inner primaries (inner primary window) (see Herring Gull 11, p. 91). Some fully spread inner primaries on flying Lesser Black-backed may appear very slightly paler than the rest of the trailing edge of the wing, but not as pale as in Herring Gull (see *middle* photo of Lesser Black-backed 12).

LESSER BLACK-BACKED GULL 13 Lesser Black-backed and Great Black-backed Gulls, immatures in summer. The plumage of these two species can be quite similar in immature birds, but note the proportionally smaller head, longer wings, and noticeably more slender, tapered body of Lesser (*right*). Great Black-backed has a bulkier body structure; larger, more oval-shaped head; and a cleaner white head and underparts compared to Lesser's more distinctly spotted or streaked ones. While this Lesser's bill appears quite heavy, it is either an effect of the turned-away angle or just a very large bill. The small head of Lesser also accentuates the impression of the large bill. Note the paler gray upper back and wings of Great Black-backed compared to the darker-centered back feathers of Lesser. Both species are in the process of replacing their 1st winter feathers. New Jersey, July

LESSER BLACK-BACKED GULL 14   Older immatures, 1st summer; 1st summer Great Black-backed Gull (*right*). Two 1st summer (one-year old) Lesser Black-backed Gulls (*left* and *center*) show a plumage that has fairly uniform, darkish upperparts of black and gray tones and a white head and underparts that show dark streaks and spots. While a whitish head, mostly dark bill, and contrasting white upper breast are fairly consistent in 1st winter Lessers, the *left* bird shows a strong white head (with concentrated black feathering around the eye) and underparts, representing a plumage often seen in midsummer. The *right* bird shows plumage that is somewhat similar to that of the *left* two birds, but it has a much larger, oval-shaped head; a bulkier overall body structure; a heavier bill with a pink base; and thicker legs, which are traits consistent with Great Black-backed Gull. Plumage differs with a paler and more extensive whitish background to upperpart feathers, and a mostly white head and underparts that are typically less streaked than on most Lesser Black-backeds. Though the *left* bird has a similar white head and chest, the streaking around the eye is heavier. New Jersey, July

SUBADULT (2nd and 3rd winter/summer) Second year birds (winter and summer) are variable and may show a plumage similar to that of 1st winter birds but with more grayish feathers on the upper back and often cleaner white underparts, or they may show a mostly solid gray upper back similar to that of adults combined with blackish-gray wing coverts. Legs may be pink or yellowish (though typically pink), and bills are either mostly dark with a pale tip or darkish overall with pale pink on the base of the lower bill.

Most 3rd year birds (including winter and summer) have mostly charcoal-gray upperparts with scattered brown feathers, or groups of feathers, in the wing coverts. Some appear to have completely charcoal-gray upperparts, but flight views of these birds usually reveal retained browner feathers somewhere on the upper wing. They have a bill that may be mostly dark with diffuse pale areas and a small, lighter (often yellow-red) tip, or they may show a pink to yellow bill with a dark band inside a small, pale tip. Bill pattern and color are highly variable in subadult Lesser Black-backed (see *left* photo of Lesser Black-backed Gull 16, with mostly blackish bill on mostly adult bird). Legs are often yellow at this age (although some 3rd winter/summer individuals may show pink). Plumage and bare parts are extremely variable on this species in this age group, although a dark gray upper back is mostly consistent.

LESSER BLACK-BACKED GULL 15   Younger subadults. These Lesser Black-backed Gulls transitioning from 2nd summer to 3rd winter are more advanced in plumage than those in the previous photos since they are a year older and have dark charcoal-gray upper back feathers coming in. Note the smallish, rounded heads; slender, straight bills; and long wings of these birds, which help separate them from similarly plumaged Great Black-backed Gulls. The white head and upper breast with moderate streaking are not uncommon in this species at this age in late summer. Birds of this age often show pink legs, but some could have yellowish legs as well. New Jersey, July 29 (*left* and *center*); New Jersey, August (*right*)

LESSER BLACK-BACKED GULL 16 Older subadults. These older subadults (3rd summer, three years old) show completely charcoal-gray upperparts and pale eyes. Note the heavy streaking concentrated around the eye and the heavily streaked head and neck that Great Black-backed never shows. Most birds at this stage show yellow legs (*left* bird has slightly yellow legs), but clearly not all. The head streaking on Lesser Black-backed is thin and dark, as if drawn with a pencil that was pressed down hard, while Herring has blurrier, browner head streaking. New Jersey, September

LESSER BLACK-BACKED GULL 17 Lesser Black-backed and Ring-billed Gulls, adults in summer. This direct comparison allows you to see how small some Lesser Black-backeds can be. This Lesser is only slightly larger than the nearby Ring-billed Gull (*right*), but it shows a longer, more uniform-shaped, straight, yellowish bill with a red spot near the tip compared to the Ring-billed's more decurved upper bill and bulge near the tip on the lower bill. The profiles of these two plump-breasted birds are somewhat similar. The pinkish legs on the Lesser, which should be yellow at this age, are possibly a result of diminished sexual hormones at this late summer date. New Jersey, August 21

IVORY GULL,
1st winter

DARK HORSE GULLS
(Rare or Unlikely Gulls)

These are gulls you are most unlikely to encounter in North America, but you should be aware of them. Some of these may be found at appropriate times of year in very remote locations that average birders don't typically visit, while others are rare vagrants whose presence cannot be predicted.

SLATY-BACKED GULL
KELP GULL
BLACK-TAILED GULL
IVORY GULL
ROSS'S GULL

SLATY-BACKED GULL *Larus schistisagus*

SIZE **24–26 inches long** WINGSPAN **57–59 inches**

It's the Far Eastern Western Gull. (PD)

PROFILE A large, robust, dark-backed, pink-legged Asian gull, it is a rare visitor to Alaska, where it has been found in coastal portions and nearshore waters of the Bering and Beaufort Seas. It bred on offshore islands of western Alaska in 1996–1997, and it may breed in the outer Aleutians (*Gulls of the Americas*, Howell and Dunn, 2007). It is roughly the same size and shape as Western Gull but has a slimmer, straighter, less bulbous-tipped bill.

STATUS AND DISTRIBUTION In winter, uncommon to rare in coastal Alaska, with occasional sightings of subadults in summer. Some birds occur very rarely south to Canada and the lower forty-eight US states, with scattered sightings across this region, including two of three records in New York State (adult in September 2002, Seneca Falls, and another adult in February 2018, Oswego). It is the most likely blackish-backed gull to be found in its normal vagrancy range (coastal Alaska), bearing in mind that Vega Herring Gulls found in northern regions are slightly darker above than typical American Herring Gulls but nowhere near as dark as Slaty-backed Gulls (see Slaty-backed Gull 4).

ADULT (combines adult and 3rd winter) Charcoal-gray above and white below with bright pink legs, a yellow bill with a red spot near the tip, and a dirty yellow eye. Typical bright pink legs are very eye-catching (Western Gull's legs are duller pink). *In winter, the adult's head and hind neck are heavily marked with gray-brown streaking, whereas the head of adult Western Gull is mostly unblemished white. Also, in winter, Slaty-backed's yellow eye is bracketed by a dark streak (a feature absent on adult Western).* In flight, multiple white spots on the blackish outer primary wing tips resemble a "string of pearls," and wings show an especially noticeable broad white trailing edge compared to Western Gull's narrower one (see Slaty-backed Gull 4).

IMMATURE (combines juvenile and 1st winter) Brown above and somewhat less coarsely patterned than very similar juvenile Western and Herring Gull. It differs from Herring Gull in its broader, longer wings and straight, stouter bill. Tail

SLATY-BACKED GULL 1 Subadult (3rd winter). This large, dark-backed gull with pink legs is a regular visitor from Asia in small numbers to western Alaska, but rare elsewhere. This species superficially resembles Great Black-backed Gull but is smaller; has a dark charcoal rather than black back; richer pink legs; and a smaller, slimmer bill that usually lacks the strong bulbous tip of Great Black-backed. Note the blackish back in this photo, which is possibly a result of the strong overhead light creating a deeper shading tone. The worn feathers in the wing panel and the black markings on the bill and the tip of the tail help to age this as a 3rd summer bird. Alaska, June

SLATY-BACKED GULL 2 This subadult 3rd summer bird is similar to the bird in Slaty-backed Gull 1 but has a heavier bill with a bulging lower outer portion and strongly hooked tip. Similar to Great Black-backed, subadults show a black and red spot near the bill tip, while full adults show only a red spot on their yellow bill. Note the pale yellowish-green to dull whitish eye, which is not as yellow as in other dark-backed gulls, and which gives older subadult and adult birds of this species a blank "zombie-like" appearance (Cameron Cox comment). Alaska, June

SLATY-BACKED GULL 3 This immature (1st winter) Slaty-backed Gull shows a large but relatively straight bill and a blackish tail. It differs from Herring Gull in its broader wings and straight bill that lacks noticeable pink at the base, as in Herring. This bird was photographed in March, so some pale color is visible on the bill. Underparts are generally more uniformly pale compared to the often splotchier pattern of immature Herring. Compared to immature Western Gull, Slaty-backed has a more slender bill that lacks the bulbous tip of Western, and the plumage is noticeably paler, especially the upperparts. Considerable identification problems occur with immature Glaucous-winged × Herring Gull hybrids, which are commonly encountered in Alaska and on Pacific coast beaches in winter. Japan, March

is all dark, and bill is distinctly thinner than in Western Gull but more robust than in Herring Gull. Otherwise, immature Slaty-backed is very similar to immature Western and Herring Gulls, but its bold pink legs, sometimes with a yellowish cast, are noticeably different in shading from those of both Herring and Western Gulls. This species is subject to pronounced bleaching on its wings by the 1st summer (turning some individuals all white, and others brown and white, or piebald).

SUBADULT (combines 2nd summer and some 3rd winter) Shows the dark back of an adult but also worn (or bleached pale) immature wings (2nd winter), which contrast markedly with the blackish back feathers. Legs are bright pink by this stage. Head, neck, and perhaps chest or belly are heavily spotted to bleached white. Yellowish bill shows a dark tip or spot. Eyes are dull yellow on older subadults. Subadults have a noticeably darker back than Western Gull, and there is little contrast between the dark back and the wing tips.

SLATY-BACKED GULL 4 Adults, breeding and nonbreeding, with Glaucous and Vega Gulls (*right*). Slaty-backed is the only dark-backed gull that occurs in its extreme northern range, although the Vega subspecies of Herring Gull has only a slightly paler gray back and could cause confusion (see *right* bird in *right* photo). The *left* photo shows a breeding adult Slaty-backed with its charcoal-gray upperparts, which are unique to this species. The *right* photo shows an advanced subadult (*center*) with typical dense streaking in nonbreeding plumage and a concentration of dark feathers around the eye, similar to Lesser Black-backed Gull. Note the black bill tip, pale eye, and dark markings in the tail. The *right* bird is a Vega Herring Gull with medium-gray upperparts and strong black outer primary wing-tip shading. The *left* bird is either a nonbreeding adult Glaucous Gull with dense markings on the head and breast and white wing tips, or a Glaucous-winged Gull. Since both of these species are found in Gambell, Alaska, where the photo was taken, there is a good chance that this bird is a hybrid Glaucous × Glaucous-winged because of its small size and white primary wing tips. Alaska, early June (*left*); Gambell, Alaska, early September (*right*)

KELP GULL *Larus dominicanus*

SIZE **21–25 inches long** WINGSPAN **50–56 inches**

A medium-large, stocky, dark-backed gull from the Southern Hemisphere with a shrimp in its mouth, standing on a dock in Maryland or gracing the beaches of Galveston, Texas, in the late 1990s. (PD)

KELP GULL
Breeds inland locally in Patagonia. Casual north to the United States.

■ resident, breeds locally

nonbreeding occurrence (can be year-round)

PROFILE This gull has a stout bill with a bulging tip, a heavy body structure, and wings that extend slightly past the tail. Legs are stout and greenish yellow to grayish green. Adult Kelp Gull is somewhat similar to Lesser Black-backed Gull in plumage, with a head and body that are strikingly white, but unlike Lesser, it has very little streaking on the head in winter. Back is solid black in adults (charcoal gray in Lesser Black-backed), with equally black wing tips. Bill is yellow, with a red spot near the tip in adults.

Immature Kelp Gull more closely resembles Lesser Black-backed Gull in plumage, but it is overall heavier bodied and compact in structure and has a much stouter, swollen-tipped bill and shorter wing tip projection. All these features contribute to the overall stockier appearance of Kelp Gull. The initial impression when you see an adult Kelp Gull on a beach or in flight is Great Black-backed Gull because of its bulky structure, black back, broad wings, and large bill. It appears similar physically to Great Black-backed Gull, but it is smaller and has different leg color (yellow versus pink on subadult and adult Great Black-backed).

STATUS AND DISTRIBUTION A very rare vagrant to North America; small numbers appeared in the Gulf of Mexico in the late 1980s and 1990s, and it bred on small islands off the Louisiana coast during this time. It is accidental to the United States, with records from the Great Lakes region and mid-Atlantic coast (thus the reference in the first sentence), and an adult bird appeared in Galveston, Texas, in the winter of 1996–1997 (see Kelp Gull 1, 2, and 3). Note that the bird in flight with a Herring Gull in Kelp Gull 2 is slightly smaller than the Herring but bulkier in structure. Breeding coastally

KELP GULL 1 Similar to a hypothetical larger-billed Lesser Black-backed Gull or a small Great Black-backed Gull, Kelp Gull is a very rare vagrant from South America. This species has also wandered to other states, most notably Maryland (thus the reference in the species heading). This bird's upperparts are basically as dark as its primaries, as in Great Black-backed Gull. The large bill and large, squarish head on this adult Kelp Gull immediately eliminate Lesser Black-backed, and its smaller size assessed in the field and yellowish versus pink legs would eliminate Great Black-backed. The nonbreeding Laughing Gull seems surprised to be seeing this South American vagrant in Galveston, Texas, while the nonbreeding Dunlin at *left* appears indifferent. Lesser Black-Backed Gull would show brighter yellow legs, a much smaller bill, and a charcoal-gray rather than black back. Texas, January 1996 (also seen in the winter of 1997, when white outer primary wing-tip spots were distinct)

KELP GULL 2 Adult with adult Herring Gull. This photo shows that this Kelp Gull (*left*) is slightly smaller than the nonbreeding Herring Gull. Great Black-backed Gull would be slightly to much larger than Herring, and most Lesser Black-backeds would appear conspicuously smaller and more slender bodied and slender winged than this Herring Gull. Texas, January

KELP GULL 3 Adult. This adult Kelp Gull shows longish wings that are broader than those of Lesser Black-backed; a much larger bill; and a lack of strong contrast between wings and wing tips, as in Lesser Black-backed. Plumage and structure are more similar to those of Great Black-backed, which was the initial identification of this bird by a very experienced birder. Adult Slaty-backed Gull is another dark-backed gull from Alaska that is similar in size to Kelp Gull, but it has paler charcoal-gray upperparts and bold white spots just inside the tips of the outer primaries that resemble a string of pearls, which is very different from Kelp Gull. Texas, January

in South America, this smaller version of Great Black-backed Gull may be undergoing a range expansion, so it may turn up anywhere. Anticipate it but don't expect it.

ADULT Upperparts are blacker than Lesser Black-backed Gull's charcoal gray (about as dark as the larger and bulkier Great Black-backed Gull). Kelp Gull's legs are also a duller greenish yellow, whereas adult Lesser Black-backed's legs are typically bright yellow, and Great Black-backed's are pink. The long, deep yellow bill has a red spot near the tip, where the bill bulges noticeably.

IMMATURE (combines juvenile and 1st winter) Mottled grayish-brown upperparts similar to those of immature Lesser Black-backed, but Lesser is much slimmer overall and has longer, narrower wings and a much more slender bill that does not bulge as much near the tip. Streaking on the breast is generally more diffuse and spotted than on Lesser Black-backed. Note that immature Kelp Gull can show the same punched-in-the-eye bruised look of immature Lesser Black-backed.

KELP GULL 4 Immature (1st winter) Kelp Gull is very similar to immature Lesser Black-backed but shows broader, less tapered wings; a stockier, more rounded body shape, and a heavier bill with a bulging tip on most birds. Immature Great Black-backed is larger overall, with a whiter head, narrower dark tail band, and upperparts that show a checkered, granite-like appearance. South America, November

SUBADULT (2nd winter) Shows the dark back of an adult but residual brown immature wings. Legs are dull greenish; nape and white underparts are lightly to heavily spotted (legs of Lesser Black-backed at this stage are yellow or dull pink).

BLACK-TAILED GULL *Larus crassirostris*

SIZE **17–20 inches long** WINGSPAN **46.5–49 inches**

A Ring-billed Gull–sized, dark-backed gull (adult) from northeastern Asia with nothing in its bill because you aren't really seeing it. (PD)

PROFILE *A graceful, long-winged, medium-sized gull with a small, rounded head and slender bill.* Note Black-tailed's very long, straight, slender, bicolored bill (pale pink or yellow with a dark tip). In all plumages it shows a white tail with a broad dark band at the tip and long wing tips that extend well beyond the tail when it is perched, so it has a physical profile most similar to that of Ring-billed Gull. Immature is most likely to be confused with immature California or Laughing Gull.

STATUS AND DISTRIBUTION Asian coastal breeder and very rare summer visitor to western Alaska; very rare elsewhere, but widely scattered records exist, primarily from the East and West Coasts (summer to winter).

ADULT *Charcoal-gray back is intermediate between dark-backed and silver gray-backed gulls.* A broad black tail band distinguishes it from other dark-backed species. The lightly streaked collar and face of the nonbreeding adult frame the bright yellow eye. The distinctive long, slender, yellow bill shows a red and black tip. Adult has yellow legs.

BLACK-TAILED GULL 1 Mostly adult plumage. Black-tailed is a medium-sized, slender, long-winged gull that occurs as a rare vagrant from Asia in North America. It is about the same size as Ring-billed Gull but has a charcoal-gray back and a black tail band. Rhode Island, late July

IMMATURE (1st winter) Overall dark grayish brown with whitish face and prominent white eye arcs. Slender, long, pinkish bill has a dark tip. Pinkish legs are unusually long. It is most likely to be confused with immature California Gull, which also has a broad, dark terminal tail band, but California Gull's tail band is brown, not black as on Black-tailed, and 1st winter California Gull has a heavily streaked, darkish upper tail, which is white on 1st winter Black-tailed Gull.

BLACK-TAILED GULL 2 Note the similarity in size and shape with nearby Ring-billed Gulls. With its yellow legs, this Black-tailed might be mistaken for a near-adult Lesser Black-backed Gull, but the bill is too slender, and it has a bold, black tail band. Adult Black-tailed shows a black bill with a small red tip, which averages longer and is slightly heavier toward the tip compared to that of Ring-billed. Rhode Island, late July

IVORY GULL 1 Adult. This stocky, medium-sized, pigeon-like Arctic gull is uncommon even in its high Arctic breeding and nonbreeding ranges, and rare south of the seasonal ice cap in winter. Our only pure white gull, this bird has a black eye that quickly distinguishes it from albino gulls, and the orange- to red-tipped, dusky, bullet-shaped bill is unique. Snowy substrate is the normal habitat for this gull. Ivory Gull often feeds on remnants of polar bear kills on the Arctic pack ice, or on carcasses of dead animals. January

IVORY GULL
Casual south to northern
United States bordering Canada.

■ seasonal, breeds locally
■ nonbreeding occurrence
  (can be year-round)

IVORY GULL *Pagophila eburnea*

SIZE **16–17 inches** long   WINGSPAN **42.5–47 inches**

It's the medium-sized, all-white gull with a proportionally large head, perched on ice with its short bill filled with polar bear scat. (PD)

PROFILE   Smaller than Iceland Gull, Ivory Gull is slightly smaller than Ring-billed Gull but stockier and plumper overall. *Ivory Gull is our only pure white gull with black legs and black eyes* (thus eliminating the possibility of albinism in other species).

Ivory Gull is often described as an aggressive and voracious feeder—a trait that serves a bird that lives very literally on the edge. It is somewhat pigeon-like on land but wheeling and nimble in flight, with quick wing beats. Mostly solitary and somewhat nocturnal, it is reported to investigate anything red. It is always found near water, even cattle watering troughs if nothing more suitable is around.

This distinctive but rarely seen all-white Arctic gull is typically found foraging around pack ice, where it makes a decent living scavenging the remains of polar bear kills. Vagrants often feed on fish scraps near fishing piers or docks where boats dump their bycatch.

STATUS AND DISTRIBUTION   Rare away from its high Arctic breeding locations with pack ice, in Greenland and extreme northern Canada. In winter, found almost exclusively near pack ice, with wintering areas in the Bering Sea and Labrador Sea to Davis Strait. Occurs casually to the Canadian Maritimes and is accidental south to New Jersey and other scattered locations. There are a few inland records, including Tennessee, with most clustered around the Great Lakes. It is very rare south of Canada.

IVORY GULL 2 Ivory Gull foraging for food. With a lack of carrion scraps to feed on in New Jersey, Ivory Gull forages by flying low over the water and dipping its bill into the surface for possible food sources. This feeding style is similar to that of Bonaparte's Gull, but without the foot-pattering or belly-dipping behavior of Bonaparte's. New Jersey, early December

IVORY GULL 3 Immature. Because this species rarely interacts with humans, it shows little to no fear of our presence when it occurs as a very rare vagrant to the United States. This birder is taking the picture with a point-and-shoot camera, and the Ivory Gull shows no reaction to his presence since it is intent upon eating fish scraps. New Jersey, December

IVORY GULL 4 This adult Ivory Gull shows the classic broad, pointy wings as well as the idiosyncratic orange-tipped bill, which is faded on this individual. The overall whiteness of this species gives it a special mystique among birders, and it is one of the most sought-after gulls in North America. This is not a small, petite gull, and some males come close to Ring-billed Gull in size, but they have much shorter, broader wings and a stocky, rounded body shape. January

IVORY GULL 5 While eye-catchingly white, this immature (1st winter) Ivory Gull also shows an array of small black spots on the upperparts and narrow black trim on the tail tip and trailing edge of the outer wings (see Ivory Gull 7). Touches of black on the face and head are also typical. Bill is mostly dark with a pale tip, and legs are black. New Jersey, late November

IVORY GULL 6 Immature. Note the round, pigeon-like head and the dusky bill that is starting to acquire the yellowish-orange tip of older immatures. The black eye and dark spotting rule out any possibility of an albino gull. New Jersey, early December

ADULT *All-white plumage is distinctive.* The adult bird's black legs and black eyes combine with a short, bullet-shaped, *two-toned*, gray to dark olive-green bill with a yellow to orange to red tip to make it unique.

IMMATURE (juvenile, 1st winter, and 1st summer) Much like adult but shows a dirty face and sparse to lavish small black flecking on folded wings. Tips of primaries and tip of tail are likewise black.

The dirty-looking, heavily marked face makes birds appear masked. Because of the bird's scarcity and very restricted range, you should give the possibility of albinism primary consideration before assigning the name "Ivory Gull" to any all-white gull you may encounter.

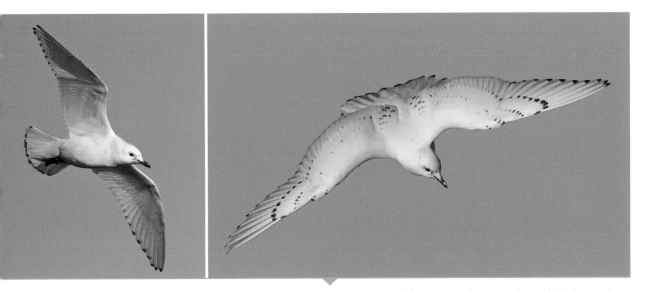

IVORY GULL 7 Immature. Fairly lightly marked, this immature (1st winter) Ivory Gull shows pigeon-like proportions with black-tipped outer flight feathers and tail. The faces of some individuals are even "dirtier" than that of this bird, and some appear almost black faced New Jersey, late November/early December

IVORY GULL 8 Immature, in comparison with Great Black-backed Gull. This immature 1st winter Great-Black-backed Gull is probably thinking, "I've never seen one of these before, but it looks edible enough." Direct comparison with this familiar species allows you to store a general size impression of Ivory Gull for future sightings. A fish carcass at *far right* was the food source for the Ivory Gull until the much larger, aggressive gull showed up. New Jersey, early December

ROSS'S GULL 1 Adult breeding. Finally, a gull anyone can identify. The small, elegant, long-winged adult breeding Ross's Gull shows pale gray upperparts with noncontrasting gray primary wing tips. The black bill is slender, and wings and tail are relatively long. Breeding birds have a unique narrow black collar and pinkish underparts (see Ross's Gull 5, *right* photo), of which this bird shows only a hint. Bright red legs break up the muted black, gray, and white appearance of this species. This beautiful gull inhabits Arctic regions and rarely strays to the lower forty-eight states. Churchill, Manitoba, June

ROSS'S GULL 2 Adult nonbreeding. Nonbreeding Ross's Gull shows a pale grayish nape, gray primaries, and a characteristic dainty overall profile. Little Gull's primaries would be white, and the head would show a black cap. Ross's pointed tail is often not evident on perched or floating birds. England, May

ROSS'S GULL 3 Adult breeding Ross's Gull shows a long-winged profile and grayish primary wing tips that match the shading of the upper back. The narrow black collar is unique and gives this bird a charm that sets it apart from other gulls. Churchill, Manitoba, June

ROSS'S GULL *Rhodostethia rosea*

SIZE **11.5–12 inches long** WINGSPAN **35.5–39 inches**

It's the small, pink-breasted gull plucking edible tidbits from the defunct walrus. (PD)

PROFILE *Ross's is only slightly larger than Little Gull, with a longer, more tapered rear body, a petite bill, and more slender and pointier wings that are grayish below, not black as on adult Little Gull. The long, wedge-shaped tail attenuates to a tapered point (Little Gull has a somewhat squarish, slightly wedge-shaped tail). Standing birds appear elegantly long winged, with short, pink to reddish legs set well forward.*

STATUS AND DISTRIBUTION You should be so lucky. For many years, one or two pairs famously nested in the vicinity of Churchill, Manitoba, and small to large numbers are noted annually migrating past Barrow, Alaska, from September to mid-October. Most birds winter at sea near pack ice, but rare vagrants to the lower forty-eight states have been found in harbors and sewage-treatment facilities, as well as far offshore. This diminutive, fairylike gull breeds on open tundra in Arctic Canada and Greenland, often close to freshwater lakes, and winters in northern seas, rarely wandering to the lower forty-eight states. When it occurs in the lower forty-eight, it is typically found among flocks of Bonaparte's Gulls and is often mistaken for the similarly plumaged Little Gull.

ADULT BREEDING Pale gray above, flushed pink below, with grayish primaries about the same color as the back (primary wing tips of adult Little Gull are contrastingly white). Also note the small black bill and the unique narrow black ring on the hind neck and the coral-colored legs (dark red on Little Gull).

ADULT NONBREEDING Neck ring is replaced by a small, shadowy collar, but white underparts may retain a pink blush. Swimming and standing birds seem particularly long tailed because of the long wings. In flight, the trailing edge of the wing (except the outer primaries) shows a fairly broad white band that contrasts with the gray underwing and upper wing (see Ross's Gull 5).

IMMATURE (juvenile) Very rarely seen. Juvenile shows very dark brown upperparts; a brownish cap and ear patch, and a dark-tipped, pointed tail. The M-shaped black upper wing pattern is similar to that on the overall paler-backed Little Gull, but note the more restricted black tip to the tail of Ross's Gull. This plumage is held for only a short time, with birds acquiring 1st winter plumage by September.

SUBADULT (1st winter) Boldly plumaged with strongly contrasting black-and-white upper wings; gray underwings with a broad white trailing edge; a gray back and collar; a black ear patch; a white tail with a tiny black central tip; a white head with a dark eye and a blackish smudge around the eye; and a tiny black bill (see Ross's Gull 5). Differs from subadult Little Gull in the uncapped white head sporting a dark ear patch (Little Gull has a darkish cap in juvenile/1st winter birds). In flight, it shows a bold black "M" pattern on the upper wing, as several other small gull species do, but it lacks the black collar of Black-legged Kittiwake or the dark cap of Little Gull.

ROSS'S GULL 4 Adult nonbreeding. While missing the black collar, this nonbreeding adult Ross's Gull still retains a hint of pink underparts and shows the gray wings. The slightly smaller or same-sized nonbreeding adult Little Gull (10.25–11.5 inches) shows white wing tips, a darker gray back, darker crown markings, and a dark cheek spot. England, May

ROSS'S GULL 5 Adult and juvenile. *Left:* The elegant, slender-winged, pointy-tailed profile of Ross's Gull is enough to incite envy among the terns. Longer and pointier winged than Little Gull, adult Ross's Gull has distinctive uniformly dusky gray underwings with a mostly white trailing edge, and a unique shadowy gray collar. Slight remnants of the thin black collar present in breeding birds are visible, along with a noticeable pink blush to the underparts. *Right:* This photo (and what a spectacular photo it is, thanks to Greg Lasley of Texas!) shows a pink-bodied, pink-headed adult (*left*) and a juvenile with its strikingly bold M-shaped dark upper-wing pattern. The large white wedge on the juvenile's upper wing extends almost to the outer wing tip, whereas juvenile Little Gull's outer upper wing is mostly black (see Little Gull 8, p. 67). Note the black tip on the pointed tail of juvenile Ross's Gull (*right*). And look, no black cap as in Little Gull, just big black eyes against a white head and a tiny black spot on the cheek. Alaska, August

LITTLE GULL with
BONAPARTE'S GULLS

HYBRID GULLS

Many gull species are closely related, with their evolutionary divergence fairly recent, and their geographic isolation is not always absolute. In fact, the ranges of some genetically similar species overlap. Because of this fertile combination of genetic similarity and physical proximity, hybridization between similar species currently considered distinct is both likely and problematic.

GLAUCOUS-WINGED × WESTERN GULL

GLAUCOUS-WINGED × HERRING GULL

GLAUCOUS × HERRING GULL

GLAUCOUS-WINGED × GLAUCOUS GULL

HERRING × LESSER BLACK-BACKED GULL

The offspring of theses hybrid combinations often show traits of both parent species, making identification challenging, or may show the physical traits of one species but some plumage features of the other species. Being themselves fertile, these hybrid gulls may then backcross—that is, breed with either parent species or with another hybrid gull—further muddying the ID picture. Hybrids are not countable as distinct species by any ornithological organization.

Common hybrids to be aware of include the following:

GLAUCOUS-WINGED × WESTERN GULL This is the most common hybrid gull encountered in North America, and it occurs mostly on the Pacific coast from California to British Columbia. In certain areas of northern Oregon and southern Washington, hybrids may outnumber pure individuals of both species. Some hybrids resemble Western Gulls, especially in body and bill structure, but show some plumage traits of Glaucous-winged, while others resemble Glaucous-winged in structure and bill shape but show some plumage features of Western Gull.

GLAUCOUS-WINGED × HERRING GULL The hybrid offspring of these two species may resemble either adult at first glance, or a combination of both species, but certain field marks and features don't correspond with the "normal" appearance of only one species. Hybrids of these two species may produce offspring that resemble Thayer's Gull, now a subspecies of Iceland Gull, but are generally larger, more robust, and thicker billed than the slighter-proportioned Thayer's Gull.

A common disparate feature is the very dark to black wing tips on birds resembling Glaucous-winged Gull that fall outside the variation seen in pure Glaucous-winged Gull. Another nonconforming field mark is pale eyes on a Glaucous-winged-type bird, which suggests Herring Gull genes intermixed. Adult Herring types with Glaucous-winged genes often show paler upper and underwing primaries, dusky eyes, and deep pink orbital rings. Hybrids of these two species typically result from interbreeding in southern Alaska, with migrants showing up along the North American Pacific coast as far south as southern California. Noted gull expert Paul

HYBRID 1 Glaucous-winged × Western Gull hybrids. The *left* bird, photographed in northern California in March, has the stocky body and heavy bill typical of Western Gull, as well as the head shape of that species with a bump on the crown. However, the back is gray like that of Glaucous-winged, but the wing tips are too dark for that species. The *right* bird, photographed in northern Oregon in June, shows the stocky body and very heavy bill with a bulbous tip of Western Gull, but a midtoned gray back that is a bit too pale for the northern subspecies of Western Gull and a bit dark for Glaucous-winged. The wing tips are black, as in Western Gull, but the pale underwing primary shading on the far wing is inconsistent with Western. California, March (*left*); northern Oregon, June (*right*)

Lehman recently told us that he sees more hybrids of these species in San Diego than he does pure Glaucous-winged.

GLAUCOUS × HERRING GULL Hybrids from these two species may be confused with Glaucous-winged Gull. This hybrid form is so widespread that it is often referred to as "Nelson's Gull." Adult birds may appear similar to Glaucous Gull but show dark slaty wing tips with bold white patterning. Immature birds, like the one pictured here, may appear similar to Glaucous Gull but have darker primaries. These two species typically interbreed in northwestern and northeastern Canada. Migrant hybrids occur mainly south to northwestern Mexico and the eastern United States (*Gulls of the Americas*, Howell and Dunn, 2007).

HYBRID 2 Western × Glaucous-winged Gull hybrids. The *left* photo shows an adult Western Gull (*right*) and a paler gray-backed Glaucous-winged type. This hybrid gull has the gray upperparts of Glaucous-winged, although maybe a bit darker than usual, and the blackish outer wing tips typical of Western and very unlike the pale gray wing tips on Glaucous-winged, which are typically the same shading as the upper back. The body structure is a bit stockier than that of a typical Glaucous-winged, which usually shows a more slender, tapered body shape. Herring Gull is eliminated on the *left* bird by the pale underwings on the left wing, a dusky rather than bright yellow eye, and the gray inner primary shading. The *right* photo shows a hybrid adult in flight from California in December with gray inner wings (upper wing coverts) on the upperparts like those of Glaucous-winged, but darker outer wings not typical of either species. The black primaries and white mirrors on the left upper wing are like those of Western Gull. This winter bird lacks the heavily streaked head and neck of nonbreeding Glaucous-winged but shows the typical lightly spotted head of Western. California, November (*left*); California, December (*right*)

HYBRID 3 Herring × Glaucous-winged Gull hybrids. These photos, all taken in the southern Kenai Peninsula region of Alaska, where these two species interbreed freely, show a variety of subtle hybrids. The *left* photo shows a bird that resembles Herring Gull with a tapered front snout look and a pale versus darkish eye, as in Glaucous-winged, but it has pale brownish-gray primaries as in Glaucous-winged versus black in Herring. The *center* bird also suggests an adult Herring Gull, but the outer primaries are too pale gray on the interior for Herring and the eye is pale dusky rather than bright yellow, as in adult Herring. The wings are too dark for Glaucous-winged, and the eye too pale for that species. The *right* photo is a male of a mated pair of Glaucous-wingeds (shown in Glaucous-winged Gull 10, *right* bird, p. 140), but his primaries are black, not very pale gray, as in Glaucous-winged. Primary wing tips on Glaucous-winged are typically the same pale gray shading as the upper back. Alaska, May (all photos)

GLAUCOUS-WINGED × GLAUCOUS GULL Inter-breeding between these two species occurs in western Alaska, and hybrids show virtually all combinations of parental plumage and structure (*Gulls of the Americas*, Howell and Dunn, 2007). Birds from this gene mix may resemble Glaucous Gull but show dusky wing tips, a dusky or dark eye, and a bill shape more like that of Glaucous-winged. Some migrants may occur south to California.

HERRING × LESSER BLACK-BACKED GULL A few examples of this hybrid mix have been documented in recent years, including a bird that was banded on a nest in Maine in 2007 and wintered in Daytona Beach, Florida, for a number of years. The bird pictured here was photographed by Kevin at Daytona Beach in January 2015, and although its plumage is similar to that of adult Lesser Black-backed Gull, its structure is much more like that of Herring Gull. Adults have a back color about midway between that of Herring and Lesser Black-backed, as in the bird pictured here. Legs are duller yellow than on Lesser Black-backed and often show a pinkish cast between the toes.

Even a cursory review of the species prone to hybridization shows that the challenge of gull hybrids is much more acute on the West Coast and especially prevalent on the outer islands of the Alaskan coast and the Kenai Peninsula. In fact, Pete does not personally recall a single encounter with a hybrid gull in his forty years of East Coast birding, while Kevin has seen two "Nelson's Gulls" (Glaucous-Herring hybrids), both in 1st year immature plumage; one Laughing–Ring-billed hybrid (all in New Jersey); and two Herring–Lesser Black-backed Gull hybrids in Daytona Beach, Florida, including the offspring of the banded bird from Maine. After a recent trip to the Kenai Peninsula in Alaska, Kevin identified a few Herring–Glaucous-winged Gull hybrids that he did not notice in the field but became aware of when he looked closely at the photos (see Hybrid Gulls 3).

HYBRID 5   Lesser Black-backed × Herring Gull hybrid, adult. This bird has plumage and leg color similar to that of an adult Lesser Black-backed Gull, with a charcoal-gray back, black wing tips, and heavy spotting around the eye in nonbreeding plumage, but the structure is much more like that of Herring Gull, with a husky, foreshortened body shape and short wings that barely extend past the tail (however, these new primaries are still growing, so they may have come to resemble those of Lesser after this photo was taken). Lesser Black-backed has a slender, athletic structure and long wings that extend well past the tail. The head is also quite large, and the bill is more typical of Herring, with its strong, overlapping hooked tip, although some larger Lessers might have a bill similar to this. The chest also lacks the plumpness seen on Lesser and instead has the slender-breasted look typical of Herring. Note the orange orbital ring, which is typical in hybrids of these two species (Lesser has a bold red orbital ring; Herring a yellow one). Florida, January

HYBRID 4   Herring Gull × Glaucous Gull hybrid, immature 1st winter. This "Nelson's Gull," which is what birders call this common hybrid mix, has the bulky body, oval-shaped head, bright pink legs, and stocky, bold pink bill with a black tip commonly found in Glaucous Gull, but darker brown primaries that are fully inconsistent with Glaucous but fine for Herring. The gull was about the same size as all the other Herring Gulls on the beach in New Jersey in May, while Glaucous would appear slightly to much larger. New Jersey, May

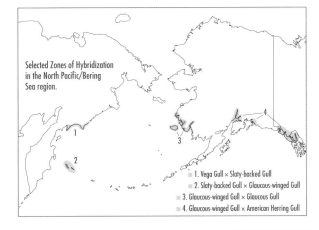

Selected Zones of Hybridization in the North Pacific/Bering Sea region.

1. Vega Gull × Slaty-backed Gull
2. Slaty-backed Gull × Glaucous-winged Gull
3. Glaucous-winged Gull × Glaucous Gull
4. Glaucous-winged Gull × American Herring Gull

QUIZ AND REVIEW

This chapter contains a number of photos that present ID challenges for both beginning and expert birders, or a review of photos previously used in the book to test your powers of retention. For a fun quiz, try to identify all gulls in the photos, and for an added challenge, try to work out the age of these birds as well. Use whatever terms you like, but if you say "immature" because the gull is mostly brownish or grayish overall, try to pinpoint the specific age, such as 1st winter, 2nd winter, 3rd winter, or adult. Or just use immature, sub-adult, or adult if you wish, since that is a simpler approach. If the bird was photographed in summer and shows the typical plumage of a bird transitioning from 1st winter to 2nd winter, we use the terms 1st summer, 2nd summer, and so forth. If you say 1st cycle, 2nd cycle, 3rd cycle, that is fine too.

In photos that show two or more gulls, you should try to find a familiar gull in the scene or use your field guide to identify one, and then use the size and shape of the now-familiar gull to help with your ID of the unfamiliar ones. A small number of photos show messy-plumaged birds that encourage you to assess their overall shape and structural features for your guess. We include the date the photo was taken, which provides important information about a gull's typical plumage at that time of year, but not the location, which would give too much away as to the correct identity of each gull. Try to pinpoint which features (physical structure, bare parts, or plumage) contributed to your guess before looking at the answers, since we give general reasons for the ID in the answers. Answers are provided at the end of this section. Good luck!

QUIZ 1

Late January

QUIZ 2

July 31: Try to guess the species of the gull in the background also.

QUIZ 3

July 9

QUIZ 4

Assorted gulls and terns, March 17

QUIZ 5

QUIZ 6

March, New Jersey (Advanced)   August 21

QUIZ 7

QUIZ 8

February 17 (Advanced)   November 11

March 17   January 28 (Advanced)   February 17 (Advanced)

August 21: Guess the identity of both gulls, and indicate what led you to your ID.   February 16

February 13: Guess the identity of the swimming duck for an added quiz.   April 11: Guess the species of the terns in the background.

Early August (Advanced)   September 5   April 2

April 2

Early August (Advanced)   July 9 (Advanced)

QUIZ 22   February

April 2   QUIZ 23

QUIZ 24

QUIZ 25

Late July   Assorted gulls and terns, March 21

QUIZ 26

QUIZ 27

Early February (Advanced)   February 17

QUIZ 28

QUIZ 29

Early June (Advanced)

May 13

January 30: Try to identify
all the gulls in this photo,
even the ones in the front.

QUIZ 30

QUIZ 31

QUIZ 32

February 15   May 15

QUIZ 33   August 25 (Advanced)

QUIZ 34   April 11 (Advanced)

QUIZ 35   April 14 (Advanced)

ANSWERS TO QUIZ PHOTOS

QUIZ 1   **Lesser Black-backed Gull, immature/1st winter, Florida, late January**

Lean, trim proportions; plump breast; longish legs; and long primary (outer wing) projection past the tail are good physical features for Lesser Black-backed Gull. This 1st winter bird also shows the typical all-black bill; pale head; and dark grayish brown–centered upperpart feathers. Sparse dark spots and streaks on the underparts with a paler upper breast are also consistent with 1st winter Lesser Black-backed. Note the overall cold brownish-gray tones to the upperparts versus the warmer brown ones on immature Herring Gull. The mostly dark-centered wing coverts (wing panel) also differ from the paler, more heavily marked ones on Herring Gull. The position in the wave zone is classic for this active foraging species.

QUIZ 2   **Great Black-backed Gull, juvenile, New Jersey, July 31**

Since you can't judge the size of this gull, you don't know that you are looking at the largest gull in the world, Great Black-backed Gull. However, the bulky body profile; large, oval-shaped head; very heavy bill with a bulging tip; and thick, pink legs all point to this species. This juvenile bird has recently fledged and shows the typical black and brown spots and streaks against a dull, white to buff background on the head and underparts; a cold granite look to the upperparts; and a piano-key appearance to the wing coverts (wing panel). A slightly smaller, more slender immature Herring Gull with a noticeably more slender, pink-based bill is shown in the background.

QUIZ 3   **Herring Gull, worn, sun-bleached immature in its 1st summer, New Jersey, July**

Ignore all the white. Severely worn, immature Herring Gulls are typically the messiest, most disheveled, and confusing birds on the beach. If you look at just the physical features, a proportionally smallish head; a long, slender, droop-tipped bill; and a pulled-taffy look to the front face are consistent with Herring Gull, as is a diffuse pink base and ill-defined dark tip on the bill in some 1st summer birds. Dark wing tips rule out a "white-winged" gull (Iceland, Glaucous, and Glaucous-winged), and pale gray (versus charcoal-gray) upper back feathers rule out Lesser Black-backed Gull.

QUIZ 4   **Assorted gulls and terns, New Jersey, March**

There are three gull species and one tern species in this photo. The largest bird is an adult Herring Gull, which dwarfs the adult Ring-billed Gull (*right center*), which in turn is noticeably larger than the surrounding nonbreeding adult Bonaparte's Gulls (which are doing their best not to let you see their heads and bills but are allowing a good look at their dark cheek spots). Now, where is the tern? It is the one with the white wing tips, more slender body, and shorter, orange legs (*lower right*).

QUIZ 5   **Black-headed Gull, 1st winter; Ring-billed Gull, adult, New Jersey, March (Advanced)**

An all-pale, gray-backed, yellow-eyed (with red orbital ring), yellow-legged gull with fine speckling (not coarse blotching) on the head: why not adult Ring-billed Gull? The smaller bird next to it could be a 1st winter Bonaparte's Gull, but the leg seems too

yellowish-orange, and the worn, retained juvenile feathers on the wing panel are brownish, not black. These field marks are more consistent with Black-headed Gull, whose orange bill is hidden. The dark markings typically seen on the head of this species in winter have worn off by late winter, and only a dark cheek spot is left. Bonaparte's would have pinkish legs and darker juvenile feathers on the wing panel and tertials, except for some worn late winter birds, which can show slightly darker brownish wing coverts and tertials.

QUIZ 6   **Herring Gull, fresh juvenile, New Jersey, August**

You see a large, warm brown gull with buff feather fringes on the upperparts on a beach in New Jersey in August. Stop. You are looking at an immature (juvenile) Herring Gull. Juvenile Laughing Gull is also dark brown, but it is much smaller overall, with a small black bill and black legs.

QUIZ 7   **Western Gull, immature 1st winter, February, La Jolla, California (Advanced)**

Yes, this is a tough one. This very small-billed immature 1st winter Western Gull is showing an especially white, possibly sun-bleached head. Note the slightly thickened tip on the bill and the pale base on the lower mandible, but the charcoal-shaded upper back feathers identify this as one of the dark-backed gulls. Range alone points to Western Gull, but Lesser Black-backed can be ruled out by the compact, stocky body structure, short wings that barely extend past the tail, and short legs. Lesser would have a slender, tapered body with very long wings and relatively long legs. The tiny bill suggests a female at the extreme small end of the size range for Western Gull. The dark feathering on the face and crown and the extensive dark bases on the greater wing coverts help to ID this bird.

QUIZ 8   **Franklin's Gulls, nonbreeding, with a Laughing Gull, nonbreeding, South Padre Island, Texas, November**

This is a fairly regular scene on the lower Texas coast in November, as hordes of nonbreeding adult and 1st winter Franklin's Gulls (showing dark rear hoods) migrate south, where they often mix with the larger Laughing Gulls. Laughing Gull at this early date shows only limited dark markings on the head and smaller white spots on the tips of longer, more pointed black primaries. Note the smaller head and bill, shorter wings and legs, and more prominent white eye crescents emboldened by the dark feathering on the head of Franklin's. The size difference between these species is normally not this dramatic, which means that this Laughing Gull is at the large end of its size range. The shorebird at the *lower left* is a nonbreeding Short-billed Dowitcher, which is identified by the thick-based, relatively short bill with a blunt tip and the uniformly pale upperparts that lack the dark internal shafts of Long-billed Dowitcher.

QUIZ 9   **Bonaparte's Gull, adult nonbreeding, New Jersey, March**

With that white wedge on the leading edge of the wing and the petite black bill, could this be anything but an adult nonbreeding Bonaparte's Gull, which is feeding along the New Jersey coast in March? The pink legs and all-black bill are typical of nonbreeding Bonaparte's, with the very similar Black-headed Gull having deeper reddish legs and a reddish-tinged bill. These very small gulls often feed in a buoyant fashion, dipping frequently to pick up small fish and invertebrates on the surface of the water.

QUIZ 10   Ring-billed Gull, immature/1st winter, Florida, January (Advanced)

No, this is not a shearwater! Kevin was confused when this bird first flew past at Merritt Island National Wildlife Refuge in Titusville, Florida, but after he watched it fly away, the ID became apparent. This photo is not an easy one, since it catches this 1st winter Ring-billed Gull flying into a strong wind, which accentuates the angled aspect of the slender wings. In the field, you would have noted the smallish size compared to Herring Gull, and the small pink bill with a black tip. This bird has retained a good deal of its juvenile plumage at this late date, including the characteristic dark markings on the underparts (sparse scallop-shaped markings). Other choices might have been Mew or California Gull, but the much larger, pink-based bill, longer neck, and longer rear body eliminate 1st winter Mew Gull, and the long, slender body, lack of strong white feathering on the smaller head, and petite bill compared to California Gull's larger bill eliminate that species.

QUIZ 11   California Gull, immature/1st winter, San Diego, California, February (Advanced)

A good first impression of this tough, head-on flight shot is a whitish cast to the small head of this gull, which also shows long, slender wings with uniformly grayish flight feathers. A relatively slender body eliminates some of the larger, bulkier gulls, and the uniform, long, slender pink bill with a black tip is a good field mark for 1st winter California Gull. Note the pale face, slender, dark-tipped pink bill, unpatterned trailing edge to the wing, and dark tail. Mew Gull would have a much smaller bill and a more compact, slender body, and Ring-billed Gull in the 1st winter has a dark trailing edge to the inner wing, paler and grayer lesser and median underwing coverts, and a sparsely streaked head that lacks the contrasting white-faced look of California.

QUIZ 12   Lesser Black-backed Gull with Great Black-backed Gull, subadults, New Jersey, late August

A mostly adult 3rd summer Great Black-backed Gull (left) has a bulkier body profile with a more foreshortened rear body and proportionally shorter wings compared to the athletic but slender-bodied, mostly adult-plumaged Lesser Black-backed Gull, which shows the classic long-winged look of this species. The size difference between these two species is not as apparent as usual because of different distances from the camera. Note the robust body, heavier bill, and less contrast between the blackish wing tips and dark back on the Great Black-backed versus the charcoal back with black wing tips and more slender bill on the Lesser. Also note the pink legs on the Great Black-backed versus yellow on the Lesser. The yellow bill with a red spot is typical on adult and some subadult Lessers. Paler feathers intermixed on the upperparts of the Great Black-backed give the back a less solid black appearance and a closer resemblance to the Lesser's back shading.

QUIZ 13   Western Gull, adult breeding, La Jolla, California, February

A large, dark-backed, preening adult gull with no visible bill in North America has only a handful of possibilities. Yellow-footed and Lesser Black-backed Gulls are quickly ruled out by the absence of yellow legs; Great Black-backed is ruled out by the paler, charcoal-shaded back that contrasts with the black wing tips. And if you really want to consider the very rare Slaty-backed Gull, note the deep yellow orbital ring on Western versus a pink one on Slaty-backed, and the dusky eye on Western differs from the whitish to grayish-green eye on adult Slaty-backed. The location of coastal California in February, where this robust, dark-backed, pink-legged gull was photographed, points strongly to Western Gull, a supposition supported by the yellow-orange-ringed dusky eye and pink gape line at the base of the bill. This is a breeding Western Gull, so there is no streaking on the head, regardless of the winter date.

QUIZ 14   Ring-billed Gulls, subadults (2nd winter), California, February

A first impression shows relatively slim-bodied and slender-winged gulls with a smallish bill that has a dark ring near the tip, which is pale. The left bird shows a pinkish bill and legs and a gray eye compared to the right bird's yellow bill and legs and pale, straw-colored eye, but this just indicates a more advanced individual, since the upper and underwings are all mostly grayish on both birds, with 1st winter birds having retained, dark juvenile feathers on upper and underwings. Also note more black feathers on the underwing of the left bird, and a few black spots on the tail of both birds. First winter birds would show a dusky tail band and more spotting on the underparts. The duck is a female Red-breasted Merganser.

QUIZ 15   Herring Gull, immature 1st winter with Royal Terns, Florida, April

This one is not as cut-and-dried as you think. A slender, droop-tipped bill and a pulled-taffy look to the front face suggest Herring Gull, but the whitish head with dark feathering around the eye could be present on Lesser Black-backed Gull. The white head on the brown body may be the result of sun bleaching, but that does not explain the concentrated dark feathering around the eye. This bird also resembles 1st winter Lesser Black-backed Gull with its slender body; long, lanky legs; smallish bill; and long wings, but the uniform, heavily dark-mottled underparts; pale gray incoming upper back feathers; and brownish cast to the strongly patterned wing panel (wing coverts) all favor Herring Gull. Lesser Black-backed typically has a whitish upper breast that contrasts with the darker belly in late 1st winter; a more uniform, nonpatterned, darker wing panel (especially the greater wing coverts); and a colder overall appearance to the upperparts. Hybrids of these two species need to be considered in birds like these, as more such birds are appearing these days. Note the variation in the orange to red color on the bills of the Royal Terns.

QUIZ 16   Ring-billed Gull, fresh juvenile, New York, early August (Advanced)

This fresh juvenile Ring-billed Gull shows delicate features compared to adults, overall uniformly mousy grayish-brown upperparts with strong, pale fringes, and a round head with a short, dark-tipped, pink-based bill that has yet to grow to full size. This bird resembles juvenile Mew Gull with its tiny bill, but Mew Gull has an even smaller, shorter bill that is mostly dark as a juvenile, with a grayish to pale pink base in early 1st winter; a smaller, more rounded head; more uniform grayish-brown upperparts that lack the strong contrasting markings of Ring-billed; and more diffuse, smudgy grayish-brown markings on the face, neck, and underparts.

QUIZ 17 **Great Black-backed Gull, fresh juvenile, New York, early September**

In juvenile plumage, Great Black-backed Gulls can be surprisingly warm toned, with a robust body, heavy black bill, thick pink legs, and oval-shaped head. The wing coverts have extensive black internal markings and a piano-key look. The bill is too thick for either Herring or Lesser Black-backed Gull. Note the adult Ring-billed gull in the *right* background with its yellow legs and a bill with a dark ring near the tip.

QUIZ 18 **Herring Gull, immature 2nd winter, New Jersey, early April**

This immature Herring Gull shows a slender pinkish-yellow bill with a dark tip; a white rump with a black tail band; pale gray flight feathers on the inner primaries (inner primary window); and incoming pale gray feathers on the upper back. These last two features eliminate Lesser Black-backed Gull, which lacks the pale gray inner primary window and which would show darker charcoal incoming back feathers, not pale gray ones.

QUIZ 19 **Lesser Black-backed Gull (1st winter); Great Black-backed Gull (subadult); and Herring Gulls (1st winter), New Jersey, early April**

This photo shows a valuable comparison of immature Herring and Lesser Black-backed Gulls, and the sometimes-subtle size and structural differences between both of these species compared to the much larger, bulkier, and heavier-billed Great Black-backed Gull.

Lesser Black-backed (*right front*) shows a contrasting whitish head and upper breast with sparse brown streaks and a pale brownish lower belly. Immature Herring Gulls (*leftmost* three birds) show mostly uniform brownish plumage (*second and third from left*); a slightly bulkier, more compact body structure with shorter wings; and a slender bill with a more bulging tip compared to Lesser. The late 1st winter Lesser (*right front*) shows a more slender, athletic body with longer wings that extend noticeably past the tail, and *a stronger contrast to the darker-centered, less patterned wing panel (wing coverts) compared to the somewhat similarly plumaged 1st winter Herring Gull (far left)*. This Herring also shows a greater amount of diffuse pink on the bill base compared to Lesser's mostly black bill with just a slight amount of pink on the base of the lower bill. The brown tail on this Herring differs from the visible black tail on 1st winter Lesser Black-backed, but the long black primaries are very similar in shading and projection past the tail.

Great Black-backed (*second from right*) has a larger, bulkier body with a heavier bill; thicker pink legs; whiter underparts and head; and a larger, more oval-shaped head. The pink on the bill base and the incoming dark upper back feathers help to age this as a 2nd winter bird.

QUIZ 20 **California Gull, fresh juvenile, California, early August (Advanced)**

Young juvenile California Gull usually retains this unique plumage condition for a short time, after which it quickly replaces the dark upper back feathers with paler ones, and the pale fringes wear off the remaining juvenile feathers. However, some birds retain this juvenile plumage until early winter. The dusky head often turns white by fall, and the bill acquires a strong bubble-gum-pink color with a black tip. Juvenile Western Gull has similar plumage, but the greater wing coverts are mostly solid blackish, and the bill is typically much heavier.

QUIZ 21 **Herring Gull, subadult, New Jersey, July (Advanced)**

This tricky photo without a head shows the tripatterned upper wing of a worn 2nd summer Herring Gull transitioning to 3rd winter plumage. The fresh pale gray adultlike feathers with bold white tips on the inner primaries (inner primary window) age this bird, with 2nd winter feathers lacking the white tip and showing dusky interiors. Lesser Black-backed Gull would show charcoal-shaded feathers, not pale gray, on the upper back and some charcoal wing coverts at this age. Another photo of this bird a second later showing its head is presented here.

This photo, taken a second after the headless photo in **Quiz 21**, shows the pale yellow eye and small-headed look of Herring Gull, as well as the adultlike inner primary feathers that are pale gray with white tips.

QUIZ 22 **Herring Gull, subadult 2nd winter, New Jersey, February**

This rather small, slender subadult Herring Gull has a petite head and a very small, straight bill that suggests a small female, and the heavy streaking on the head and smudgy spotting on the underparts is consistent with nonbreeding subadult/adult Herring. Striking are its piercing, pale yellow, mean-looking eyes. While this bird may suggest a 1st winter Ring-billed Gull because of its smallish features, plumage patterns, and yellowish bill with a dark tip, Ring-billed lacks the heavy smudges on the underparts and would not show gray feathers in the brownish wing coverts, as this bird does. The larger and obviously bulkier dark gull in the background is an immature Herring Gull with noticeably longer legs.

QUIZ 23 **Lesser Black-backed Gull, immature 1st winter, New Jersey, early April**

This immature 1st winter Lesser Black-backed Gull shows a contrasting whitish face and upper breast against a lightly streaked belly and head. Typical of this species are the long wings with uniformly pale grayish-brown flight feathers that lack the pale inner primary window of Herring Gull; the lightly marked white rump; and the black tail band. The punched-in-the-eye black feathering around the eye is also evident in this young bird. An all-black bill with a very small pink spot at the base is also typical of this age, while most immature/1st winter Herring Gulls in April show more extensive diffuse pink on the bill base. A uniform cold brownish-gray tone to the upperparts differs from Herring's warmer ones.

QUIZ 24   **Ring-billed Gull, immature (fresh juvenile plumage), Rhode Island, late July (Advanced)**

Since the fresh juvenile plumage of this species is usually seen from midsummer to early fall at or near northern breeding sites, many birders are unfamiliar with it. Some birds retain juvenile plumage into late fall, but this is uncommon. So a good starting point is to note the slender body structure, smallish head, small pencil-stub bill, and relatively slim wings that taper on the outer half. By late summer to early fall on average, the brown upper back feathers are replaced with adultlike pale gray ones. The heavy brown mottling and spotting on the head and underparts will also begin to wear and sun bleach to show whitish feathers by fall, but this transition does not follow a consistent timetable; some birds show mostly white underparts and head by late fall, while others show remnants of juvenile head and underpart markings into spring.

The similar juvenile Mew Gull has a less contrasting brownish-gray back and head; a darker, more heavily barred upper tail; and underparts that show smudgy spots and fine streaks. Mew Gull is also less distinctly marked overall. Mew Gull shows less contrasting markings on its upper wings, with plainer, paler feather centers, and it typically shows a pale thin rear collar. Although the bill with a pink base and black tip appears smallish, Mew Gull's bill is noticeably smaller and mostly black in juveniles. A wide black tail band with small gray tips and pale upper tail coverts add to the strongly contrasting upperparts of juvenile Ring-billed Gull.

QUIZ 25   **Assorted gulls and one tern species, New Jersey, March**

Immediately obvious are the two larger gulls in the background and foreground, but size differences are difficult to assess because the *front* gull is much closer to the camera. Differences between these two large gulls include a bright yellow bill with red and black markings near the tip versus a duller yellow bill with an all-black ring near the tip; a clean white head and underparts on the *rear* gull versus a heavily marked head and white underparts on the *front* gull; and yellowish legs on the *front* gull versus pinkish-gray ones on the large *rear* gull. The *rear* Herring Gull has a blockier body structure versus the slender, evenly balanced body shape of the *front* Ring-billed Gull. If both birds were standing side by side, you would notice the smaller head, shorter legs, and longer, tapered rear body on the Ring-billed. Both are adult birds, but the Herring has achieved breeding plumage much earlier than the Ring-billed, which still shows the heavily spotted and streaked head and hind neck of a nonbreeding adult.

Now for the other birds. The smallest five birds on the sand with short orange legs; black head streaks with a slender, darker, rectangular black mask behind the eye visible on some birds; a long, black, dagger-like bill (some with reddish color on the base); and long, whitish-gray wings are Forster's Terns transitioning from nonbreeding to breeding plumage.

The other three birds with wet feet that are a bit larger than the Forster's Terns are Black-headed Gulls, with the dark-hooded one on the *left* a mostly breeding-plumaged adult. The other two with retained worn, brownish wing coverts and tertials are subadult 1st winter Black-headed Gulls, with the *left* one considerably larger than the *right* one. Size differences between small gulls are rarely this obvious, and most birds are best left unsexed.

For more information about the plumage of immature Black-headed Gulls, see the Black-headed Gull species account. Leg color ranges from dull reddish (adults) to yellowish-orange (immatures), but the legs of some adults may appear black in dull light or at a distance. The deep orange-based bill on the young Black-headed also separates this species from 1st year Bonaparte's, which has an all-black bill.

QUIZ 26   **Iceland Gull (Thayer's subspecies) or possible Thayer's x Iceland Gull (Kumlien's subspecies) intergrade, adult, Cape Ann, Massachusetts, February (Advanced)**

This gull, showing a plump breast; petite, bullet-shaped bill; round head; and dark eye caused confusion among some gull experts in North America in the late 1980s when Iceland and Thayer's Gulls were separate species. The darker gray back, rich pink legs, and black primaries (which are too dark for Kumlien's) support Thayer's, as does the extensive white underside to the far primary feather, which can be similar in the variable Kumlien's. Kumlien's would show whitish to gray primaries and a pale ice-blue back. Probable hybrids between Thayer's and Kumlien's Iceland Gulls have been reported from low Arctic Canada on eastern Baffin and eastern Southampton Islands (*Gulls of the Americas*, Howell and Dunn, 2007), but this bird appears to be a good candidate for Thayer's.

QUIZ 27   **California Gull, immature 1st winter, California, February**

This is a tricky photo of a young gull because the angle of the wings does not reflect the true shape that you would see in real life. This is a relatively long-winged gull with somewhat broad-based wings and tapered outer wings, but the mostly long, slender pink bill with a black tip is a good feature for immature/1st winter California Gull. The strongly hooded look of this species in its 1st winter, with a concentration of streaking on the rear head and neck, is also not obvious because of feather wear, but the uniform strong dark markings on the underparts and underwing coverts and a collared nape combined with the bill pattern point to immature California Gull. Herring Gull would typically show a longer body profile, especially in the rear; a paler, more pronounced inner primary window; and a more slender neck and chest. The underwing and bill pattern and underpart markings at the late date of February rule out the similar underpart markings of early 1st winter Ring-billed Gull.

QUIZ 28   **Iceland (Thayer's) Gulls and Herring Gulls, adults breeding, Churchill, Manitoba, June 5, 1986 (Advanced)**

Location, time of year, and the white heads and underparts, gray backs, black primaries, and pink legs narrow your choices to either Herring or Iceland (Thayer's) Gulls. The *front left* bird shows a dark eye with a dark red orbital ring, deep pink legs, a rounder head with a steeper forehead, and a slightly smaller bill that lacks the can-opener tip of the two Herring Gulls *in front of* and *behind* it. An extensive white outer primary feather on the underside of the far wing also supports this as a Thayer's Gull, since Herring lacks this extreme white outer primary pattern on the underside. These Herring Gulls have pale yellowish eyes with pale yellow orbital rings; paler pink legs; a deeper, flat-topped head with a shallow forehead (giving the birds a pulled-taffy look to the front of the head); and larger, stockier bodies compared to the plump-breasted, more-compact look of Thayer's Iceland Gull. The bird in the *rear* is also a Thayer's Iceland Gull since it most resembles the *front* bird, with deep pink legs, a small bill, and a dark eye (if you zoom in close). In 1986, when Kevin took this photo, Thayer's was a distinct species. A major storm with strong winds and snow pushed a group of Thayer's Gulls back to Churchill, where they are typically found into late May. Most of these thirty-plus birds showed dark eyes with deep red orbital rings, deep pink legs, a smaller bill, and long wings, but a handful of Herring Gulls were mixed in.

QUIZ 29 **Ring-billed Gull, subadult/1st winter, Florida, May**

With the head turned toward the camera, it is hard to clearly see the important bill pattern of this species. If you had a side angle on the slender bill, you would see a pinkish-yellow bill with a distinct dark ring just short of the tip, which is typical of subadult/1st winter Ring-billed Gull. The very slender wings rule out the larger gulls, and the unmarked white head rules out the "hooded gulls," even in nonbreeding plumage. The worn nature of the flight feathers is a result of the late date of May 13, since this species and the similar slender-winged Mew Gull retain most of their juvenile wing feathers through the 1st year. Mew Gull has more uniform gray underwings in its 1st year and lacks the contrast and dark markings shown in this photo. Immature (1st winter) California Gull differs with its dark upper underwing coverts, which Herring Gull also shows, but they are not as strongly contrasting on Herring.

QUIZ 30 **Glaucous Gull, Herring Gull, Lesser Black-backed Gull, and Laughing Gulls, Florida, January**

Your first impression of this photo should be of a very large, whitish gull compared to the much smaller, browner one behind it. The big, bulky, white gull is an immature 1st winter Glaucous Gull. Note the large size, robust features, all-white plumage, bubble-gum-pink bill with a crisp dark tip, the beady-eyed look, and the white primaries (exposed outer wings) that extend only modestly beyond the tail. It is much larger than the exceptionally small immature 1st winter Herring Gull in the background, which shows a mostly dark bill with very little pink at the base.

While the size difference between these two species is dramatic, a small female Glaucous Gull could be roughly the same size as a large male Herring Gull. The overall white plumage with brown mottling below and pure white primaries points to Glaucous Gull. The dark eye ages this bird as an immature 1st winter, with 2nd winter Glaucous showing a pale eye (see Glaucous Gull account). Similarly plumaged Iceland Gull in its 1st winter would have a much thinner, black bill (some can show an ill-defined pink base), a more slender body, and long wings that extend well past the tail.

Laughing Gulls (mostly heads only) at *lower right* and *center* are perennial on the beaches of Florida in January, and they are much smaller than either of the other two species. If you picked out the 1st winter Lesser Black-backed Gull at the *lower left*, you deserve a star because the head-on angle makes this ID difficult. It is noticeably larger than the Laughing Gulls and has a heavier, dark bill; larger, bulkier body; and dark spotting on the sides of the upper breast and lower belly. Also note the bruised-eye look to the Lesser. Two other images show this bird in side profile, with no doubt as to its identity (see Intro 17, p. 24, and Glaucous Gull 9, p. 133).

QUIZ 31 **California Gull, subadult, California, February**

This gray-backed, white-headed gull is heavily streaked on the head and neck, but its general size can be determined by the adjacent American Coots. Several of the larger gray-backed, white-headed gulls would be noticeably bigger, which narrows the choices to Ring-billed or California Gull, since the bill is too large for Mew Gull, and the bill markings, including a red spot, also differ from those of Mew. The red spot connected to the black one on the bill rules out Ring-billed, so this must be a California Gull.

Note the overall slender profile of this subadult nonbreeding California Gull. A slender bill with a bold black ring inside the pale tip and a connecting red spot is typical of this species. The dusky eye and dense streaking that is heaviest on the nape are good features of nonbreeding California. Subadult Herring Gull at this stage would have mean, bright yellow eyes, a paler gray upper back, and coarser and more lavish streaking on the head and neck, as if applied with a putty knife.

QUIZ 32 **Iceland Gull, very worn immature/1st winter, Florida, May 15**

This gull with an injured left leg is totally bleached by the strong Florida sun, with most of its flight feathers worn to shafts and just a few feathers still attached. However, note the petite bill with the dull, pinkish base, the plump breast, and the white wing tips projecting well past the tail. The injured leg explains its presence in May in Florida, because a healthy bird would be long gone to northern breeding areas by this date. The similar Glaucous Gull is ruled out by the small, rounded head versus a large, blocky head on Glaucous; the small, slender bill with diffuse dull pink at the base versus a large, heavy, strongly bubble-gum-pink bill with a well-defined black tip; and the slender rear body with long wings versus an overall heavy, bulky body shape with wings that extend just past the tail. Leucistic (pigment-deficient) Herring or Ring-billed Gull can be ruled out by the dusky mottling on the lower belly that is out of the sun's reach, and by the darker underwing coverts in the flight photo of this bird in the Iceland Gull account (see Iceland Gull 14, p. 125).

QUIZ 33 **Yellow-footed Gull, immature/juvenile, Salton Sea, California, August 25 (Advanced)**

If you knew the location of this photo, you might not confuse this species with the very similar juvenile Western Gull, which does not typically occur at this location as of this printing, but some Westerns have been seen at the Salton Sea, so care should be taken at all locations.

Both species show heavy, brownish-gray mottled plumage, pinkish legs, and a very heavy bill with a bulging tip. Similarly plumaged immature 1st summer Herring Gull is ruled out immediately by the heavy bill with a large, bulbous tip and the feather patterns on the upperparts. Yellow-footed differs from similarly aged Western Gull by its noticeably paler head and underparts; more defined two-toned bill with a pale base (Western has an all-dark bill at this age); and paler pinkish legs, rather than the deeper pink legs on Western.

QUIZ 34 **Mystery gull photo, assorted gulls at Bolivar Flats, Texas, April 11, 2017 (Advanced)**

The assortment of gulls in this photo would cause many birders to walk away from this group of birds without trying to identify anything other than the obvious small, displaying, hooded Laughing Gulls. The large brownish-gray gull *behind* the white gull is an immature Herring Gull, with dark flight feathers and a more robust body structure compared to the noticeably smaller, more slender, plump-breasted adult Ring-billed Gull to its *right*. The Ring-billed also differs from Herring in its yellow legs (Herring has pink legs). The background gulls are all Herring Gulls.

The tough gull is the white one whose primary flight feathers are totally worn off, with just shafts remaining, but its size, structural features, and overall white plumage narrow your obvious choices to Iceland (either Kumlien's or Thayer's subspecies) or Glaucous Gull. The bill appears too slender for Glaucous Gull, and the diffuse pink base might be a bit crisper on Glaucous as well, which would show a strong bubble-gum-pink base with a defined black tip. So possibly an Iceland Gull?

Not so fast: What about a leucistic (pigment-deficient) Herring Gull, if the feather pigment on this bird lacked the dark tones typical of this species? An albino gull is ruled out by the dark markings on the underparts, which are not exposed to the harsh Texas sun, and the pale, thin brown barring in front of and behind the legs, which might suggest Kumlien's, with Herring or Thayer's typically showing heavier, less defined markings on the underparts, similar to the Herring Gull behind the white gull. Three of the top gull experts in the country reviewed this photo with the following results: (1) Kumlien's Iceland Gull, not the Thayer's subspecies;

(2) leucistic Herring Gull, with the body and bill shape of this bird quite similar to that of the immature Herring Gull behind it; and (3) "I won't put a name to this bird."

Sometimes it is best to walk away from birds like this and not try to identify them to species based on the bleached-out, worn plumage with missing flight feathers (just shafts are left). There are no diagnostic plumage field marks to analyze, which is why these three experts offered different opinions. Another gull expert recently commented that it more closely resembled the Herring Gulls nearby and was possibly a bleached-out, partially leucistic Herring Gull. The jury is still out. After much deliberation, Kevin thinks it could be a Kumlien's Iceland Gull because of the bill shape, strong pink legs, small rounded head, pink bill with dark tip, and similar fine barring and spotting on the underbelly (best seen in zoomed-in views).

QUIZ 35   **Mystery gull from Bolivar Flats, Texas, April 14, 2017**

This second photo of the previous bird shows it a bit closer, but also with direct comparison to nearby Laughing and Herring Gulls. The disheveled head is due to a heavy rainstorm that just occurred, making it even harder to compare to Herring Gull. It's probably best to leave this one as either immature/1st winter Iceland Gull or leucistic immature Herring Gull.

APPENDIX

Answers to the quiz questions in the book are listed below in order of appearance.

1. **INTRO 4**, p. 14 – The two larger gulls in the *center* of the photo with heavily marked underparts are immature Herring Gulls in late 2nd winter plumage. Note the pale eye on these birds, which helps to age them as 2nd year birds. First winter immatures have dark eyes.

2. **INTRO 16**, p. 24 – The bird is a subadult Lesser Black-backed Gull.

3. **INTRO 17**, p. 24 – The large white gull that is lying down in the *center* is a 1st winter Glaucous Gull, and the smaller gull in *dead center* with a petite black bill and charcoal-gray back is a subadult Lesser Black-backed Gull.

4. **INTRO 23**, p. 28 – The two birds on each side of the photo are Laughing Gulls, as is the small, dark brown, juvenile-plumaged bird in the *center* of the photo. The slightly larger gray-backed bird *left of center* is an adult Ring-billed Gull that is missing its tail, while the larger gray-backed bird *right of center* is an adult Herring Gull. The very large gull to the *right* of the Herring Gull with a blackish back is an adult Great Black-backed Gull. These are the four commonest gulls in the eastern United States.

5. **LAUGHING GULL 10**, p. 40 – The sleeping shorebird is a Black-bellied Plover transitioning into breeding plumage. This is a relatively large shorebird (11–12 inches) that frequents beachfronts in migration and during winter, and this profile shows the very bulky, chest-heavy body structure that differs noticeably from that of American Golden-Plover. The brownish back shows black-and-white breeding feathers coming in, and a contrasting whitish belly. By contrast, American Golden-Plover shows breeding dark-centered upperparts with golden edges, and a uniform dusky wash to the underparts in nonbreeding plumage.

6. **FRANKLIN'S GULL 3**, p. 45 – The sleeping bird is an adult Franklin's Gull.

7. **FRANKLIN'S GULL 8**, p. 48 – The white tern with a partial rear hood and yellow bill tip is a Sandwich Tern.

8. **FRANKLIN'S GULL 4**, p. 46 – There are 12 Laughing Gulls in this photo (*below*).

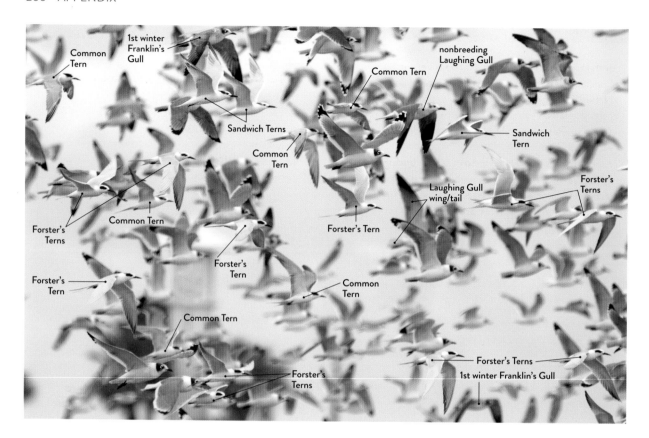

9. **FRANKLIN'S GULL 9**, p. 49 – (*see* photo *above*)

10. **BLACK-HEADED GULL 2**, p. 59 – This is a very difficult quiz, since both Bonaparte's and Black-headed Gulls have similar upper wing patterns. It is an adult Bonaparte's Gull because the black trailing edge to the outer wing is fairly narrow, and the black trailing edge of Black-headed is wider and less neatly arranged. The feet are a deep pink, which could apply to both species in March. The outer part of the bill appears all black, while adult Black-headed usually shows some red on the outer bill.

11. **GLAUCOUS GULL 9**, p. 133 – The smallest, most numerous gulls with charcoal-shaded backs are non-breeding Laughing Gulls. The other charcoal-backed bird at *left* that is larger than Laughing Gull is a subadult Lesser Black-backed Gull. The brownish gull behind the Glaucous Gull, which is very similar in size and shape and in bill size, shape, and color to the Lesser Black-backed, is a very small 1st winter immature Herring Gull (possibly a female because of the very small size compared to the other Herring Gulls). Also Herring Gulls are the large gull at *rear center* (2nd winter Herring Gull) and the adult at *far right*.

BIBLIOGRAPHY

Alderfer, Jonathan, ed. 2006. *National Geographic Complete Birds of North America*. Washington, DC: National Geographic Society.

Howell, Steve N. G., and Jon Dunn. 2007. *Gulls of the Americas*. Peterson Reference Guide Series. Boston: Houghton Mifflin.

Karlson, Kevin T., and Dale Rosselet. 2015. *Birding by Impression: A Different Approach to Knowing and Identifying Birds*. Peterson Reference Guide Series. Boston: Houghton Mifflin Harcourt.

North Dakota Game and Fish Department. Brice. 2003. "Franklin's Gull." https://gf.nd.gov/wildlife/id/shorebirds/franklins-gull.

Olsen, Klaus M., and Hans Larsson. 2004. *Gulls of North America, Europe, and Asia*. Princeton, NJ: Princeton University Press.

Sibley, David. 2014. *The Sibley Guide to Birds, Second Edition*. New York: Alfred A. Knopf.

PHOTOGRAPHER CREDITS

INDEX